D0090259

ADVANCE PRAISE FOR *LEADERSHIP BS*

"*Leadership BS* goes directly to the soul of leadership practices, exposing both the rewards and penalties of contemporary notions. You'll be challenged to look at qualities such as narcissism, vulnerability, immodesty, and ego, and to consider why these too are important traits of effective leaders."
— Curt Coffman, coauthor of *First, Break All the Rules*

"A fascinating inquiry into why the 'leadership industry' has failed to develop better leaders. Pfeffer turns conventional wisdom about leadership upside down and challenges us to rethink why and how leaders behave. It's an indispensable book for every leader, executive coach, and anyone else who seeks to help leaders."
— Morten T. Hansen, professor, University of California, Berkeley, and coauthor of *Great by Choice*

"Pfeffer offers no nostrums, no feel-good solutions; instead, he offers unvarnished insights and dry-eyed suggestions. Anyone who is seriously interested in leadership should read this book."
— Stephen Kosslyn, founding dean, the Minerva Schools of Arts and Sciences at the Keck Graduate Institute

"Jeffrey Pfeffer has done it again. He forces us to confront uncomfortable questions about ourselves and our culture. This book reminds us of the dangers of pursuing comforting messages instead of practical truths."
— Kent Thiry, CEO, DaVita Healthcare Partners

"*Leadership BS* persuasively attacks the simplistic, glib generalities that masquerade as leadership analysis and advice. Pfeffer offers many examples of when such advice can actually hurt leaders and their effectiveness. By turning some of our assumptions concerning authenticity, trust, and humility on their heads, this book is essential reading for anyone who would rather rely on scientific evidence than on merely cool stories."
— Sim B. Sitkin, faculty director, Fuqua/Coach K Center on Leadership and Ethics, Duke University

"In this wonderful book, Jeffrey Pfeffer takes on sacred cows and conventional wisdom, showing us a different path to the leadership excellence we all desire yet find so elusive. It should be required reading in every business school."
— Herminia Ibarra, the Cora Chaired Professor of Leadership and Learning, INSEAD

"Challenges conventional thinking and traditional bromides, underscoring the importance of being evidence-based if you want to make an impact in developing leadership."
>—Barry Z. Posner, PhD, Accolti Endowed Professor of Leadership, Santa Clara University, and coauthor of *The Leadership Challenge*

"Pfeffer shatters the self-interested myth-making of the leadership industry consultant and the romantic ideologies of the high priests of the leadership religion. Anchored in research and concrete public case histories of leaders, his book reveals the uncomfortable hard truths about power, impact, and success, and uncovers the often buried moral paradoxes."
>—Jeffrey A. Sonnenfeld, senior associate dean for leadership studies and Lester Crown Professor of Leadership Practice, Yale School of Management, and author of *The Hero's Farewell*

"Pfeffer explores what is most typically a feel-good field with ferocious tenacity and the tools of a statistician. Preferring evidence over anecdote, Pfeffer exposes bold truths, even when they are inconvenient. It turns out the meek often do not inherit the earth, or much else, for that matter."
>—Strauss Zelnick, partner, ZMC, and chairman, Take-Two Interactive Software

"Pfeffer provides detailed and systematic evidence for how far apart the rhetoric and the reality are in the world of leadership. This hard-hitting book may not give you a warm, fuzzy feeling about leadership, but it offers practical advice for coping with the realities of work in today's organizations."
>—Julian Birkinshaw, professor of strategy and entrepreneurship, London Business School, and author of *Becoming a Good Boss*

"Jeffrey Pfeffer's writing is the apotheosis of challenge, and there is much to be challenged and changed in what Pfeffer characterizes as the 'leadership industry.' This accessible and yet scholarly book will irritate some, inform others, and challenge us all. But why the unclassy title for a book with such profound and practical messages?"
>—Andrew Pettigrew, professor of strategy and organisation and Senior Golding Fellow, Brasenose College

"As much nonsense has been written about leadership as dieting and sex, and the debunking Pfeffer awards the leadership industry is long overdue. His focus is on the truth."
>—Carl Stern, former CEO, Boston Consulting Group

LEADERSHIP BS

ALSO BY JEFFREY PFEFFER

Power: Why Some People Have It—and Others Don't

*What Were They Thinking: Unconventional
Wisdom About Management*

*Hard Facts, Dangerous Half-Truths, and Total Nonsense:
Profiting from Evidence-Based Management*

*Hidden Value: How Great Companies Achieve
Extraordinary Results with Ordinary People*

The Knowing-Doing Gap

The Human Equation: Building Profits by Putting People First

Organizations and Organization Theory

Competitive Advantage Through People

Managing with Power

Power in Organizations

*The External Control of Organizations:
A Resource Dependence Perspective*

Organizational Design

LEADERSHIP BS

Fixing Workplaces and Careers
One Truth at a Time

WITHDRAWN

Jeffrey Pfeffer

HARPER
BUSINESS

An Imprint of HarperCollinsPublishers

HarperCollins books may be purchased for educational, business, or sales promotional use. For information, please e-mail the Special Markets Department at SPsales@harpercollins.com.

FIRST EDITION

Designed by Renato Stanisic

Library of Congress Cataloging-in-Publication Data has been applied for.

ISBN 978-0-06-238316-7

15 16 17 18 19   OV/RRD   10 9 8 7 6 5 4 3 2 1

Contents

Preface

If we want to change a world with too many leadership failures, too many career derailments, and too many toxic workplaces, we must begin by acknowledging the facts and understanding why we are where we are. Only then will we begin to enjoy long-delayed progress. Myths and inspiring stories can be comforting, but they are worse than useless for creating change.

I came to understand this truth from experience. Whenever I teach my MBA class, The Paths to Power, or give talks about my book *Power: Why Some People Have It—and Others Don't*, I often get the same comment: Your material contradicts much of what others say and teach about leaders and leadership. At the same time, many former students tell me that over the course of their careers, they frequently confront a huge disconnect between what the leadership industry tells them to do and what they have learned from me and also from watching others—ideas that have made them more effective and successful. My response to these comments: much of the oft-repeated conventional wisdom about leadership is based more on hope than reality, on wishes rather than data, on beliefs instead of science.

The shibboleths of modern leadership loom large and influence how people navigate their careers, often to their detriment. And people's uncritical acceptance of the feel-good stories told about leadership prevents them from apprehending reality and taking action to make things better. So I decided to engage directly with the topic of leadership and examine why all the writing, blogging, and speaking about leadership and all the money spent on leadership development has been so manifestly unsuccessful in changing workplaces or helping people be more successful in their careers.

Thus, this book is, in a sense, a prequel to *Power*. *Leadership BS* explores why so much of the conventional wisdom about leadership and so much of the activity aimed at developing leaders do not fit the facts on the ground. This reality means we need a different way of apprehending human behavior. And we particularly need a different way for teaching and coaching people to be effective in navigating the organizational world in which we all live. These are precisely the objectives of *Power* and also the class on power in organizations that I teach at Stanford.

I began the writing of *Leadership BS* with a simple, albeit ambitious, goal: to cause people to rethink, to reconceptualize, and to reorient their behaviors concerning the important topic of leadership. My purpose in all of this is for the next decades of what goes on in workplaces and in people's careers to be, optimistically, a lot more humane and beneficent than the last decades have been.

I proceed from a historical analogy. Around the turn of the twentieth century, medical practice and medical education in America were pretty dismal. People were hawking untested and unproven "cures," with their financial success dependent more on their slickness and persuasiveness than on the actual science or medical efficacy of what they were pushing. Almost anyone could practice medicine, as there was no license required. And while there were some outstanding doctors and scientists building the foundations of modern medicine, charlatans and quacks abounded. Many medical schools were proprietary, for-profit entities with little concern with science, lots of concern for financial gain, and little interest in doing evaluations of what they, or their students, were accomplishing (or, more accurately, the harm they were doing).

Into this morass, the Carnegie Foundation sent Abraham Flexner, who was notably a teacher and not a doctor, to survey the landscape of American medical education. His report, published in book-length form in 1910, transformed the training and also the science and practice of medicine. As a result of that report, one-third of the existing medical schools closed, formal licensing for doctors was instituted, and the biomedical, scientific foundation of medical practice—a goal still not perfectly achieved but widely embraced and something that has been responsible for so much progress in the prevention and treatment of disease—was put into place.[1]

The parallels with the current state of the leadership industry are striking. Want to be a leadership coach? You can go to an institute or enroll in one of many programs, of varying quality and rigor, that train coaches with varying degrees of skill, but you don't have to even do that. You can be a coach tomorrow.

Want to be an expert on leadership? You could get training and exposure to the relevant research literature, but it's not necessary. If you are persuasive enough, articulate enough, or attractive enough, if you have an interesting enough, uplifting story or some combination of these traits, you are or can be a very successful leadership blogger, speaker, and consultant—whether or not you have ever read, let alone contributed to, any of the relevant social science on the topic.

To be sure, these days there are many fabulously fantastic people with exceptional credentials and ethics working mightily to improve organizational workplaces and leaders' careers. But the leadership industry also has its share of quacks and sham artists who sell promises and stories, some true, some not, but all of them inspirational and comfortable, with not much follow-up to see what really does work and what doesn't. And much like the field of medicine prior to Flexner, what speaks the loudest in the leadership industry seems to be money, rather than evidence-based, useful knowledge. The way leadership gurus try to demonstrate their legitimacy is not through their scientific knowledge or accomplishments but rather by achieving public notoriety—be it the requisite TED talks, blog posts, Twitter followers, or books filled with leadership advice that might or might not be valid and useful.

I have no illusions that this book will have anything like the impact of the Flexner report in its effects on the leadership industry. But in a world with too many disengaged, dissatisfied, disaffected employees, and workplaces with too many leaders and aspiring leaders losing their jobs, I feel compelled to make the best case I can for what's wrong with leadership and what might be done to change things for the better. By calling BS on so much of what goes on, this book gives people a closer, more scientific look at many dimensions of leadership behavior. Most important, it encourages everyone to finally stop accepting sugar-laced but toxic potions as cures.

Jeffrey Pfeffer

Introduction: Things Are Bad—Here's Why

Leaders fail their people, their organizations, the larger society, and even themselves with unacceptable frequency. Every day, in the news, are more stories of leaders failing.

Leaders fail themselves: Dominique Strauss-Kahn, possibly on his way to being president of France before his arrest for sexually assaulting a New York hotel housekeeper; Brendan Eich, the CEO of Mozilla, the Firefox browser company, resigning because of his political contributions to antigay activities; the former Yahoo CEO Scott Thompson, booted out for claiming on his résumé that he had a computer science degree when he didn't.

Leaders fail their customers: airline executives who have created an experience so unpleasant that their best customers flee for private options and others avoid flying if they can; Amazon, by not carrying some bestselling books and popular DVDs in spats with suppliers; banks inaccurately foreclosing on properties and also debiting customers' checking accounts for withdrawals in ways that generate the highest overdraft fees.

Leaders fail their stockholders: Rick Wagoner leading General Motors into bankruptcy, Richard Fuld leading Lehman

Brothers into oblivion, and Ed Lampert taking the retail icon Sears into irrelevancy.

Most perniciously, leaders fail their employees: Stan O'Neal taking the venerable Merrill Lynch over a cliff, costing thousands of jobs; Carly Fiorina, Mark Hurd, and, most recently, Meg Whitman doing round after round of layoffs at Hewlett-Packard; and, except for Southwest Airlines, airline leaders slashing employees' wages, cutting the number of workers, and eviscerating employee pensions as the companies follow one another into restructurings.

This is but a very small sample drawn from a huge, almost unimaginably vast, list of leadership catastrophes.

How can this be—all this failure—after the thousands of leadership books, talks, blogs, classes, and leadership-development programs seeking to make leaders more effective? How can this be, after more than a century of research seeking to figure out how to select better leaders? I'm going to tell you part of the story of how this can be and, more important, why things aren't getting better and what might be done to make some improvements.

But first I need to be clear: This is *not* a book describing the manifest and many failures of leaders. It is a book to help you understand some of the *causes* of those failures.

There are two ways to understand the many leadership failures that fill the daily news. One is what might be called the "bad apple" theory. This approach argues that organizations have done a poor job of selecting the right people for leadership roles, schools have failed to instill ethical leadership behaviors in their students, and some leaders themselves have developed the wrong values. Although I would not for a minute deny the plausibility of all of this, the bad apple explanation not only fails to make sense of the pervasiveness of the problem, but it also offers an explanation that would never be used in other contexts.

For instance, when General Motors recalled millions of cars in 2014 because of a problem with the ignition system such that when a key was accidentally jostled, the engine shut off, also cutting off the electrical power used to deploy air bags in accidents, observers correctly attributed this decades-old issue and its cover-up not just to the fifteen GM employees who were fired but to the company's culture.[1] No reasonable person would accept that a few bad actors on their own accounted for the initial problem and its fallout, events that unfolded over more than a decade. After all, this is the same company that almost fifty years earlier had produced the unsafe Corvair model and then hounded Ralph Nader when he had the temerity to call attention to that car's miserable safety record.[2]

There is a second way to understand the many leadership failures that fill the news: to explore the systemic processes that produce leaders who often behave differently from what most people might like or expect. Such processes include the social psychology that makes the actual traits and behaviors that cause leaders to be successful in their careers and attain senior-level positions quite different from the qualities we hear about or might desire in leaders. And such processes also include the way we talk about—tell stories about—leaders and leadership, how we measure or fail to measure workplace conditions, and even how we teach leadership. We often measure (or fail to measure) conditions, tell heroic leadership tales, and use simplistic methods of understanding behavior in ways that becloud effective diagnosis and, as a consequence, forestall actions that might make things better.

I adopt this second approach. My objective is to help you understand *why* these leadership failures continue to occur with unacceptable frequency, to understand the systemic and psychological processes that produce what we observe every day in the world, in spite of all the leadership-development efforts, training programs, books, TED talks, and so forth. Once we understand some of the underlying causes of what we see occurring inside company workplaces, we have a better chance of making effective changes.

THE FAILURE OF THE LEADERSHIP INDUSTRY

This book originated with an observation, followed by a conclusion, and finally an insight. The observation: on the one hand, there is an ever-growing, enormous leadership industry consisting of an almost limitless number of books, articles, speeches, workshops, blogs, conferences, training sessions, and corporate leadership-development efforts, activities that have existed for decades. Over that time, a largely unchanging, sometimes research-based set of recommendations for how to improve group and organizational performance emerged. The recommendations include, but are not limited to, that leaders inspire trust, be authentic, tell the truth, serve others (particularly those who work for and with them), be modest and self-effacing, exhibit empathic understanding and emotional intelligence, and other similar seemingly sensible nostrums. And on the other hand, there sits ample, even overwhelming evidence of workplaces filled with disengaged, dissatisfied employees who do not trust their leaders and whose oft-expressed number one desire is to leave their current employer. What's the upshot? Not only is the world filled with dysfunctional workplaces, but leaders themselves are not doing so well, as they confront shorter job tenures and an ever-higher probability of suffering career derailments and getting fired.

My conclusion that follows from these two sets of facts: *The leadership industry has failed.* Good intentions notwithstanding, there is precious little evidence that any of these recommendations have had a positive impact. Indeed, many prescriptions for leaders are often more problematic and invalid than generally acknowledged. And as a consequence of all this failure, both workplaces and many individual leaders are in bad shape. Even worse, there are few to no signs that things are getting any better.

Others share my conclusion. Two consulting psychologists surveying the leadership landscape concluded that "there is scarcely any evidence that all this spending . . . is producing better leaders."[3] Barbara Kellerman, a lecturer on leadership at Harvard's Kennedy School and the founder of the Center for Public Leadership, agrees. She recently wrote that the leadership industry "has failed over its roughly forty-year history to in any major, meaningful, measurable way improve the human condition" and that "the rise of leadership as an object of our collective fascination has coincided precisely with the decline of leadership in our collective estimation."[4]

For a while I thought this paradox/predicament was just an interesting and possibly coincidental discontinuity between a large set of feel-good leadership activities on the one hand and too many toxic workplaces and disrupted careers on the other. But then came the insight: It is not just that all the efforts to develop better leaders, decades of such effort notwithstanding, have failed to make things appreciably better. I realized that much of what was and is going on almost certainly, although sometimes inadvertently and unintentionally, makes things much worse. There are ways to remedy all of this, but the solutions will not be easy or readily implemented, for reasons I will make clear.

If one cares about the enormous psychological and even physical toll exacted on employees from bullying, abusive bosses and work environments filled with multiple sources of stress, if one is at all sensitive to the human costs incurred as leaders flame out and lose their jobs—cares and concerns that I and, I suspect, many others share—then the continuing failure of the leadership industry in all of its forms and activities to make things better needs to be both explained and remedied. This book represents my best efforts to accomplish that task.

Here's the plan. In this introductory chapter, I lay out evidence demonstrating four things: (1) the leadership industry is large and prominent, but, notwithstanding its magnitude and reach, (2) workplaces in the United States and around the world are, for the most part (as there are obviously exceptional places on best-places-to-work lists), filled with dissatisfied, disengaged employees who do not trust their leaders; (3) leaders at all levels lose their jobs at an increasingly fast pace, in part because they are unprepared for the realities of organizational life, and thus, (4) the leadership industry has failed and continues to fail in its task of producing leaders who are effective and successful, and it has even failed to produce sufficient talent to fill leadership vacancies.

I also suggest some reasons for the failures. One big problem is that much leadership training and development has become too much a form of lay preaching, telling people inspiring stories about heroic leaders and exceptional organizations and, in the process, making those who hear the stories feel good and temporarily uplifted while not changing much of what happens at many workplaces. In chapter 1, I explain why inspiration is a very poor foundation on which to build substantive change, and why and how the leadership tales we hear, stories that often have only modest amounts of validity, routinely make things worse, and possibly *much* worse.

Then in the ensuing chapters I examine some, although certainly not all, of the most commonly recommended traits and behaviors for leaders—modesty in chapter 2, authenticity in chapter 3, telling the truth in chapter 4, being trusted in chapter 5, taking care of others in chapter 6. These are all wonderful qualities, and if leaders consistently displayed them, workplaces and the employees who fill them would undoubtedly be doing better. But in each instance, I show first that few leaders, even some of the most prominent and successful, exhibit those qualities or do these recommended things. Then I lay out the evidence for and logic of why sometimes doing the *opposite* of what has been prescribed makes sense, at least for leaders seeking to advance their own careers. And this fact is at the core of the argument—that the qualities we *actually* select for and reward in most workplaces are precisely the ones that are unlikely to produce leaders who are good for employees or, for that matter, for long-term organizational performance.

Chapter 7 draws one important lesson from all this evidence: first, you need to take care of yourself. Although it might be cathartic to bemoan the evidence that positive leadership qualities often go unrecognized and unrewarded while their opposite produces career advancement and wealth, such moralizing changes nothing about organizational decision-making and also does little to help you in your own career challenges. Furthermore, the pursuit of individual self-interest just might be, as virtually all economics writing and theory since the time of Adam Smith teaches, good not just for you but also generally beneficial for the social systems including the work organizations in which you live. The alternative—hoping for some beneficent, godlike parental figure to look out for and take care of you at your place of employment—seems like a risky bet at best.

Chapter 8 concludes the book by developing a simple but important message: to change the world of work and leadership, we need to get beyond the half truths and self-serving stories that are so prominent today. Throughout each of the chapters, including this introduction, I offer recommendations and suggestions about what leaders and, for that matter, others might do to fix the problems discussed. But I am, above all, a realist. If these recommendations were comfortable and easily implemented, they already would have been.

My purpose is straightforward. Rather than giving you yet one more book to reassure you and make you feel good, while nothing changes in most workplaces and meanwhile you un-knowingly cruise to a career disaster, perhaps it is time to muster some evidence about what is really going on with leaders and leadership and why. Even if such insight does not motivate you to change things, at least it will leave you much better equipped to understand the realities of day-to-day organizational life, and therefore better able to cope with them. So let's proceed to dissect the essence of the leadership endeavor—that large set of activities that have mostly failed to help either workplaces or leaders themselves.

THE LEADERSHIP INDUSTRY IS LARGE

"Leadership," is a popular term, and the set of activities focused on leadership are enormous. When I searched for the term "lead-ership" on Google Scholar, a search engine that accesses scien-tific research literature, I found 2,640,000 entries. Searching on Google itself revealed 148 *million* links to the term. On Amazon, entering the term "leadership" produced 117,000 entries.*

The word "leadership" is prominent in part because many people, both scholars and practitioners, view leadership as a construct important if not fundamental to explaining business and organizational performance. This unequivocal belief in the importance of leadership persists, even if the scientific evidence on this point is much more mixed.[5] The late business school pro-fessor James Meindl referred to this emphasis on leadership as

---

* *I conducted this search on December 12, 2013.*

an explanation for organizational outcomes as the "romance of leadership." He and his colleagues noted that "the social construction of organizational realities has elevated the concept of leadership to a lofty status and level of significance. Such realities emphasize leadership, and the concept has thereby gained a brilliance that exceeds the limits of normal scientific inquiry."[6] Meindl and his colleagues showed that the proportion of mentions of leadership in the popular press was positively related to economic performance—there were more mentions and studies of leadership when economic times were good. Examining the variation in the use of the term "leadership" across industries and individual companies, Meindl once again observed a positive relationship between mentions of leadership and performance. Meindl's conclusion was that the construct of leadership was invented to account for unusually good—or unusually bad—performance as a way of creating a relatively simplified account of the world that made personal control seem possible. In other words, if things aren't going well, just scapegoat the leader and bring in a replacement.

If "leadership" is an important term and a prominent way of apprehending the world, we should find it scarcely surprising that the institutions of higher education, seeking both applicants and donations, would emphasize the development of leadership skills in their students. And this is precisely the case. Universities frequently claim that they develop leadership capabilities, a set of skills so apparently sought-after and desirable that virtually all business schools, many other professional schools, and numerous undergraduate colleges and universities make developing leaders a prominent part of their mission statements. For instance, Harvard Business School's mission is to "educate leaders who will make a difference in the world." Wake Forest University's mission statement includes the phrase "providing students an example of the world they will be called upon to lead." A study in the *McKinsey Quarterly* notes, "Colleges and universities offer hundreds of degree courses on leadership."[7] Meanwhile, leadership centers proliferate in colleges of all sizes and orientations, in part to organize leadership-development activities and in part to serve as a focus for fund-raising.

Another measure of the leadership industry's girth is the amount of time and money it consumes. Kennedy School lecturer Barbara Kellerman estimated that about $50 billion is spent on corporate training and development annually.[8] The American Society for Training and Development's (ATSD) 2012 state of the industry report estimated that $156.2 billion was spent on employee learning and development during 2011. Of course, not all training and development is leadership training; some training focuses on technical skills, total quality management, or various technical processes and procedures. Nonetheless, according to ASTD, managerial and supervisory content constituted some 12.6 percent of the total amount spent, which would mean that almost $20 billion was spent on leadership education and development.[9] Three McKinsey consultants estimated that U.S. companies spend about $14 billion annually on leadership development, an amount echoed by other estimates.[10]

WORKPLACES ARE MOSTLY HORRIBLE

Regardless of the time and money spent on leadership, the situation in workplaces, not just in the United States but around the world, is dire, with disengaged, disaffected, and dissatisfied employees everywhere. Here are a few representative examples to help make the case.

A few years ago, management professor (and Stanford colleague and occasional coauthor) Robert Sutton wrote a book entitled

The No Asshole Rule.[11] The book became a bestseller all over the world because it touched a chord. People told Sutton about how they would buy copies to place on their boss's desk (anonymously, of course). People also purchased the book for themselves to make sense of the abusive work environments that so many faced and to learn what to do to cope with harmful work situations. After the book appeared, Sutton received numerous e-mails describing, sometimes in heartrending detail, the slights, bullying, and ill treatment heaped on all too many employees in contemporary workplaces. One way to read the market's positive reaction to Sutton's book and the many personal anecdotes he received is that the so-called leaders whom many people work for are either abusive bullies or just out of touch with their subordinates.

And indeed, systematic data on workplace bullying report widespread verbal abuse, shouting, berating others, and the general creation of a climate of intimidation. One study of part-time, more mature students at Staffordshire University in the United Kingdom found that half of the sample reported having been bullied at some point during their careers.[12] Another study of 1,100 employees in the National Health Service in Great Britain reported that some 38 percent of employees had experienced one or more incidences of workplace bullying in just the previous year.[13] A study of nurses working in the National Health Service found that 44 percent of the nurses had experienced bullying in the previous twelve months.[14] Two management professors reported that 10 percent of employees in the United States said they witnessed incivility *daily* in their workplaces, and 20 percent of the people surveyed noted that they were targets of workplace incivility at least once a week.[15]

There are consequences for both employees and their employers from people working in abusive environments for bullying, difficult leaders. Employees experience stress and depression, with adverse effects on both their physical and mental health. And "because of their experiences of workplace incivility, employees decrease work effort, time on the job, productivity, and performance" and are also more likely to quit.[16]

Employees, confronted with harsh work environments and bad leaders, are not surprisingly dissatisfied with their jobs. According to a national survey conducted by the Nielsen Company for the Conference Board, fewer than half of employees (47.2 percent) reported being satisfied with their jobs. The survey, which began in 1987, shows a striking decline in job satisfaction, from 61.1 percent in 1987 to 47.2 percent some twenty-five years later. Moreover, except for a few upticks during recoveries from recessions, the decline in job satisfaction has been consistent and steady.[17]

Another study of job satisfaction, conducted by Right Management in 2012 in the United States and Canada, reported that only 19 percent of people said they were satisfied with their job, with two-thirds of the respondents saying they were not happy at work. Susan Adams, a writer for *Forbes* magazine, reported on a survey conducted by Mercer, the human resource consulting firm. Mercer surveyed some thirty thousand employees worldwide and reported that between 28 percent and 56 percent of employees wanted to leave their jobs.[18]

Maybe job dissatisfaction is not your favorite indicator of workplace health. Consider, then, the data on employee engagement. The Gallup Organization, drawing its conclusions based on extensive surveying, reported in 2012 that only 30 percent of the U.S. workforce was engaged and inspired at work, with 20 percent of people reporting that they were actively disengaged, roaming the halls spreading discontent and seeking to undermine their employer.[19] Things are even worse elsewhere. A Gallup study of 142 countries reported that only 13 percent of employees were engaged at work, with some 24 percent actively disengaged.[20] Moreover,

Gallup noted that although the economy had undergone substantial changes over the preceding decades, employee engagement levels remained almost completely unchanged. If for some reason you don't like the Gallup research, virtually all of the numerous studies and reports regularly emanating from the various human resource consulting firms portray the workplace situation similarly, finding that the vast majority of employees are unhappy with their work, disengaged, and hoping for a different job.

Even more to the point, employees are unhappy with their leaders. Very, very unhappy. In the summer of 2012, *Parade* magazine released a poll of the American workforce. Fully 35 percent of U.S. employees reported that they would willingly forgo a substantial pay raise in exchange for seeing their direct supervisor fired.[21]

Taken all together, these data show that workplaces are often toxic environments that are bad for the people working in them, with negative consequences for employers, also. And there is absolutely no evidence that these conditions are substantially different in other countries or that things are getting better over time. So whatever other things the leadership research, writing, speaking, blogging, and programs are doing, making workplaces better is clearly not one of them.

Because the focus of much leadership research is precisely on demonstrating the connection between leadership and leader behavior on the one hand and outcomes such as job satisfaction, employee engagement, and turnover on the other, these data reveal the abject failure of the leadership enterprise. As one study commented, "Leadership style and employee satisfaction are hot questions of leadership theory research in recent years,"[22] while another noted that "management and leadership are pivotal to staff satisfaction."[23] And a study of nurses noted that "quality nursing leadership is an important determinant in itself as a predictor of job satisfaction."[24] If, as scores of studies demonstrate, leadership affects engagement, satisfaction, and turnover, the sorry state of these workplace indicators provides compelling evidence of leadership failure.

LEADERS REGULARLY LOSE THEIR JOBS AND DERAIL

Things are no better for the people in leadership roles. At breakfast, "Matt" tells a story of being fired first by one famous Silicon Valley firm and now another. Fortunately, Matt, a graduate from a very prestigious business school, an individual with fabulous strategic skills and business acumen, and a hard worker who is also a very nice human being, reports that he has found an even better job at yet another up-and-coming technology company.

As Matt jokes about failing upward, he relates how he lost his previous jobs, essentially by focusing on doing a great job technically but being largely oblivious to the political dynamics and particularly the requirement for managing his relationships with his bosses by doing whatever they wanted and flattering them endlessly.

Maybe Matt is just an anomaly, but I don't think so. Another graduate of a very high status, highly selective business school related story after story of classmates who were fired within the first couple of years of graduating. As he told me, "Getting fired is something people from great academic programs don't talk about, but it is more common than people think." His estimate, based on the anecdotal experience of people in his personal network, was that between 10 and 20 percent of his talented and highly credentialed classmates left their jobs involuntarily within the first couple of years postgraduation. Again, the predominant cause of the firings: people believed in the world described to them in business school and in the prescriptions for leader behavior. Consequently, they were surprised by and completely unprepared for what they actually encountered at work. And when their leaders failed to live up to the expectations of these new hires, many of those folks let the leaders know, either directly or indirectly, how they were failing and how the subordinates were feeling, thereby completely sealing those subordinates' fates.

It's not just junior-level leaders who suffer career derailments. Senior leaders also face ever-tougher conditions that they seem to have difficulty navigating, as evidenced by decreasing lengths of tenures and the ever-growing incidence of getting fired. The Conference Board's 2012 report on CEO succession documented a decline in CEO tenure since 2000.[25] Research by the consulting firm Booz also showed declining tenure for CEOs today compared with the past, with a higher proportion of CEOs getting fired. In 2011, some 14 percent of CEOs of the largest 2,500 companies in the world were replaced, with the turnover rate being highest among the 250 largest companies as measured by market capitalization.[26] And according to the annual Booz reports on CEO tenure and departures, the trends for shorter tenures and more frequent firings are evident not just in the United States but also around the world.

Experienced executive coaches tell the same story—of otherwise smart, motivated, interpersonally competent, hardworking people with great credentials who derail at unexpectedly high rates. One critical time for derailment is when, in their first jobs postgraduation, people move from positions where they can succeed mostly on the basis of their individual performance and into more interdependent roles where political skills become more important. The next critical time comes around twenty years later, when, if successful, people have reached very senior hierarchical levels where everyone around them is smart and accomplished. At that point, the differentiating factor is the ability to navigate increasingly politically charged environments that are peopled by those who mostly do not fulfill the leadership industry's prescriptions.

TOO FEW GOOD LEADERS, TOO MANY BAD ONES

If unhappy workplaces and short-tenured leaders suffering career derailments (a nice-enough euphemism) aren't enough to convince you that things are bad, there are yet additional data that show that the profusion of leadership talks, workshops, books, blogs, courses, and trainings have failed to improve the state of leadership. Bill Gentry, a researcher at the Center for Creative Leadership, has summarized numerous research studies conducted and published over decades. Gentry concluded that "one of every two leaders and managers" is "estimated to be ineffective (that is, a disappointment, incompetent, a mishire, or a complete failure) in their current roles."[27] In other words, this leadership expert, working from extensive research, concluded that 50 percent of leaders were failures. Yet another review of the research literature on leadership concluded that "the base rate for managerial incompetence in any organization is quite high,"[28] while still a different summary concluded that about half of the occupants of leadership positions are falling short.[29]

A McKinsey article noted that even though most executives identified leadership development as a high priority, "only 7 percent of senior managers polled by a U.K. business school think that their companies develop global leaders effectively, and around 30 percent of US companies admit that they have failed to exploit their international business opportunities fully because they lack enough leaders with the right capabilities."[30] An Accenture survey reported that only 8 percent of the executives felt their company was proficient in developing leaders, while a Corporate Leadership Council study found that "people management training improved productivity by only 2%."[31]

The Institute for Corporate Productivity's 2014 *Critical Human Capital Issues Survey* of some 1,367 respondents reported that even in the best, highest-performing companies, 66 percent of those companies reported that they were ineffective at developing leaders and that they were getting *worse* in this critical process. Not surprisingly, low-performing organizations were even more challenged, with 89 percent indicating that they were deficient in leadership development. The same study found that even in top companies, only 27 percent had successors ready to fill executive-level roles, as might be expected if companies are ineffective in developing leaders.[32]

A survey of more than fourteen thousand human resource professionals and line managers "found that only 26% of HR and 38% of leaders reported that the quality of leadership across their company was 'excellent' or 'very good.' Future prospects were even worse, with only 18% of HR and 32% of leaders reporting that their bench strength to meet future needs" was either strong or very strong.[33]

In 2012, the Center for Public Leadership at Harvard University's Kennedy School reported that 69 percent of Americans believed that America had a leadership crisis—with the only good news being that in the prior year, some 77 percent of those surveyed had said the same thing.[34] The Harris Poll reported that since 1996, "the percentage of people reporting at least *some* confidence in the leadership of government, corporations, and Wall Street has plummeted from around 90% to 60%."[35]

And why shouldn't respondents believe there is a leadership

crisis and report declining confidence in leaders when, among other indicators, organizational malfeasance is incredibly common? Donald Palmer, a professor at the University of California, Davis, wrote, "Organizational wrongdoing is prevalent. Ronald Clement tracked firms listed among the Fortune 100 in 1999 and found that 40 percent had engaged in misconduct significant enough to be reported in the national media between 2000 and 2005."[36] Yes, that's four out of ten of large firms engaging in significant wrongdoing in just five years; and note that this finding predates the economic meltdown and financial crisis that began in late 2007.

It's not just that others, such as researchers or the public at large, give organizational leaders low marks; the leaders themselves do, too. Development Dimensions International (DDI), a forty-year-old company in the business of consulting on the attraction, hiring, and retention of talent, published a white paper on leadership based on a survey the company conducted. The report noted, "In multiple studies, including DDI's 2011 Global Leadership Forecast, leaders are, by their own admission, falling short. . . . Over a period of many years, leaders have consistently given low marks to the quality of leadership in their organizations. . . . despite all of the effort and investment in leadership development—innovative new modalities, up-to-date content, business simulations, acceleration pools, 70/20/10 approaches, better diagnosis of strengths and areas for development— widespread improvement in leadership effectiveness remains elusive."[37] That is an understatement. DDI's survey of almost 1,300 people around the world found that more than one-third did not consider their own manager to be effective in his or her job. More than half of the respondents, some 55 percent, reported that they had considered leaving a job because of their leader, and 39 percent said they had done so.

WHY ALL THIS FAILURE?

When lots of well-intentioned effort expended over decades produces nothing except ever-worse workplaces and more frequent career flameouts of leaders, there must be an explanation. Actually, there are many ways of understanding why leadership doesn't seem to improve. Here are some of them, and we will explore others throughout this book.

Diverging Interests

One day at lunch, a thoughtful senior executive, knowing that I am writing a book about leadership and how bad things are in many workplaces, says, "All right, so tell me what to do to be a better leader." My reply: "Tell me what criterion you want to measure 'better leader' by. Performance? And if so, over what time period and using what metrics? Holding on to your job as a leader? Obtaining the highest-possible salary for yourself? Moving on to a more prestigious position in another company as quickly as possible? Increasing employee engagement and reducing turnover?" The simple but important point: the oft-observed divergence in interests between individual leaders and the organizations they lead means that any prescription of what someone should do has to begin by both acknowledging the trade-offs and sorting through that person's real priorities and the multiple, often poorly correlated measures of a leader's outcomes.

This divergence in the interests between corporate leaders and the groups in which they are members appears prominently in the growing literature on sociobiology, an evolutionary approach to understanding social behavior that speaks to the discrepancy between what's good for individuals and the groups in which they are members. Individuals maximize their own survival chances by acting selfishly to acquire, at all costs, the resources necessary for their survival. Group survival, however, often depends on individuals sacrificing their own well-being for that of the group, such as soldiers' throwing themselves on hand grenades to save their colleagues' lives, or parents forgoing food so their children can live. As one article in this theoretical tradition noted, "The problem is that for a social group to function as an adaptive unit, its members must do things for each other. Yet, these group-advantageous behaviors seldom maximize relative fitness [for a given individual] within the social group."[38]

Social psychologists also have long acknowledged the inherent tension between the need for leaders to help groups function effectively, and the personal interests of group leaders to maximize the power differences they enjoy over others and hold on to and exploit for their own benefits.[39] Leaders frequently focus, hopes and blandishments notwithstanding, primarily on their own careers and what's good for them. Consider the following example:

When the technology entrepreneur Dick Costolo was recruited from Google to come to Twitter as chief operating officer, his first tweet as he prepared for his first day at his new job was: "First full day as Twitter COO tomorrow. Task #1: undermine the CEO, consolidate power." Note that he didn't say, "First full day, figure out what to do to make the company more successful." That tweet, written on September 13, 2009, was taken by some as a joke, and maybe even intended that way. But the tweet was nothing if not prescient. In October 2010, barely thirteen months later, Costolo did take over as CEO from the then-CEO Evan Williams, a cofounder of the company. While Williams was gracious, issuing a statement saying, in part, "I am most satisfied while pushing product direction. Building things is my passion. . . . Starting today, I'll be completely focused on product strategy," few founders give up power voluntarily, and there is no evidence that Williams, who was soon gone from Twitter, was the rare exception.[40]

Was Costolo's ascension to power, and for that matter the comings and goings of another company cofounder, Jack Dorsey, good for Twitter? Who knows? Twitter's stock price has been stagnant. But there are many factors that might account for the company's struggles and ongoing management shakeups, such as the 2014 resignation of its chief operating officer.[41]

Contrary to what many people seem to believe—and, moreover, one of the core foundations of much leadership thought—there is far from a complete correspondence between what is good for a company, or for that matter, a unit within that company, and what is good for the company's or unit's leader. In case you have been asleep during the last decade, plenty of CEOs and board members took their companies over a cliff even as those same CEOs left with enormous severance packages, and board members mostly kept their board seats and even obtained new ones.

The distinction between group and individual interests becomes evident in what the numerous studies and the inspiring leadership stories invariably focus on—mostly if not exclusively some measure of group or organizational performance, or the satisfaction and engagement of the people in the work unit. Leadership stories and much leadership research seldom explore the leader's qualities, behaviors, and characteristics that affect the well-being of the leader, rather than the organization. Leader well-being includes outcomes such as job tenure, salary, and getting into a leadership role in the first place. This neglect of what's good for the individual interests of leaders might be one reason so many recommendations have so little traction in the real world: while leadership research may not be that interested in leader (as opposed to group or organizational) well-being, leaders almost always are.

Little Measurement of the Base Rate of Desirable
Leader Behaviors

A second problem with the numerous recommendations about what leaders should do is that too many of them emphasize the causal relationships between various leader behaviors and work-unit outcomes, but show remarkably little concern with base rates, that is, the extent to which desirable, effective leader behaviors *actually* occur in the world and, furthermore, if they are as rare as they seem to be in spite of being widely recommended, *why*, and what to do about it. Here's an analogy to help you understand why this distinction between prescriptions and actual implementation is important:

In 1847, Dr. Ignaz Semmelweis, a Hungarian physician, noticed something interesting. Mothers who delivered their babies in a Viennese maternity hospital died at a rate many times that of mothers who delivered their babies at home. Semmelweis came to the conclusion that the problem occurred because physicians went from one woman to the next without taking any sanitary precautions such as washing their hands, thereby spreading infection. After he introduced hand washing with a chlorine solution, mortality fell from an average of 10 percent to about 1.5 percent. Semmelweis was ostracized and ultimately fired for pushing people to implement the results of his discovery. But once Louis Pasteur developed the germ theory of disease, the idea that sanitary practices were important in health care became generally accepted.[42]

So far, so good. But, as much systematic evidence demonstrates, hundreds of years after the development of the germ theory of disease and its implications, sanitary practices in hospitals and doctors' offices remain woefully deficient. A Center for Disease Control report noted that studies of adherence to hand-washing guidelines in health care settings averaged just 40 percent.[43] After giving a tour of the Minneapolis Heart Institute to a group of directors from a medical device company, Dr. Robert Hauser, a noted cardiologist, asked the group to guess which of the things they had seen during the tour, which had included some amazingly advanced equipment, had made the most difference in patient outcomes. The answer: the signs posted on plain sheets of paper outside each room that said in large, bold letters, "Wash Your Hands."

Note the medical profession's response to this fact of the divergence between what is known about how better sanitary practices improve health outcomes and the incomplete implementation of that knowledge. In the first place, there are not many additional studies to demonstrate the well-established causal relationship between sanitary practices and disease—no point reiterating what people already know. Nor do health care organizations assume that, since everyone knows these facts, good practices must be automatically occurring, so measuring the frequency with which they are implemented is unimportant. And there aren't lots of inspirational TED talks, blogs, or speeches about doctors who wash their hands.

Instead, health care policy makers and organizations do two important things: First, many sites where medical care is delivered now measure the extent of adherence to good sanitary practices, thereby establishing a base rate so that improvement can be tracked over time as different interventions are implemented. And second, the medical profession and other scholars study interventions that increase the rate of hand washing and the implementation of other germ-prevention strategies as they seek to understand why good practices do not get used.

Compare this example with the leadership industry, with its inattention to assessing the implementation of its recommendations and to understanding why so little has changed. The leadership industry is so obsessively focused on the normative—what leaders *should* do and how things *ought* to be—that it has largely ignored asking the fundamental question of what actually is true and going on and why. Unless and until leaders are measured for what they really do and for actual workplace conditions, and until these leaders are held accountable for improving both their own behavior and, as a consequence, workplace outcomes, nothing will change.

No Credentials, Experience, or Even Knowledge Required

Numerous other problems help account for why there has been so little positive change in workplaces or careers. Here's one of the more important: There are no "barriers to entry" into the leadership industry; no credentials, rigorous research, knowledge of the relevant scientific evidence, or anything else required to pass oneself off as a leadership expert. Anyone and everyone can write a book, be a leadership speaker or a blogger, offer consulting and advice, or start a leadership-development or consulting firm. And there are days when it seems that virtually everyone does.

Rich Moran, a former senior partner at Accenture and now the president of Menlo College, has commented that many of the people offering leadership advice have (a) either never held a leadership position, or (b) if they have, were notoriously unsuccessful in their leadership role, or (c) often promulgated leadership prescriptions almost completely inconsistent with their own behavior. In a similar vein, Robert Gandossy, formerly a very senior executive at the human resources consulting firm Hewitt who ran their Top Companies for Leaders research and ranking, noted that many of the people offering leadership coaching and advice were formerly compensation consultants. As he said, "There's nothing wrong with compensation consulting, but I don't see how providing advice on pay systems necessarily makes someone an expert on either leadership or leadership development."

But it's even worse. Not only do many of the leadership industry's participants have no particular qualifications or training germane to their activities, but many also seem to possess little of the interest or intellectual curiosity that would cause them to do the work required to read and learn so as to build their expertise.

And as near as I can tell, there is not much of a connection between actually knowing something about leadership and being successful as a leadership guru. To take only one of countless examples that come to mind, one group seeking a leadership speaker for a conference told me they hired a particular speaker because, according to an inside source on the hiring committee, he was good-looking. This tale is completely consistent with the view that much of leadership education, even in academic classrooms, let alone inside companies and at those omnipresent conferences and conventions, reflects the fact that the goal is as much about delivering entertainment ("edu-tainment," as one experienced consultant called it) as it is helping leaders or remediating workplace problems.

Conceptual Imprecision

A related problem is that in part because of the backgrounds and qualifications, or lack thereof, of some practitioners, and also in part because of the normative focus and wishful thinking in general, conceptual confusion and imprecision abound in the leadership industry. The imprecision results in recommendations that are often incorrect and also so ambiguous as not to be implementable.

Consider the idea of charismatic or transformational leadership. Charisma seems to be a desirable trait. Charismatic political candidates such as Rick Perry of Texas, former president John Kennedy, and, of course, Barack Obama, have big advantages over less charismatic opponents. The early and enduring success of companies such as Southwest Airlines and Apple is frequently attributed to the charisma of their CEOs, Herb Kelleher and Steve Jobs respectively. Charismatic leadership is often argued to be a particularly effective form of leadership because it engages others' emotions and deepens their connections to both the leader and the organization.[44] Some studies show that charismatic leadership has profound transformational effects on followers. Followers of charismatic leadership display greater reverence, trust, and satisfaction with their leaders as well as a heightened sense of collective identification with their group.[45]

However, as nicely demonstrated in a devastating critique by Daan van Knippenberg and Sim Sitkin, two organizational behavior scholars, the study of charismatic leadership lacks a precise definition of the term and also an understanding of the psychological and behavioral mechanisms that presumably produce results from charisma. They go on to note that much of the research on charismatic leadership suffers a great deal of confusion between causes and their effects; they also note that there is a great deal of invalid measurement of the concept of charismatic leadership.[46] One cannot build a science this way, and, more important, it is impossible to develop valid recommendations that leaders can implement given the sloppy thinking about leadership that is so much in vogue.

FIXING THESE PROBLEMS

There are some ways for the leadership industry and its practitioners to improve their performance. These recommendations follow quite directly from the problems enumerated in this chapter.

Measure and Hold People Accountable for
Workplace Outcomes

One of the core principles coming out of the quality movement is that what gets inspected gets affected. Measurement focuses attention and, if nothing else, makes problems salient. The measurement of leadership improvement activities is pathetic. Much of this effort is simply not evaluated at all, as the HR consultant Robert Gandossy argues, and that includes a number of corporate- and university-sponsored leadership-development programs, executive coaching, and, except quite informally, the various books, blogs, and conferences that continue to proliferate.

To the extent there are evaluative measures, some of these merely ask about the amount of activity—the number of sessions, speakers, events, hours of training, number of attendees, and so forth, in other words, the resources expended or consumed on leadership training and development, not whether anything happened as a consequence. Or, in the case of books or speakers, measures of sales figures and revenues are examined, under the assumption that the market is good at separating the wheat from the chaff. We know this is not the case, as decades of leadership writing and speaking have produced no discernible betterment in either workplaces or leaders and their careers.

And then there are those ubiquitous "happy sheets" that people fill out to report on whether or not they enjoyed their experience at some conference, training session, or other event, or the reviews and recommendations that assess whether people liked some book or blog. As the Institute for Corporate Productivity noted in a report on global leadership development (GLD), in 2012 the number one way of assessing leadership programs was participants' self-reported satisfaction, which the document appropriately referred to as "smiley-face" indicators of success.[47]

This should not be a surprise. Self-reported satisfaction with the experience is how most universities and conferences evaluate their activities. Indeed, students' evaluation of teaching is incredibly common, with more than 99 percent of all business schools using student evaluations in some form. However, a recent review of the evidence concluded that there is a very small and statistically insignificant relationship between student evaluations and learning, and that "the more objectively learning is measured, the less likely it is to be related to the evaluations."[48] Another review also concluded that "teacher ratings and learning are not closely related" for many reasons that ought to give pause to anyone relying on such evaluations, including in cases of adult development.[49] As J. Scott Armstrong of the University of Pennsylvania noted, "Learning implies change, and this can be a trying experience, especially if it involves important attitudes and behavior."[50] Because leadership development almost certainly involves engaging with important attitudes and behaviors if it is to be successful, a large body of empirical research conducted over decades suggests that student evaluations are more than unhelpful; instead, they are likely to change the behaviors of presenters in ways that make learning and personal growth less likely. That is one reason why Armstrong concluded that "teacher ratings are detrimental to students."[51]

In 2013, participants' self-reported happiness with their leadership-development experience was still ranked second in importance as a criterion of the experience's success. The Institute for Corporate Productivity's report noted that observable changes in the specific behaviors of participants had moved up in importance in evaluating GLD efforts. But engagement scores of the leaders' direct reports or department ranked just sixth in importance and were used by only 36 percent of the companies responding to the survey.[52]

No wonder workplaces remain in such a bad state. Instead of evaluating the books, blogs, talks, events, and all the similar sorts of activities on whether they actually improve workplace functioning and well-being, most evaluations focus on whether those exposed to the various products of the leadership industry— the leadership industry's "consumers" if you will—like them, and whether they are having a good time and are feeling good. When three McKinsey consultants sought to understand why leadership-development programs failed, one of the four causes they uncovered was the failure to measure results. They noted that companies paid only lip service to developing leadership skills and did not invest in measurement to track actual changes. They commented, "Too often, any evaluation of leadership development begins and ends with participant feedback."[53]

But it's even worse. Measuring the wrong thing is often worse than measuring nothing, because you do get what you measure. So if the assessments focus on how much people "enjoy" the experience—be that reading a book, watching a talk, or going to a training session—those same books, talks, and trainings will respond to those measurements by prioritizing the wrong outcomes: making participants feel good and giving them a good time. Simply stated, measuring entertainment value produces great entertainment, not change; measuring the wrong things crowds out assessing other, more relevant indicators such as improvements in workplaces. Improvement comes from employing measurements that are appropriate, those that are connected to the areas in which we seek improvement. In the case of leadership, that appropriate measurement would include assessing the frequency of desirable leader behaviors; actual workplace conditions such as engagement, satisfaction, and trust in leadership; and leaders' careers— measures that are notable by their absence not only in use but even from much of the discussion of leadership-development activity.

Not only is the leadership industry unaccountable for the condition of workplaces, leaders aren't either, at least in many places. Years ago, when Hewlett-Packard had a positive and strong organizational culture and senior leadership cared about that culture, people were held accountable for the results of anonymous employee surveys conducted throughout the company and reported on a work-unit basis. Some individuals lost promotion opportunities because even though their financial results were good, their survey results, which assessed employees' engagement and trust in them as a leader, were not.

There are still companies like DaVita, a kidney dialysis provider, that measure adherence to values, and that care about those results. At DaVita, people actually get fired for behavior that is counter to the company's culture and inconsistent with its focus on the importance of dialysis centers and the people who work in them. There are places like the privately owned software company SAS Institute, where the cofounder and CEO Jim Goodnight evaluates managers by their ability to attract and retain talent, and where people can lose their jobs if their units experience excessive voluntary turnover. But this commitment to workplace culture is the exception rather than the rule. Certainly there is lots of talk about the importance of culture and people, but there are not many actions consistent with such talk. More typical are the stories I hear all the time about companies in which the senior leadership, not liking the results of employee surveys measuring engagement or trust or satisfaction, simply decides to stop doing them. After all, as one CEO reportedly said, "If we're not going to change things, why raise people's expectations by asking them their opinions about aspects of the work culture that we really don't care about."

Measuring results, measuring leader behaviors, and assessing whether or not prescriptions get implemented would go a long way to both highlighting and then altering the current sad state of affairs in most workplaces. Without baseline measurements of leader and workplace conditions, it is simply impossible to understand what to do to make improvements.

Acknowledge the Different Interests of Leaders and Their Companies

This step requires expanding evaluations and measurement to incorporate not just unit performance and even customer or employee satisfaction but also what happens to leaders' careers, including their jobs, their salaries, and their career progress. And when we see, as we will frequently throughout this book, the different effects of a leader's traits or behaviors on a company's performance versus his or her own success, we will see the need to understand *why* there is the divergence in interests and how to make things work better for both sides.

Use More-Scientific Methods and Worry about Credentials

When medicine began its quest to become an evidence-based science, with a concomitant improvement in treatment outcomes and the rate of medical progress, the medical profession worked—and still works—assiduously to promulgate professional standards of practice. Such standards include prioritizing systematic evidence over stories or examples, basing practice to the greatest extent possible on the best evidence, and, most important, seeking to ensure that practitioners are knowledgeable and have at least some requirement to keep up with the progress of medical science. That's why medical schools were founded in the first place and why people seeking to practice medicine must pass some licensing requirements and engage in continuing education in order to ply their trade.

It is hard to believe that because someone happened, in a particular instance, to perform some effective medical treatment, that that individual would then go all over the world telling people how to practice medicine absent any formal training. But precisely that happens all the time in the case of leadership, where unsubstantiated accounts of heroic acts of leadership seemingly qualify people to instruct others in how to be a leader.

This is not to say that there aren't numerous well-trained and highly experienced people doing leadership research and education—of course there are. But as noted already, the field has no barriers to entry and the relationship between scientific rigor and success in the leadership industry is somewhere between small and negative.

We have seen in this chapter that the leadership industry presumes that if people follow all its feel-good prescriptions, unit performance and employee morale will be higher and that leaders, in turn, will be more successful. But neither of these premises is correct. Sometimes—not always, but some of the time—doing precisely the opposite of what the leadership industry prescribes produces better outcomes. What's more, doing the opposite of what the leadership industry advocates is sometimes a much better, more reliable path to *individual* success. There are, in this domain as in many others, trade-offs, and the frequently unacknowledged trade-off between what is good for the individual and good for the group needs to be front and center in understanding why there is so much leadership failure over such a long time.

Before taking on some of the most prominent prescriptions and showing how they do not describe many leaders and that they often don't work, one other issue must be addressed: how the lay preaching, storytelling, inspirational, and aspirational character so common in leadership makes things worse in numerous ways. That is the topic of the next chapter.

CHAPTER 1

Why Inspiration and Fables Cause Problems and Fix Nothing

May 2013, and I am at the closing dinner for an executive program in Barcelona, Spain. As with other such programs, I have taught material on power in organizations—mastering organizational dynamics. The topic of power remains, unfortunately, much as the Harvard Business School professor Rosabeth Moss Kanter described it more than thirty years ago, the organization's last dirty secret—something that nice people don't talk about, let alone teach to executives.[1] And my approach, describing organizational reality as it *is* rather than as we wish it to be, can be particularly challenging. As *Publishers Weekly* commented on a book I wrote on power (a description that also applies to my classes), "The book has a realpolitik analysis of human behavior that isn't for everyone but its candor . . . and forthrightness are fresh and appealing."[2]

A participant, who over the course of the evening has had too much to drink, decides to come over to the table where I am sitting. His inhibitions sufficiently lowered, he begins to berate me for the material I have taught, but mostly to complain about what I have failed to do. "I want to be inspired," he says. "Sure, I understand you have taught us what the research literature says and how to navigate organizational reality, but I came to this program for inspiration. It is the job of teachers to inspire their students." My reply: "If you want inspiration, go to a play, read an inspiring book, listen to great music, go to an art museum, or read some of the great treatises on religion or philosophy. I am a social scientist, not a lay preacher." "No," he insists, "it is your job, as a teacher of management, to inspire me." Or, as a former MBA student put it slightly differently when we had dinner, "I have a soul-crushing job. I need hope."

As the data reviewed in the last chapter demonstrate, many people have soul-crushing jobs and work for ineffective or even abusive leaders, and they apparently think the job of business schools and professors is to provide inspiration and hope. So many leadership players provide what the "customers" want. For instance, if you go to the website of the Belgium-based Vlerick Business School, there, on the very first page, is the headline "Looking for an Inspiring Management Course?"[3] Vlerick isn't alone. The Australian Graduate School of Management, part of the University of New South Wales in Sydney, also highlights on its website the fact that "we create inspirational learning opportunities."[4] "Inspiring" (or "inspirational") seems like an unusual and possibly surprising adjective to describe a class or a program of study. I don't see many medical schools, architecture programs, physics departments, engineering schools, law schools, or computer science departments advertising their classes as "inspiring." Useful, rigorous, well-delivered, innovative, scientifically based courses and programs that provide a foundation of knowledge for effective professional practice—certainly. But "inspiring?" Probably not.

If you are a leader seeking to actually change a workplace's conditions so as to improve employee engagement, satisfaction, or productivity, or if you are an individual seeking to chart a course to a more successful career, inspiration is not what you need. What you need are facts, evidence, and ideas. Cheering may be helpful at sporting events, but not so much in the nitty-gritty job of fixing workplaces and careers. This chapter lays out the many reasons why inspiration is not only a poor basis from which to attempt serious organizational change but also useless for figuring out how to have more personal success inside work organizations.

My view about inspiration is clearly in the minority. Inspiration of the sort that participant in the executive education course was seeking is precisely what the leadership industry mostly delivers—providing good feelings if not always enlightenment, entertainment if not invariably education, and, most important, (at least to the consumers thereof), hope rather than despair. And why not? Real life is difficult and depressing enough. Who wants to attend an executive program or hear a speech or read a blog post and not feel happier and more enthused as a result? So the leadership industry delivers what the customers want. Whether it is what they *need* is an entirely different matter.

MYTHS AND FABLES, AND WHY INACCURACY IS INEVITABLE

To build a science of leadership, you need reliable data. To learn from others' success, you need to know what those others did. The best learning, simply put, comes from accurate and comprehensive data, either qualitative or quantitative. But the leadership business is filled with fables. In autobiographical or semiauto-biographical works and speeches, in the cases and authorized biographies leaders help bring into existence, and in their prescriptions for leadership, leaders describe what they want to believe about themselves and the world and, more importantly and strategically, what they would like others to believe about them. The stories leaders tell or have others tell about themselves on their behalf are primarily designed to create an attractive legacy. Sometimes such accounts are, to put it delicately, incomplete. Because these tales are designed to build an image and a reputation, they do not constitute qualitative data from which to learn. In fact, they aren't data at all, any more than advertising is data or evidence. There are many examples of this phenomenon. Here are some.

Some years ago, the former Medtronic CEO and now Harvard Business School professor Bill George wrote *True North* with the former Stanford MBA student and now consultant and speaker Peter Sims.[5] This bestselling book, like many in the genre, advocated the importance of authenticity as a leadership trait. At the time the book came out, I was serving on the board of directors of a publicly traded company with someone who had been quite senior in the financial function at Medtronic. When I commented to this individual on the publication and success of *True North*, fully expecting to hear how its principles were reflected at Medtronic, the person replied that the Bill George and the prescriptions in the book and the Bill George who had worked his way up the corporate hierarchy and then ran Medtronic were not quite the same.

Another person with long experience in the pharmaceutical industry, an individual who knows Medtronic and Bill George well, commented that the principles laid out in *True North* probably held more for the culture built by George's predecessors than for George himself. And then he made another insightful statement: "Bill George today [as a Harvard faculty member teaching leadership] is probably closer to the principles in the book than he was while he was at Medtronic. The ideas in *True North* are undoubtedly closer to what he currently believes than to the behavior he engaged in while he was there."

This example is not meant to criticize Bill George, who is a sincere and talented individual genuinely interested in making the world a better place and improving leadership. He is scarcely the only leadership-industry figure who has described a more aspirational than veridical version of himself and the company he led.

You can read Jack Welch's books about General Electric and his management approach and never encounter the phrase "GE jerks." Yet that is a term I first heard from a now-retired GE senior executive who reported directly to Mr. Welch. He used it to describe the kind of workers GE's hard-driving culture created with its politics, competition, and forced-curve ranking. The phrase and that description of GE were shared by this former executive's wife, someone who had worked in GE in a very senior role in human resources for many years. And it is an observation I have heard frequently from others who worked at General Electric. Nor do Welch's writings about his management approach and accomplishments dwell on (or even mention) the pollution clean-up suits, price-fixing, or defense contract frauds that occurred at GE during his tenure.[6]

Motivated cognition is one factor that explains the unreliability of the stories we read. Not surprisingly, people are motivated to think well of themselves. Therefore, not only do individuals perceive themselves to be above average for most positive attributes and believe that the qualities in which they excel are the most important—the so-called above-average effect[7]—but individuals will also selectively remember their successes and forget their failures or shortcomings. In general, leaders want to remember their accomplishments and not remember some of their most negative behaviors, let alone disclose such things even if they did remember them—so they don't.

But it's worse than that. Even in the absence of motivational reasons to misremember and misreport, people invariably recall past events with considerable error, even if they try to be as honest and accurate as possible. The large literature concerning the unreliability of eyewitness accounts of accidents or crimes attests to the fact that even when people want to recall and report things accurately and have no incentive to do otherwise, memory plays tricks and makes recall frequently unreliable.[8]

Moreover, for the leaders who talk or write or blog about their leadership experience, the problem becomes even more pernicious. In telling their stories, leaders create and re-create their own reality so often that soon it becomes almost impossible for them to distinguish the actual truth from what they recall as being true, even if they wanted to do so. As the writer Ben Dolnick perceptively commented:

> William Maxwell wrote, "In talking about the past we lie with every breath we draw." I misunderstood this sentence, when I first read it, as a statement about the fallibility of memory; now I see it as a statement about the distorting power of speech—or of speech's pretentious cousin, writing. Because one of the strangest things I've learned . . . is how the things you write begin to blend with, and then replace, the things you experienced.[9]

And there is another potential process that works to make the leadership stories told by leaders unreliable. An extensive research literature in evolutionary psychology speaks to the advantages—and therefore the pervasiveness—of self-deception. The evolutionary benefit of self-deception is clear: if you can deceive yourself, you can much more easily and convincingly deceive others, and thereby obtain the benefits that accrue from being able to successfully fool people. Summarizing this research and these theories, Robert Trivers, an anthropologist at Rutgers University, and William von Hippel, a psychologist, noted, "Our biased processing perspective suggests that the individual can self-deceive in a variety of ways, some of which prevent even unconscious knowledge of the truth."[10]

What this means is that the stories one hears from leaders (or, for that matter, from anyone) may be untrue but not known to be untrue by the person telling the tales, because that person has so successfully deceived him- or herself. Between motivation to self-present and the unconscious ways in which people misremember and self-deceive, believing the accounts of leaders or anyone else without a lot of fact-checking would seem to be singularly unwise.

In spite of these cognitive biases, we nevertheless accept and indeed embrace the fables about leaders and leadership because the stories are so consistent with what most people would *like* to believe about the world. Many of the stories are consistent with the just-world phenomenon—a social science idea that, to paraphrase a wonderful line from the movie *The Best Exotic Marigold Hotel*, things will be all right in the end, and if they aren't all right, it's not yet the end.[11] Many of the stories offer morals that fit what we want to believe, and many offer hope. We often engage in astonishingly little due diligence to assess the accuracy of what we hear.

The problem isn't the storytelling per se. Indeed, as Chip and Dan Heath remind us, stories are often much more memorable and persuasive than cold statistics.[12] The problem is that the leadership stories are often exaggerated or fabricated out of whole cloth, and their listeners don't bother to do any fact-checking.

If the morals and the heroic nature of leadership stories remind you of myths, as they should, they might also remind you of many aspects of religion. For good reason: just as religion seeks to provide believers a sense of personal control, a belief in the fairness of the world, and a feeling of meaning and purpose, so, too, do the leadership myths and fables passed off as truth, often using remarkably similar means. That's why I refer to these activities as a form of lay preaching.

In his essay about religion, Sigmund Freud commented on religion's functions in ways that nicely parallel how and why the myths of leadership are created and persist whether or not they are true:

> These [religious ideas] . . . are not the residue of experience or the final results of reflection; they are illusions, fulfilments of the oldest, strongest and most insistent wishes of mankind; the secret of their strength is the strength of these wishes. We know already that the terrifying effect of . . . helplessness aroused the need for protection. . . . Thus the benevolent rule of divine providence [or a benevolent leader] allays our anxiety in face of life's dangers, the establishment of a moral world order ensures the fulfilment of the demands of justice, which within human culture have so often remained unfulfilled.[13]

But believing in the myths and stories about leadership and leaders has few positive consequences and lots of negative results. Understanding these costly consequences can help us understand why and how so much of what goes on in the omnipresent feel-good talks, books, and blogs makes things worse—in many cases much worse—for both workplaces and the people who lead them.

ONE CONSEQUENCE: CYNICISM

Does it really matter if leaders and others who tell their stories burnish the truth? Actually it does, in several ways and for a variety of reasons. First of all, as already noted, inaccurate accounts of leader behavior constitute a poor foundation from which to offer advice. And there are other problems as well.

At a cocktail party, someone who knows many leadership teachers quite well, an entrepreneur and a former business case writer, pulls me aside to relate instance after instance in which one particular individual, an experienced senior executive who also teaches classes on leadership, has presented himself, his companies, and his interactions with peers and subordinates in ways that are demonstrably false. When I ask this entrepreneur the same question I just posed, "What difference does this make?" the reply is immediate. The entrepreneur, seeing the enormous discontinuity between the espoused behaviors and what this person actually does, is, first of all, deeply disappointed and upset. More than that, he argues that the all-too-frequent examples of people who profess one set of behaviors and act the opposite produce cynicism on the part of those who see the hypocrisy. His telling conclusion: In our quest for inspiration over insight, we wind up with neither. We get no inspiration, as we learn that the leadership stories are more fiction than fact. And we obtain no insight, because we do not gather the data on which to build an understanding of effective leadership.

And there is yet another adverse consequence. Confronted with a leadership industry that promulgates a set of prescriptions that many employees come to see in their daily lives as having little resonance with the reality they experience, people become tainted and cynical, not just about the leadership industry but about social science research and its conclusions more generally. After all, if you can't trust the leadership trainings, speeches, and books, many of which have garnered wide publicity and are featured on major television talk shows and in the media, why should you trust any other material delivered in similar formats to similar acclaim, even if that material covers different topics? Such distrust of what passes for social science in the study of leadership contaminates people's reactions to other social science research, thereby making it all the more difficult to build evidence-based management practice.[14]

A SECOND CONSEQUENCE: PEOPLE LOSE THEIR JOBS—OR JOB OPPORTUNITIES

A woman who works in one of those iconic Silicon Valley companies sits in my office, telling me about the behaviors of three people: a peer, her boss, and the head of human resources for the company. She has run a marketing analytics exercise that has resulted in making the company about $4 million. Because of her success and, more important, because of her background and skill level, she has been promoted to head her own marketing analytics team, a position that leaves her as the youngest, least-senior leader in terms of company tenure, and as the only woman directly reporting to her boss. A peer has gone to their mutual boss and suggested that her unit be moved under him—a smart way for him to not only expand his domain but also get more talent working in his unit so the unit's performance will appear better in the future.

"What was your response to all of this?" I ask. Her reply: to use her learning and ideas from a leadership course on interpersonal dynamics, colloquially referred to as "touchy-feely," to attempt to repair the relationship with her peer. "Why did you do that?" I inquire. "Because," she responds, "I have been taught to build relationships of authenticity and trust at work." When I ask how her efforts went, she comments that of course they didn't work at all, because her peer was not interested in "repairing a relationship" or behaving with trust and authenticity; he was interested in taking over her team for his own advantage—a not-uncommon situation.

When she went to her boss and later to the head of HR to explain what was going on, in each instance reminding them about how her colleague's behavior was inconsistent with the company's espoused values and with its many leadership-development activities, their response was to do nothing except to sensibly remind her that she needed to become able to effectively look after herself (a theme to which we will return in chapter 7). Today that woman works for another organization in a different part of the country.

People not only have problems in their current positions, but they also lose out on attractive job opportunities by believing in the prescriptions so frequently proffered for how leaders should behave. Another example: A South American executive (let's call him Martin) was the CEO of a health care organization until he was forced out of his position by the company's founder and some private equity investors. One complaint about him, even though he was extremely talented and intelligent—he had graduated from a leading U.S. business school—was that he was perceived as not being forceful enough. I had coached him to negotiate an exit that left his reputation intact, and he had subsequently moved on to run the country operations of a very large pharmaceutical company.

Now the company he had once run was being bought by a very rich health care leader, but, because that person was in his seventies, he would need someone to run the firm on a day-to-day basis. Could it be Martin? Not likely. At a dinner with a person who for years has overseen a large purveyor of management training events and who knows the situation well, I asked about Martin's prospects. His immediate reply: the new owner had no respect for Martin, because he "isn't a leader."

When I pressed this person on what that meant, his reply didn't address Martin's culture-building or business-analysis skills, or his trustworthiness and authenticity, which, everyone agreed, Martin had in profusion. Instead, he spoke of Martin's failures to show anger, be forceful, and advocate for himself. These comments seemed particularly surprising because they came from someone who runs seminars filled with speakers who advocate precisely the strengths that Martin has, and someone who would never, because of the audience's response, have presenters on stage to advocate the opposite. Nonetheless, he agreed with the new owner about Martin's unsuitability. What irony— someone who oversees large leadership seminars that feature people who promulgate one set of leader qualities and behaviors basing his evaluation and judgment of a possible executive on precisely the opposite set of qualities!

I know too many similar examples. People suffer career troubles because they believed what they were told in the books, blogs, and talks. One such person was told to build closer, more personal relationships with his subordinates, in a quest to build more authenticity into his leader-follower interactions. His reward? Some of his subordinates used the personal information he shared to undermine his reputation and his authority, not just in the unit he managed but also more widely within the company.

It is examples such as these, and the hundreds or thousands of others just like them that people encounter every day, that led the chief technology officer for a major media organization to provide the following shockingly direct advice to some students in my Paths to Power class in February 2014: "Go home and throw out the numerous leadership books—or better yet, give them to career competitors."

There is still another way in which all this mythmaking and storytelling creates career troubles: the leaders who are the progenitors and the subjects of these stories sometimes believe the veneration and adulation they have successfully garnered. In the belief that they are, as great leaders, "bulletproof," the leaders are insufficiently attentive—or paranoid—and sometimes lose their jobs as a result.

Case in point: George Zimmer, who in 1973 with about $7,000 founded the Men's Wearhouse, an off-price retailer of tailored men's clothing that more recently has expanded into the tuxedo rental and uniform businesses. In 2013, the company was doing about $2.5 billion in business with a market capitalization of $2 billion. Zimmer had filled the board of directors with people he knew and liked, had hired the senior executives and watched them grow with the company, and, most important, was the face of the company's ubiquitous television and radio advertising, well known for his signature line, "You're going to like the way you look. I guarantee it." In 2011, when Zimmer had reached his early sixties, he and the board promoted Doug Ewert, a longtime company employee, to be the CEO, as Zimmer stepped into the role of chairman of the board of directors. In June 2013, Zimmer was summarily fired. How could George Zimmer be thrown out of the company he founded, whose brand he personally embodied, by people he had himself hired and known for decades?

There are many answers to this question, and a lot of them revolve around the belief in the mythical qualities of leaders. When the company's stock price was depressed in 2012 and early 2013, the board was concerned about a hostile tender offer. As Zimmer explained to me, he had told the board that because of the personal nature of the company's brand and its connection with its customers, embodied in him, and because of the strong, people-centered culture that was an important component of the company's original success, also embodied in him, and his strong, emotional connection to the company's fifteen thousand employees, he did not think anyone would or could mount an unfriendly bid for the company. Of course, the more Zimmer believed this, the even more inconceivable it would be for the company itself to get rid of him.

One of the elements of the company's culture when Zimmer was the CEO was a compressed pay distribution between the executives and the frontline employees. One of the first things Ewert did when he became CEO was to raise the CEO's pay significantly. And there were disagreements with Zimmer over the fate of K&G, a small chain of stores with an even lower price point that was not as profitable as the core brand.

Zimmer had ceded formal control of the company, but he was reluctant to just accept decisions with which he strongly disagreed. And in part because he had hired and brought the senior leadership onto the board, he was less deferential and at times could even be rude (or just bluntly direct) with those who disagreed with him. If you are a mythical, heroic, larger-than-life figure used to getting your way, rules and social conventions and corporate governance tenets don't apply. In the showdown in which he was fired, George Zimmer was completely surprised when his opposition mobilized in secret, got others on board with their sense of momentum, and presented Zimmer with a fait accompli.

There is yet another problem with the mythmaking besides the disinhibition and overconfidence that come from having power and having held it for a long time that can cost leaders their jobs. Mythical, heroic leaders become vulnerable to losing their jobs because after a while, regardless of their business skills and leadership capabilities, they find it impossible to live up to the hype, as it would be for anyone. With great expectations and high hopes come, naturally enough, great disappointments.

When Carol Bartz, the former CEO of Autodesk, replaced Yahoo's cofounder Jerry Yang as CEO in 2009, she came into a company that was going nowhere and struggling to define itself. She arrived surrounded by great expectations. "Her hiring was initially met with optimism by Wall Street, which saw her as a tough-talking savior who could whip the company into shape."[15] Some two years later, without even having a successor in mind, the board fired her—by phone. Under pressure from the first day on the job and hired as a savior, Bartz was doomed unless she had managed to perform a turnaround miracle that her successors had also failed to accomplish.

A THIRD CONSEQUENCE: UNREALISTIC EXPECTATIONS FOR OURSELVES

The leadership stories we tell, and the mythology of superperformance they create, produce other problems also. As we build up leaders to be larger-than-life, three things happen, all of which are harmful: (1) people invariably see themselves as not measuring up to these mythical leadership figures and therefore either don't try or excuse themselves from seeking to do things because of their perceived deficiencies compared with these heroic figures; (2) individuals are reluctant to accept, let alone seek out, stories of failure or imperfection among the leaders who have come to be venerated, a lack of due diligence that produces an inability to see, let alone learn, from failure and setbacks; (3) in setting up people who are admittedly rare and unusual as exemplars, the leadership business falls into the problem of trying to learn from rare and in many instances random events, thus failing to develop recommendations that can be readily implemented by regular people and generate predictable results. Consider each of these problems in turn:

On the first point, humanizing leaders and acknowledging their imperfections can go a long way toward getting all people to acknowledge that even if they are fallible and imperfect, so were some of the most interesting and productive people in history; therefore, there is no reason for "ordinary" people not to try to accomplish great things. In this regard, Michael Dyson, an author and teacher, uses the example of the infidelities of Martin Luther King Jr. to illustrate the importance of not mythologizing leaders. After detailing the many ways in which King has been put on a pedestal, Dyson notes that after King's womanizing became known, "I felt for the first time I was able to grasp what King accomplished in its true proportions. . . . Investing in King's perfection allows us to dismiss the humanity of the underregarded. . . . With a more nuanced view of King in play, we should be inspired to create social change within our own communities, armed with the belief that good things can be done by imperfect people."[16]

Nelson Mandela, sometimes called the father of modern South Africa, was also venerated almost as a saint, particularly toward the end of his life. While Mandela is someone to be admired and was an individual who accomplished a great deal, the mythmaking in many respects derogates his actual achievements. Mandela was a pragmatic politician who, as Pierre de Vos noted, was "among the most transformative of his era, but still a politician."

Nelson Mandela was not a saint. We would dishonor his memory if we treated him as if he was one. Like all truly exceptional human beings, he was a person of flesh and blood, with his own idiosyncrasies, his own blind spots and weaknesses.[17]

People's desire to see and hear only good things, to ignore contradictory or negative evidence, and thereby build portrayals of leaders on incomplete information, is at once understandable but also unfortunate. A second problem that arises: In the desire to learn only from success, people miss the opportunity to learn from failure, which is often a more promising and interesting teacher. The admonition to "learn from failure" is common and well known but mostly ignored.[18] Amy Edmondson, a professor at Harvard Business School who has extensively studied health care settings, has argued that "healthcare organisations that systematically and effectively learn from the failures that occur in the care delivery process . . . are rare"; she has maintained that this creates significant obstacles to improving the results produced by these systems.[19] Two management professors have noted that "failures may lead to ultimate success in both nature and business. Just as dynamic ecosystems depend on death to replace senescent organisms with vigorous growth, the termination of uneconomic activities is essential to wealth creation."[20]

And the third problem: Amid all the mythologizing that besets leadership, people try to generalize and learn from exceptional cases. Holding aside the fact that such cases don't hold up too well on closer inspection in many instances, learning from rare events is a singularly problematic endeavor. Research by Jerker Denrell, a professor at Warwick business school, shows that in many instances the relationship between skill and observed performance is surprisingly weak. That is because of the effects of luck and other random variations on observed outcomes, among other things.[21] Denrell argues that in many circumstances, people who perform well but are not at the very, very top are actually better people to learn from. That is because their performance is more likely to be a result of their true abilities and actions instead of chance events, and therefore such individuals offer more reliable and valid examples from which to draw conclusions about how to become successful.

INSPIRATION DOES NOT PRODUCE CHANGE

Even leaving aside the empirical accuracy, logical rigor, and usefulness of the leadership stories we tell and so uncritically accept, I have a more pragmatic concern with all of this inspiration-seeking: whether such inspirational storytelling is an effective way to produce change. It is not.

Of course, precisely *because* inspiration does not work very well to produce tangible change, one can make a good living doing it again and again.

We know a lot about how to change behaviors, and inspiration is not high on the list of effective strategies for doing so, for several reasons. First, inspiration works to increase the motivation to do something with more intensity or differently. But the motivational effect is likely to last only briefly, when the emotional uplift from the inspiration is still fresh.

Even more fundamentally, inspiration and the motivation it engenders do nothing to change the situations in which people work—how they are measured and evaluated and paid, whom they work with and what those people tell them, and so forth. When the inspiring event is over, people return to the same work environments they previously inhabited, and they probably interact with the same people both inside and outside work. They may react and respond somewhat differently postinspiration, but I wouldn't bet on it, given the potency of situations to affect behavior in a sustained fashion.

This is particularly true if little changes in the informational environment that people confront. From an extensive social science research literature, we know that priming—the salience of information, including physical cues—has a large effect on people's attitudes and behaviors. For instance, people vote more favorably on school bond issues when they happen to cast their ballots at a school instead of at a firehouse or some other location.[22] People exposed to fast food logos are more impatient.[23] Individuals who wear fake (counterfeit) branded sunglasses cheat more often across a number of different tasks.[24] People working in a somewhat darker room also cheat more, as if the darker environment brings out their darker nature.[25] The amount we eat depends in part on the size of the plate the food is served on.[26] In all cases, the information—the cues—in our environments profoundly affects what we do. Reading an inspiring leadership book or blog or hearing an inspiring speech changes those environments not at all—at least not in enduring ways that cue different workplace behavior.

Effective methods of personal change and self-improvement recognize the importance of changing the information that people see and experience. Research shows that having people sign an honor code—an act that entails both making a moral commitment and making moral action salient—reduces unethical behavior.[27] Want to walk more to burn up more calories and get more exercise? Get one of those devices that hang on your belt and measure how many steps you take per day. Want to change what you eat? Get and keep a diary of what you eat. Most devices and tools focused on changing people's behavior proceed from a set of simple, evidence-based principles: you change people's behavior by having them set some specific, measurable goals, reminding them of what they have committed to do, measuring their activities and providing frequent feedback, and providing positive reinforcement for progress.

Effective programs of personal change also recognize the importance of changing people's social environment—changing the individuals with whom they regularly interact. People are profoundly influenced by those with whom they have contact, as these others provide information and also models for their behavior. For example, an evaluation of a network of more than twelve thousand people over a thirty-two-year period found that an individual's weight gain was dependent on the weight gains of others with whom that person was socially tied.[28] Alcoholics Anonymous (AA) works in part by providing social support—not inspiration—to people who are trying to stop drinking. As with the case of weight gain, research shows that not having pro-drinking others in people's social networks increases their likelihood of abstinence, net of the effects of their involvement in AA.[29]

Keith Ferrazzi, a consultant and management speaker, related that a talk on how companies can accomplish cultural change prompted a manager in the audience to note the similarities in Ferrazzi's prescriptions to elements of addiction programs.[30] For good reason: Successful efforts at change at the individual or the organizational level have many elements in common, including emphasizing the importance of peer support and pressure, providing sponsors or mentors to help maintain accountability and encourage progress, acknowledging small improvements, and understanding that "you are the company you keep."[31] So while inspiration can make people feel motivated and good in the moment, it typically does nothing to change their networks of relationships or the informational cues with which they are bombarded. Consequently, inspiration is unlikely to produce enduring or even temporary behavioral change.

In a similar fashion, organizations do not improve their quality through lots of moving speeches and meetings about how important quality is. They seldom improve even by listening to tales of other places that have made great progress in improving quality. Rather, companies improve their quality by defining what the idea means in terms of specific operational measures, then routinely and frequently assessing those aspects of performance, sharing the outcomes with everyone (often in graphical form), and holding people accountable for improving the measures that are under their control.

When Amir Dan Rubin arrived as the CEO of Stanford Hospital and Clinics in 2011, the hospital had a history of underperformance along many indicators ranging from patient satisfaction to the incidence of hospital-acquired infections. In less than two years, Rubin and has colleagues transformed Stanford Hospital. Measures of patient satisfaction rose from the fortieth to the ninetieth percentile, waiting times in the emergency room decreased dramatically, and a hospital that had been rated as among the lowest in the Bay Area was now winning national awards for its measures of quality of patient care. The remarkable transformation had little to do with inspiration, although Stanford Hospital did adopt a mission statement ("To care, to educate, to discover") and a vision statement as well ("Healing humanity through science and compassion, one patient at a time"). The improvement mostly occurred because Rubin built a robust operating model around a performance management system and installed a leadership team with a performance-improvement orientation. For every aspect of operations, the question was "Do you have a standard?" Standards and measurements, made visible through charts in every unit, were what drove the remarkable performance improvement—not nice words or inspiring stories.

These recommendations are not news. Indeed, the research on goal setting, which is both voluminous and in some cases decades old, shows that setting specific, measurable goals is much more effective for changing behavior and improving results than are general blandishments meant to inspire people to perform better by increasing their motivation through stories and examples.[32]

To his credit, the famed executive coach Marshall Goldsmith

has made the idea of reflecting on specific behaviors on a daily basis to accomplish change and to improve behavior as a leader the foundation of his coaching practice; it is also an integral part of a leadership improvement program developed by Taavo Godt-fredsen of Skillsoft. Goldsmith's and Godtfredsen's programs require a daily question process whereby at the same time each day (in the morning or evening, for example), individuals rate themselves on how well they have progressed on the five or six questions that have the greatest impact on their personal and professional objectives. Systematically and regularly reflecting on behavior, and even better, *measuring* such behavior, is much more likely to produce substantive change than mere storytelling and emotional uplift is.

SANCTIMONY CREATES PROBLEMS

If these problems aren't enough, developing the unwarranted belief that you are becoming a better leader can also be quite counterproductive in several ways.

Some years ago, the social psychologists Benoît Monin and Dale Miller described the idea of moral licensing. This elegantly simple concept, which has been empirically demonstrated numerous times, shows that if people display moral or ethical behavior in one given instance, they then feel freer to behave less prosocially or less ethically at a subsequent time. Having displayed to others and themselves their moral credentials, and having thereby established their identity as good and moral people, individuals feel freed from having to prove their morality again. Instead, they are inclined to do more of what they really want to do, because having demonstrated their morality and their character, they are now freer of moral constraint.

In one study, people who first had the opportunity to

demonstrate that they were nonprejudiced were subsequently more willing to express attitudes that showed bias.[33] A second study suggested that when people disclose conflicts of interest, they then feel freer to provide exaggerated, biased advice— because, so the reasoning goes, having made their conflict of interest apparent, they consider themselves relieved of the obligation to act as ethically.[34] Another experiment demonstrated that when people were able to write a self-relevant story using words that referred to positive traits, they subsequently donated just one-fifth as much to a charity as those who wrote a story referring to negative traits did.[35] As a review summarizing the extensive research on moral licensing noted, "Past good deeds can liberate individuals to engage in behaviors that are immoral, unethical, or otherwise problematic, behaviors that they would otherwise avoid for fear of feeling or appearing immoral."[36]

The implications of this psychology for the leadership industry are clear: once people believe they are better leaders—possibly because they have given talks or written about positive leadership, have attended lots of leadership trainings, or because they were once acknowledged for their good leadership—they are less likely to be as vigilant about their subsequent behavior, having already demonstrated their leadership credentials. These findings don't merely explain *why* hypocrisy occurs; they account for why hypocritical behavior is *produced* by the very actions that demonstrate morality (or good leadership) and that thereby free people to not behave that way subsequently. It is perhaps not that surprising, then, that some of the most harmful and hypocritical leaders are those who enjoy the most favorable leadership reputations and do a lot of teaching and writing about leadership— actions that then provide them the discretion to not actually live up to those reputations in their real behavior.

All this sanctimonious talk about great leadership creates one additional problem: people, overconfident in their leadership abilities, let talk about leadership substitute for action. Bob Sutton and I described a similar phenomenon, the mission statement problem, in our book on the knowing-doing gap.[37] We observed that companies seemed to think that once they had developed a mission statement and had promulgated it by posting it on walls and printing it on little cards, they were done. Having said something and maybe even repeated it, the companies believed they were living their mission statements—but of course, they often were not. A parallel phenomenon besets leaders and bedevils the leadership industry: having heard about leadership, studied leadership, talked about leadership, and espoused great leadership values, people believe they must be doing what they are saying. The activity makes people confident, even grossly overconfident, in their abilities and in the belief that they are doing what they are talking about.

Because talking often substitutes for reality, one ought to be quite skeptical about what actually goes on at places run by people who think they are leadership experts. One ought to be skeptical, for instance, about taking advice on leadership and human resources from someone from the senior leadership of a firm with a turnover rate hovering around 30 percent—a rate that characterizes some consulting firms offering leadership advice.

Indeed, there often seems to be a negative relationship between leaders' contributions to the leadership industry and their actual leadership behavior. In part, that's because of the moral licensing effect, but yet another process is at work. People can and do produce talks, books, and other promotional materials to proactively head off or otherwise divert attention from their real behaviors, which may be nothing like what they write or speak about. Their need to engage in such activities is often greater to the extent that their leadership behavior is worse—sort of like the worst polluters and the companies that pay their workers the least running advertisements touting their environmental bona fides and how wonderful a few employees think their careers are. Put another way, much wisdom can be found in that famous line from Shakespeare's *Hamlet*: "The lady doth protest too much, methinks."

GETTING BEYOND HERO WORSHIP

The recommendations about how to move the teaching and practice of leadership forward, and how employees can avoid career problems resulting from leaders who don't do what their companies (or maybe even they) espouse, follow logically from the discussion of the problems and their causes. None are particularly difficult to implement, but nonetheless they remain unfortunately rare in practice.

Do Due Diligence on Leaders

Virtually no intelligent or even semi-intelligent person invests financial resources without doing some amount of diligence to ensure that the claims being made on behalf of the investment are true. That does not mean investment fraud never occurs or that people don't get misled, but most individuals spend some effort checking out what they are told. But somehow such behavior disappears when it comes to leaders and leadership. People hear all kinds of stories, and ironically, the more heroic and therefore implausible the story, the more strongly individuals seemingly want to and therefore do believe such tales without doing *any* checking. Simply put, the motivation to believe in heroes and a just world circumvents people's critical faculties. So people join organizations and sign up with leaders only to be disappointed, or worse.

Here's one example: The head of a small management

consulting and leadership-development company in San Francisco persuaded a talented, experienced executive to work for the company in a senior administrative and leadership role to help the business grow. The consulting firm's leader was extremely intelligent, articulate, and charismatic, with sound ideas about organizational change and with great business-development skills; he also espoused great leadership values. But soon after the talented executive signed on and began working, she recognized that although the firm's leader could speak gracefully and convincingly about many positive leadership qualities and did great consulting work, his own leadership was almost completely inconsistent with his recommendations. He did not walk the talk, to use the common phrase, and in fact, pretty much walked the opposite of his talk. Not only did the new hire leave after a short time to find another job, but she was also involved in litigation regarding her tenure and quick departure. And yet she could have easily prevented the problem by doing due diligence and taking the results of such diligence seriously. The firm at one time had four partners, yet now there was just one, and some of the prior partners knew the problems well. Moreover, the firm had gone through a number of consultants and staff over the preceding few years. Talking to those people and triangulating on the issues uncovered in those conversations would have prevented a bad choice of employment and the resulting psychological and economic costs.

Take your favorite leaders, someone about whom you have heard amazingly wonderful things (often, by the way, from the person him- or herself). Then spend even thirty minutes doing a search to see if the claims hold up—whether it involves visiting websites such as Glass Door and others that report employees' opinions of the leadership they encounter, or reviewing social media profiles or even the public records of legal actions filed. Do some research before you believe, and, more important, act on your beliefs, about leaders and leadership. And in your research efforts, try to use multiple, independent sources. Confirm the information you receive, just as you would do if you were reference-checking a prospective employee. You are reference-checking someone much more important—someone you are possibly going to work for—so do the task well.

Get beyond the hype *before* you begin, so you can figure out the strengths and weaknesses, the good and the bad, you will confront. No one—not Martin Luther King Jr., not Nelson Mandela, not Gandhi—is without fault or imperfection. True, you won't embark on this new endeavor with the rose-colored glasses so many people seemingly desire, but you will be better prepared to navigate your environment, and you will be much less likely to be profoundly disappointed.

Stop Chasing "Inspiration"

Life is often about trade-offs, and the leadership industry cannot provide all things to all people. The leadership industry has clearly been better at providing heroes, myths, stories, and inspiration than it has been at making workplaces better or leaders last longer in their jobs. At some level, that's not completely the leadership industry's fault. If audiences want inspiring stories and will pay for them, the market will work at least moderately well and provide those stories. If people prefer excitement to education, emotional uplift to intellectual insight, then they will get what they prefer.

This means that the leadership industry's faults and failings come in large measure from that industry's clientele, the human resource executives and CEOs who hire the leadership gurus—and the employees who fill out all of those smiley-face surveys based on how good the leadership industry's infotainment has made them feel. It was only when consumers demanded

higher-quality, safer, more reliable automobiles that the car industry responded. Similarly, when shoppers demanded organic food,
they got it, not only from new chains like Whole Foods Market but
even from more conventional food retailers. Only when and if the
consumers of leadership products and services stop craving inspiration and instead pursue insight, only when people demand organizational measures and leadership practices that help improve
the condition of organizational workplaces, will anything change.

To this point, I have shown the enormous disconnect between
decades of leadership writing, development, speaking, blogging,
and so forth and the sorry state of workplaces and leadership. I
argued that the emphasis on sentiment over science and on good
feelings over reality contribute to the persistence of workplace
and career problems.

In the next five chapters, I turn my attention to five attributes
that are often asserted to be useful, and indeed essential, for effective leadership: modesty, authenticity, truthfulness, trustworthiness, and concern for the welfare and well-being of others,
particularly those being led. Without for a moment denying the
extensive, maybe even overwhelming, research connecting these
attributes (and others) to various dimensions of group or organizational performance, and while acknowledging that these are
great qualities and that work environments would be in much
better shape if more leaders had them, I want to pose two simple,
pragmatic and important questions. First, is there evidence that
these qualities do in fact characterize most, or maybe even many,
leaders? And second, since they often do not, are there both
theory and data that can help us understand why doing the *opposite* of what the leadership industry recommends might be much
more sensible, certainly for individuals and their careers but in
some cases even for other outcomes?

I ask you to put aside your judgments and feelings to the

extent possible and try to confront, as clinically as you can, the logic and the evidence. If we are going to build better leaders and create better working conditions, we need to understand the current state of play and, most important, the forces that have produced the world that we actually live in.

CHAPTER 2

Modesty: Why Leaders Aren't

Bill Bradley, the retired National Basketball Association star and former New Jersey senator, undoubtedly summarized the sentiments of many people when he said, "Leaders should be collaborative, modest, and generous."[1] Unfortunately, few leaders, particularly leaders of large organizations, seem to have many or even any of those qualities, particularly modesty.

Consider Donald Trump, listed by *Forbes* as the 417th richest man in the world, with a net worth approaching $4 billion. Trump ran for the Republican nomination for president in 2012 (at least for a while), tweets constantly, is all over the media, had his own television show, and, most famously, names all of his buildings after, of course, himself. Most recently, Trump got into a spat with Rahm Emanuel, the mayor of Chicago, when Trump put up giant stainless steel letters, more than two hundred feet high, on the ninety-six-story Trump International Hotel and Tower, Chicago's second-tallest building. The letters spell "Trump"—what else? Emanuel thought that "this was an architecturally tasteful building scarred by an architecturally tasteless sign."[2]

Trump provides fodder for many late-night comedians, and, among others, Jeffrey Sonnenfeld, a Yale management professor, questions Trump's leadership style. Sonnenfeld, commenting on the now-defunct Trump-centric television program *The Apprentice*, noted that it was "not the model for great leadership" and penned an editorial in the *Wall Street Journal* that described the show as a combination of "puffery, pushiness and deception."[3] Many observers have questioned Trump's business acumen and financial performance, in part because his casinos have gone into bankruptcy.[4] But one thing Trump has done for sure is build a brand that is worth a fortune. Everyone knows his name, more important, his projects receive enormous media coverage. All of this is extremely valuable in real estate; Trump's ultimate job is to sell hotel rooms, casino experiences, and living quarters in very competitive markets. Maybe Trump knows something about leadership not widely appreciated but nonetheless useful.

Notwithstanding Trump and legions of CEOs and ex-CEOs now writing books about themselves and their many wonderful qualities and accomplishments, research on high-performing organizations and leaders frequently emphasizes the personal quality of *modesty*. For instance, in his bestselling management book *Good to Great* and in articles based on the research done for that book,[5] Jim Collins writes about Level 5 leaders. Level 5 leaders represent the highest performing executives, those rare individuals who create extraordinary results over long periods of time as they transform average-performing companies into those earning exceptional returns. Collins argues that although leaders are not the only factor required to transform a company's performance, good-to-great transformations are pretty much impossible without Level 5 leaders.

One of the most important qualities Collins identifies that distinguishes these highly successful leaders from others with executive capability is their extreme personal humility—their modesty. This quality of personal humbleness entails giving others sincere credit for the collective accomplishments of the company. Collins notes that Level 5 leaders do not like to talk about themselves, preferring instead to speak about the company and the contributions of other executives. The Level 5 leaders Collins describes are, for the most part, not well known outside their companies and have little to no visibility in the general business press, a fact consistent with their tendency not to self-promote or claim the limelight. This quality of modesty also entails acknowledging one's limitations and fallibility, understanding that no one, regardless of how extraordinary his performance, knows everything, and that thus collective wisdom is often superior to the insights of a single individual. Acting on that insight involves including far more people in decision-making, and listening with humility to their advice and feedback.

It's not just Collins who has emphasized humility as a desirable leadership trait. Modesty and concomitant respect for the abilities of others appear *regularly* as a prescription for becoming an effective leader.[6] One treatment of ethical leadership from both Eastern- and Western-based philosophical perspectives listed moderation orientation as one of four important qualities.[7] Because modesty, or at least appearing to be modest, is so desirable for people in power, some research has examined various strategies for reducing perceived power differences and conveying modesty to others, such as the use of self-deprecating humor.[8]

WHY MODESTY MIGHT BE A USEFUL LEADERSHIP TRAIT

The emphasis on modesty seems sensible, and the logic behind the prescription to be humble appears to be sound. After all, if you are sunlike in your domination of every aspect of organizational life, everything and everyone else gets blotted out. One reason people leave companies is because they do not feel acknowledged or recognized for their contributions, and one behavior that provokes irritation is when others take credit for another's work. Modest leaders are less likely to claim credit for the accomplishments of others and also are more prone to acknowledge what others have done—so modesty should reduce voluntary turnover.

Moreover, people are unlikely to work as hard for "your" project or "the boss's project" as they are for "our" project or, even better, for their "own" project. This fact derives from at least two psychological processes. One process is sometimes referred to as *implicit egotism*. This idea refers to the principle that we like things that remind us of or are identified with ourselves. Implicit egotism is premised on the idea that because we like ourselves, we like things that remind us of or are associated with the self.[9] In turn, projects will induce greater effort to the extent that they become identified with the individuals working on them.

The second principle that suggests that people will prefer that which they feel ownership of is the *endowment effect*. This phenomenon describes how and why we more highly value what we have simply because it is ours.[10] For instance, in one classic study conducted at the University of Victoria, some people were given a choice between a coffee mug and a 400-gram Swiss chocolate bar. Of the total, 56 percent chose the mug and 44 percent chose the candy. But, when people were first given the mug—it was now theirs—and then asked whether they would be interested in trading it for the candy, only 11 percent were interested in making the switch. And when people had the candy, just 10 percent wanted to trade for the mug.[11] These and other studies demonstrate that people prefer and are willing to pay more to keep something once they are given an object so it is theirs and has become associated with them. The relevance for modest and self-effacing leadership is clear: sharing credit and giving people a sense of ownership would be expected to increase their commitment and identification with a workplace or specific projects or tasks.

Furthermore, if people see that they never get sufficient recognition for their good work because the leader hogs all the credit, they may reduce their efforts. They will reasonably conclude that they should not bother expending effort if nothing they do will matter in terms of obtaining rewards and recognition for their work. All of these dynamics make it unsurprising that reviews of leader effectiveness often show that the opposite of modesty, narcissism, correlates negatively with numerous aspects of leader performance as assessed both by the affective reactions of subordinates and also actual group performance.[12]

The prescription for leaders to be modest is also consistent with the principle that people do not like others who self-promote and are self-aggrandizing. Research shows that people who self-promote are perceived negatively by others,[13] and those who are modest about their abilities and performance are better-liked than individuals who boast about their accomplishments.[14] Other research demonstrates that boastful presenters are the least effective, while people who display an intermediate level of modesty receive the most positive evaluations from others.[15] Because likeability is an important basis of interpersonal influence, humble people, who are more likeable as a consequence of their humility, will be more influential, other things being equal.

And there is yet another mechanism that argues in favor of the advantages of modest, humble leaders. Jim Collins noted that time is a finite and, particularly for leaders, very scarce resource. Leaders who spend lots of time promoting themselves and their accomplishments steal valuable time and attention from working to maintain their companies' competitive success. This is sort of like the old *Fortune* magazine cover curse, in which the folk wisdom said that if a CEO appeared on the cover of a major business magazine, poor results for that person's company were likely to follow, because the person was spending more time with journalists than with customers, employees, and suppliers. Jim Collins used Lee Iacocca, the former CEO of Chrysler, as an example of this issue:

> Lee Iacocca saved Chrysler from the brink of catastrophe. . . . The automaker's stock rose 2.9 times higher than the general market about halfway through his tenure. But then Iacocca diverted his attention to transforming himself. He appeared regularly on talk shows . . . starred in more than 80 commercials, entertained the idea of running for president of the United States, and promoted his autobiography. . . . Iacocca's personal stock soared, but Chrysler's stock fell 31% below the market in the second half of his tenure.

WHY IMMODESTY MIGHT BE EVEN BETTER

Notwithstanding all this evidence and logic, there are some significant problems with the recommendation for leaders to be modest. First of all, modesty is a rare, and possibly extremely rare, quality among leaders. Indeed, if one takes the data in *Good to Great* seriously, the odds of making the transition required to significantly increase performance are obviously overwhelmingly long, to put it simply. Of the 1,435 companies that appeared on the Fortune 500 list between 1965 and when Collins did his study, only 11 made the transition from good to great—fewer than 1 percent. Collins apparently found only 11 modest and humble leaders (who also had fierce resolve) in the almost 1,500 companies he studied. Of course, Collins was not primarily studying leaders; his research began with a goal of downplaying the role of leaders. But even if the proportion of modest leaders is many times that uncovered by Jim Collins, it would still compose a tiny fraction of the CEOs running major companies.

Second, Collins talks about the important leadership qualities of people who had *already attained* the role of CEO as they improved their companies' economic performance. This raises the question of which qualities might be useful to get to the top in the first place. The evidence suggests that modesty may not be such a good thing for getting to the top or staying there.

And third, as Michael Maccoby notes in his book *The Productive Narcissist,* the pioneering innovation that, almost by definition, breaks with convention and reinvents products, industries, and business models requires the kind of disdain for the constraining views of others and persistence in the face of adversity and naysaying that characterize narcissists.[16] Indeed, Maccoby almost equates visionary leadership with leaders who have at least some reasonable degree of narcissism.

Narcissism

While there is not much research evidence about modesty and its effectiveness as a leadership quality, there is an extensive literature on a very closely related, albeit opposite, concept: narcissism. Studies of narcissism can help us evaluate the usefulness of prescriptions for leaders to be modest and also see the extent to which leaders are narcissistic on the one hand or modest on the other.

Although sometimes considered a form of personality disorder, narcissism and narcissistic behaviors are quite common, particularly among leaders. Michael Maccoby has noted that many of the most well-known and well-regarded CEOs, including Bill Gates of Microsoft, Steve Jobs of Apple, and Jack Welch of General Electric, exhibited narcissistic traits and behaviors. Maccoby also includes John D. Rockefeller; Robert Johnson, the founder and leader of Black Entertainment Television; J. Craig Venter, the CEO of Celera Genomics; and Jim Clark, the founder of Silicon Graphics and the onetime CEO of Netscape among a long list of narcissistic business leaders. Other narcissistic leaders include David Geffen (cofounder of the Dreamworks movie studio), Michael Eisner (Disney), Kenneth Lay (Enron), and many politicians, including Joseph Stalin and President George W. Bush. For all these individuals, attention-seeking and a sense of entitlement nearly define their personalities.[17]

Narcissism has been defined in the psychology research literature as a grandiose sense of self-importance; arrogant behavior or attitudes; a lack of empathy for others; a preoccupation with fantasies of unlimited success or power; belief in one's special or unique status, including a fixation on associating with high-status people or organizations; an unreasonable sense of expectations or entitlement; and a desire for excessive admiration from others, among other characteristics.[18] Narcissism can be measured by a validated paper-and-pencil measure, the Narcissistic Personality Inventory (NPI).[19] It can also be assessed indirectly and unobtrusively. For instance, one study of the effect of CEO narcissism on companies examined the prominence of the CEO's picture in the annual reports, the CEO's use of the first-person singular pronoun ("I") in interviews, the CEO's prominence in the company's press releases, and the CEO's compensation compared with the number-two ranking executive's to assess narcissism.[20] The use of first-person pronouns can be particularly revealing of narcissism, such as CEOs talking about themselves when they should be referring to their companies or executive teams.

You can use these and other similar indicators of immodesty and hubris to help structure your observations of the leaders you encounter, and to help answer the question for yourself: How does hubristic self-absorption affect the careers of people in work organizations? I believe that your own observations can be at least as convincing as any evidence I present. If you become attuned to assessing narcissism as exhibited in natural settings, you can learn a great deal about when, how, and why self-aggrandizement is or is not effective.

We know a lot about narcissism. One thing we know is that narcissism levels have increased significantly among college students over the past several decades.[21] Narcissism levels are higher for Americans than for citizens of many other countries and regions,[22] in part because narcissism is related to an individualistic orientation that is more characteristic of American culture. Men tend to be more narcissistic than women, possibly because men are somewhat more competitive and women are more communal, and also because narcissistic behavior would be much more gender-role discrepant for women than for men.

Business school students seem to be particularly narcissistic, an important fact because many leaders in both the for-profit and the nonprofit world come from business school backgrounds, particularly in the more recent past. One study comparing 560 undergraduate business and psychology students in the United States found that measured narcissism was (a) higher than historical averages, which is consistent with the idea that narcissism levels are increasing over time, and (b) significantly higher for business school students compared with psychology students.[23]

IMMODESTY AND SUCCESS

As we will soon see, immodesty in all of its manifestations—narcissism, self-promotion, self-aggrandizement, unwarranted self-confidence—helps people attain leadership positions in the first place and then, once in them, positively affects their ability to hold on to those positions, extract more resources (salary), and even helps in some, although not all, aspects of their performance on the job. At first this might seem counterintuitive. After all, people who self-promote are less likeable, and likeability is an important basis of interpersonal influence and a reason for others to prefer the likeable individual. Furthermore, immodesty and self-aggrandizement can harm the self-esteem and rewards received by peers and subordinates of the person engaging in such behavior. This is all true. But so is the following:

Many, possibly most, leadership roles are ambiguous—there is uncertainty about what the leader should do, uncertainty about who would be best in that position, and frequently even a lack of clarity about how people are performing in their leadership roles. All of that uncertainty means the so-called confirmation bias operates with a vengeance. Confirmation bias, an old and venerable idea in social psychology, refers to the tendency of people to both seek out and also interpret evidence and experience that are consistent with their preexisting beliefs and expectations.[24] Confirmation bias helps explain why first impressions persist; once people form an impression, they ignore discrepant information and seek out and overvalue confirming evidence. In the case of leadership, if you project confidence and claim competence with enough conviction to be credible, observers will tend to assimilate any information about you in ways consistent with the idea that you know what you are doing and are deserving of a position of leadership.

And another process operates as well. In order for you to be selected for a leadership role, either by peers or by bosses, it is necessary, albeit insufficient, that those doing the selecting *notice* you. No one who is unmemorable is going to be chosen for an important job, because one cannot select what one cannot remember. That's why in marketing, evidence shows the importance of the mere exposure effect,[25] the idea that because people choose what feels familiar and therefore comfortable to them, being noticed, getting remembered—the sine qua non for assessing advertising effectiveness—is essential. The same is true for leaders and leadership. It helps to be known, to have a brand, to, simply put, stand out.

To engage in self-promotion requires eschewing modesty and engaging in behaviors that draw attention to an individual's positive qualities, past accomplishments, future plans, and also deservingness of jobs, money, or promotions.[26] Research consistently shows that self-promotion is positively correlated with interviewers' evaluations of job candidates as well as with hiring recommendations.[27] This is not surprising. Self-promotion is one manifestation of self-confidence, and self-confidence frequently leads others to share the confidence that someone exudes.

Cameron Anderson, a professor at the University of California, Berkley, business school, conducted research with some colleagues that showed that not just confident, but *overconfident* individuals achieved higher social status, respect, and influence in groups.[28] Of course, one interpretation is that in possibly ambiguous situations, other group members conflated overconfidence with actual ability. If someone seems confident in his or her abilities, maybe this just reflects his or her actual competence. To examine this possibility, Anderson and some other researchers provided people with data that suggested that the overconfidence was unwarranted— observers of the overconfident individual received actual performance data that showed the claims of competence were exaggerated. Nonetheless "even after groups gained clear, objective information about individuals' actual task performance, they did not penalize overconfident individuals with lower status."[29]

Furthermore, even though people perceive self-promotion with a jaundiced eye, observers will also expect an individual to advocate on his or her own behalf. Consequently, self-deprecation and modest self-presentation work mostly for those who already have such well-established positive reputations that the modesty is seen as charming rather than indicative of some insecurity or incompetence. Consistent with this line of reasoning, studies of the selection of military officers show that "the confidence, charisma, and optimism associated with . . . narcissists are positive leadership traits" leading to "higher leadership ratings from peers and supervisors."[30]

A meta-analysis summarizing the results of 187 studies of individual differences presumably related to effective leadership showed seven traits associated with leader effectiveness. Four of those traits were energy, dominance, self-confidence, and charisma. The research literature shows that narcissists exhibit more of these four traits than do others, which further supports the connection between narcissism and the selection of people for leadership roles.[31] Because most researchers, like people in general, do not like immodest, self-aggrandizing, narcissistic behavior, these findings are all the more notable.

Because narcissists are more extraverted and have higher self-esteem, they are more likely to be chosen as leaders and to be seen as having leadership potential. For instance, an article on three experiments reported that people with higher narcissism scores were more likely to emerge as leaders during four-person initially leaderless group discussions. The third study in the set used expert raters who observed interactions among executive MBA students (working adults). As in the first two experiments, narcissism predicted leadership ratings, and did so even after gender and sociability were statistically controlled for.[32] Another article studying fifty-six teams found that, regardless of the type of task, narcissists were more likely to be chosen as leaders than non-narcissists were.[33] These results are not surprising. Narcissists are more likely to engage in behaviors that make them more noticeable and noteworthy. And because of their heightened sense of entitlement and positive expectations for themselves, they are more likely to push their own point of view and advocate in their own interests more aggressively—behaviors that help them come to dominate the social groups in which they are members.

Malcolm Gladwell's article describing the talent preoccupation inside the Enron Corporation prior to its ignominious implosion noted that Enron was a narcissistic company, but that narcissism could be functional in attaining leadership positions. Gladwell cited material from an essay, "The Dark Side of Charisma," which noted:

> Narcissists typically make judgments with greater confidence than other people . . . and because their judgments are rendered with such conviction, other people tend to believe them and the narcissists become disproportionately more influential in group situations. Finally, because of their self-confidence and strong need for recognition, narcissists tend to "self-nominate"; consequently, when a leadership gap appears in a group or organization, the narcissists rush to fill it.[34]

Students with higher narcissism scores have greater salary expectations and also expect it to be easier for them to find a job after they graduate. Other research shows, not surprisingly, that salary expectations are related to someone's salary, if for no other reason than the higher the salary expectations, the more likely it is for an individual to push for and negotiate for a higher salary.[35] Thus, we would expect that narcissism is positively related to salary and rates of promotion.

Research finds that narcissism produces higher levels of short-term likeability, possibly because of the greater extraversion and flamboyance that narcissists exhibit. And narcissism also produces enhanced performance on public evaluation tasks and in competitive tasks.[36] Because of the operation of confirmation bias—people see what they expect to see—and the self-fulfilling prophecy in which expectations produce responses on the part of others that help confirm those original expectations, there is little reason to believe that the short-term advantages of immodest, self-aggrandizing behavior would not be sustained over time.

Finally, the evidence demonstrates yet another mechanism that may explain the positive effects of narcissism on obtaining and holding on to leadership positions, namely, the correspondence and overlap "between narcissistic characteristics and the prototypical attributes associated with effective leaders, such as authority, confidence, dominance, and high self-esteem."[37] The extensive and ever-growing research evidence is overwhelmingly clear—narcissists are more likely to be selected for leadership roles and also to seek such positions in the first place.

What about Women and Minorities?

The fact that women and other ethnic minorities, such as Asian Americans, are on average more modest and self-effacing and less narcissistic than typical white males, in part because of gender role and cultural expectations, may help explain their worse career outcomes. As summarized in an article on gender and self-promotion:

> While negotiating, women focus on what is fair whilst men plan to win. . . . Several studies have shown that women tend to underrate their achievements, and have

less confidence in their abilities than their line managers have for them.[38]

That article also reports that women are less likely to use impression-management strategies than are men—to their detriment, as impression management affects evaluations and hiring decisions. One reason women are less frequently chosen for leadership roles has to do with their unwillingness to display confidence. The idea that women, when offered a promotion, would question (even if privately) if they were ready for and deserving of it while men would generally think "Why did this take so long?" finds support in empirical research. Not thinking that one is deserving and therefore possibly being less willing to ask for promotions and salary increases hinder career progress for anyone, regardless of gender or ethnicity.

A recent report on Asians in U.S. companies noted that only 2 percent of Fortune 500 CEOs and corporate officers are Asians and that Asians earn less money than Caucasians, even after other factors affecting salary are statistically controlled for. One factor affecting these outcomes is the importance of executive presence, which, the report noted, often requires behaviors seemingly at odds with Asian (and female) behavioral norms:

> Asians admit that their culture inculcates them with different communication and networking styles, as well as a pronounced emphasis on performance and technical competency. . . . Asian professionals are frequently held back from senior positions by the perception that they don't have "executive presence," a factor that similarly operates against other minority groups in the workplace, including women.[39]

And what constitutes executive presence? Certainly not modesty:

> Corporate culture in the U.S. places a high premium on assertiveness and individualistic thinking, values that can be at odds with those prized in the Asian tradition . . . the self-effacement and modesty emphasized by many Asian cultures is at direct odds with the realities of the contemporary workplace where assertiveness and direct-ness are central. . . . Cautionary proverbs such as "the loudest duck gets shot" (a Chinese saying), or "the nail that sticks out gets hammered down" (a Japanese saying), signal a deep suspicion of behaviors that make one stand out from the crowd. Clearly, these values are diametri-cally opposed to the self-advocacy and self-assurance that are essential leadership qualities in the American corpo-rate environment.[40]

Although focused on explaining the career issues faced by Asians and women, these findings and insights apply to every-one: although modesty may be valued in the leadership literature, self-promotion and assertiveness seem to produce better career results in the real world.

THE EFFECTS OF IMMODESTY

Thus far we have seen that narcissism and immodesty, including self-promotion, help people be selected for leadership roles, both in naturally occurring groups and in more structured selection situa-tions, including the military. Another important outcome worthy of our attention is the effect of narcissism on people's survival and success in leadership roles once they attain such positions.

Many studies of leaders focus, naturally enough, on out-comes such as organizational performance and the attitudes and turnover intentions of subordinates. Possibly surprising to some, given the oft-stated preferences for modesty in the leadership in-dustry, narcissists often lead organizations that do better than others. One study of 173 high-technology manufacturing com-panies in the Midwest found that CEOs who were more nar-cissistic tended to have more of an entrepreneurial orientation and to take bolder and more aggressive strategic actions, which resulted in higher levels of variability in performance. Another study of 203 corporate professionals found that while narcissism and guiltlessness created problems with subordinates because of the leader's management style, this personality profile was pos-itively related to having better communication skills, creativity, and strategic thinking.[41]

A study of 392 CEOs during the financial crisis beginning in 2007 found that, because narcissists tend to be self-absorbed and overconfident, firms led by more narcissistic CEOs did worse at the beginning of the crisis. However, because narcissists have a stronger bias for action and risk-taking—again a result of their higher levels of self-confidence—the study also found that more narcissistic CEOs led firms to bounce back more successfully during the post-crisis recovery.[42]

A study of U.S. presidents involved 121 expert raters evaluating the personality of 41 presidents. One investigation used the ratings of the presidents on their fearless dominance, a validated psycho-logical measure incorporating glibness, narcissism, and guiltless-ness. That study reported that fearless dominance and its associated boldness predicted "better rated presidential performance, leader-ship, persuasiveness, crisis management, Congressional relations," and objective levels of performance such as initiating new programs and being viewed by expert raters as a world figure.[43]

A second study of forty-two U.S. presidents employed data on expert ratings of presidential personality, historical surveys of presidential performance, and a set of objective indicators of presidential performance. Recognizing the dual effects of narcissism—on the one hand, narcissists do well in the evaluations made by others, are effective at becoming celebrities, and are skilled at persuading others that their ideas are innovative even when they are not; on the other hand, narcissists are overconfident in their decision-making and therefore often fail to learn and also alienate others who work with them—the study examined the dual effects of narcissism on presidential performance. The authors concluded that grandiose narcissism "is tied to independently rated and objective indicators of presidential success . . . [and] is associated with several indicators of negative presidential performance, especially in the ethical domain . . . [and] is more elevated in U.S. presidents than in the general population." The authors also concluded that the level of narcissism has increased in presidents over time.[44]

In addition to organizational and group performance, leader survival and acquisition of resources also matter. Without for a moment denying the importance of group and organizational performance, leaders themselves undoubtedly evaluate their success at least partly by whether or not they hold on to their jobs as well as by the perquisites such jobs provide them. Social pressures may cause leaders not to admit to these personal objectives, but these goals are important, as evidenced by the amount of effort leaders spend pursuing them.

So what is the effect of narcissism on the leaders rather than the led? The business school professor Charles O'Reilly and three of his colleagues conducted an innovative study on the CEOs of thirty-two companies in the high-technology industry that each employed at least twenty alumni from one of three leading

West Coast business schools. Of the firms, thirty-one were listed in the Fortune 1000, and collectively the thirty-two companies generated 67 percent of the revenues coming from all the high-technology companies in the Fortune 1000 in 2009. The researchers contacted the schools' alumni and asked them if they would be willing to anonymously rate their CEOs using a checklist of characteristics, some of which came from the Narcissistic Personality Inventory. On average, eight people with an average company tenure of more than seven years provided ratings of the personality of their CEO.

Here's what O'Reilly and his research partners found: "Pairwise correlations show that CEO narcissism is significantly correlated with CEO total compensation, the gap in compensation between the CEO and the senior team, and the total value of the CEO's share holdings. Narcissism is also positively related to CEO tenure."[45] Using more sophisticated statistical techniques and controlling for numerous other factors that might affect CEO compensation and tenure, the researchers discovered an interaction between narcissism and tenure in the job such that over time "more narcissistic CEOs who have longer tenure claim more compensation and have greater variance in pay within the senior management team than do CEOs who are less narcissistic, shorter in tenure, or both."[46] In short, narcissists earn more money and remain in their positions longer, even in high-technology companies.

The extensive research literature that includes both experimental and field data paints a consistent picture. Regardless of what one may believe about the virtues of modesty, several facts emerge from considering leaders in the real world. First, modesty is rare, while narcissism, in its productive or unproductive variants, is common among leaders, even among some of the most prominent, iconic, and celebrated of such leaders, including U.S. presidents and corporate CEOs. In fact, the most celebrated leaders are particularly likely to be narcissistic and immodest, which is one of the reasons they became so well known and celebrated in the first place!

Second, narcissism and self-aggrandizement and the behaviors associated with these constructs reliably and consistently predict the selection of leaders, the evaluations made after interviews, and the selection of emergent leadership. And third, narcissistic CEOs seem to earn more compared with others in the top management team, and last longer in their jobs—probably because they are more ready and willing to eliminate their rivals. Furthermore, narcissistic individuals are often superior performers in at least some dimensions; they are great at selling their ideas and vision, effective in attracting the support of others (particularly outside others), good at getting attention and its attendant benefits, and often effective at getting things done. The many benefits of immodesty help explain why modest CEOs are so rare, the leadership industry's blandishments notwithstanding.

SUPPOSE WE ACTUALLY WANTED MODEST LEADERS

For all the reasons just discussed, it is far from clear that we actually ought to want modest leaders. In fact, in this as in many other leadership topics explored in this book such as authenticity and truthfulness, the evidence suggests that what people *say* are the qualities they value in leaders is frequently inconsistent with their actual decisions and behavior when confronted with leaders or potential leaders exhibiting various behaviors and traits.

Rather than chalk up this discrepancy to simple hypocrisy, I attribute it to a fundamental ambivalence. On the one hand, people understand the desirable and socially desirable and approved qualities in leaders, and they articulate those views and values when asked about them. On the other hand, people are attracted to the grandiose and the unusual. And individuals also come to understand, often firsthand, the many benefits that come from following leaders who don't exhibit the traits and behaviors, including modesty, that are so often prescribed for leaders, but who instead do the opposite.

Nonetheless, if we or work organizations wanted to select modest leaders, it would be fairly easy to do so. The Narcissistic Personality Inventory is a validated scale, and it can be used not only by leadership candidates as part of a personality assessment, but also, as the studies of Silicon Valley CEOs and U.S. presidents demonstrate, by knowledgeable observers to rate people on narcissism with a high degree of reliability. Furthermore, the studies of CEO narcissism provide anyone who wants to use the results with even more unobtrusive indicators, such as the inappropriate use of the first-person pronoun, the size of pictures, and various ways in which people claim credit and seize the limelight in otherwise interdependent situations.

The fact that most companies not only don't use such selection techniques but their selection decisions also seemingly reflect precisely the opposite preference—a preference for immodest, grandiose, and narcissistic leaders—stands as an important barrier to having leaders who might create workplaces quite different from most contemporary work environments.

CHAPTER 3

Authenticity: Misunderstood and Overrated

Alison Davis-Blake is currently the dean of the Ross School of Business at the University of Michigan, a top-ten ranked business school and frequently the highest-ranked public business school in the United States. Prior to joining Michigan, Davis-Blake was the dean of the business school at the University of Minnesota. She is the first woman to hold either of these positions, and it should scarcely be news that there aren't loads of women serving as business school deans or, for that matter, in senior roles in higher education. Alison Davis-Blake achieved much in just her first two years at Ross, including hiring twenty-one new faculty members, expanding the number of bachelor's students by 20 percent, introducing new master's programs, increasing the school's visibility in India and Southeast Asia, and, most important, facilitating the raising of one of the largest gifts in the history of the University of Michigan, $100 million for the business school and another $100 million for the athletic department during her first year on the job.[1]

But if you were to ask people who knew Davis-Blake when she was still Alison Davis, a doctoral student in organizational behavior in the 1980s, if they expected her to become a business school dean, they would all tell you the same thing: No way. Out of any set of possible people who might become a future dean, she would have ranked last on that list. Alison Davis-Blake was an introvert, very quiet and unassuming. She was so quiet that at her first-year doctoral student evaluation, her adviser told her that while she was doing great in her courses, the faculty were wondering when she was going to speak up in class. "You need to speak," he said.

Obviously, being a business school dean would seem to require qualities and behaviors pretty much the opposite of introversion and a reluctance to speak. In fact, deans and other leaders speak all the time—it's sort of the primary component of their job. For Davis-Blake to become the effective leader that she clearly is, she has had to master an important skill, to behave in ways that, to at least some degree, are inconsistent with her natural inclinations and predispositions. Although she will tell you the many ways in which being less outgoing can be helpful—for instance, being a better listener helps in listening to people talk about their favorite topic, themselves, and it also facilitates learning important insights about those you need to influence—Davis-Blake will also talk about her journey of personal development in which she has acquired the behaviors and skills required of a leader.

Leaders must be able to put on a show, to display energy and pay attention to others, regardless of how they may feel at the time. On the day in the winter of 2004 that Gary Loveman, the CEO of the casino company Caesars, attended a business school class where students were discussing him, he had the flu and was running a temperature of about 101 degrees. As a sentient, normal human being, Loveman would probably have preferred to be anywhere but in front of not one but two successive sections of students from 8:00 a.m. until 12:00 noon. But Loveman was well prepared for his performance that day. As the leader of a company with tens of thousands of employees, he understood that many people in the company would see him at most once a year, and often for only a brief moment of interaction. Loveman knew that those small interactions were important, and that, regardless of how he felt, what else was going on in his life or in the company, or how tired he was, he had to be fully present and engaged in those interactions. He had to show people he had energy, both intellectual and sheer physical energy, that he was engaged and committed, and that he could lead the company to success. So, regardless of how he felt in the moment or what he wanted to be doing, Loveman, just like Davis-Blake, had to be able to put on the public face of a leader.

These two leaders, and many others, understand that the last thing a leader needs to be at crucial moments is "authentic"—at least if authentic means being both in touch with and exhibiting their true feelings. *In fact, being authentic is pretty much the opposite of what leaders must do.* Leaders do not need to be true to themselves. Rather, *leaders need to be true to what the situation and what those around them want and need from them.* And often what others want and need is the reassurance that things will work out and the confidence that they are on the right track.

Gina Bianchini, who cofounded Ning with Netscape's Marc Andreesen, and who more recently started Mightybell, both companies in the social networking space, is a Silicon Valley entrepreneur and a woman listed in *Fortune*'s list of most powerful women. As an entrepreneur, Bianchini well understands the importance of exuding confidence to attract employee talent and, for that matter, customers and capital. Start-ups invariably experience ups and downs, and there are times that Bianchini, just like any other founder, feels frustrated and discouraged and is confronted with difficult problems that test her considerable competence. Although she has a few confidants with whom she can be completely candid, she is relentlessly upbeat and positive in public. Partly that reflects her genuine enthusiasm about her company's mission and partly that's because being enthusiastic and confident is an essential quality for entrepreneurs, regardless of what they may be feeling on the inside.

But it's not just leaders who have to exhibit qualities they may not be feeling. The ability to not succumb to personal feelings or predilections seems like a crucial trait for high performers in many domains. In sports, players often "play through the pain," in that they put aside the aches, pains, exhaustion, and discouragement and summon reserves of strength they may not have even known they had to surmount obstacles. Great achievement frequently requires surmounting, not giving in, to situational exigencies—not to mention resisting the urge to be entirely oneself.

The sociologist Arlie Hochschild has written about the many occupations in which frontline people such as salespeople, customer service agents, flight attendants, and, for sure, employees at Disneyworld (which bills itself as the "happiest place on earth," even though its employees may not be)[2] are called upon, as part of their everyday work, to display positive emotions that they may not be feeling at the time.[3] She notes:

Emotion . . . can be and often is subject to acts of management. The individual often works on inducing or inhibiting feelings so as to render them "appropriate" to a situation. . . . Meaning-making jobs . . . put more premium on the individual's capacity to do emotion work. A reexamination of class differences in child rearing suggests that middle-class families prepare their children for emotion management more and working-class families prepare them less.[4]

Hochschild's research shows that jobs that require employees to display (positive) emotions that they may not actually be feeling can be psychologically demanding and stressful. But she also shows that such work is often financially rewarding. Hochschild argues that one of the ways in which social class reproduces itself is by middle-class families doing a better job than lower-class families of preparing their children to manage their emotions, particularly the emotions they display to others.

None of this is intended to say that learning to manage one's emotions and self-presentation is always good and that inauthenticity is desirable—only that inauthenticity is incredibly common and seemingly an important requirement for effective leadership.

THE AUTHENTIC LEADERSHIP MOMENT

Authentic leadership seems to be yet another leadership craze, as evidenced by numerous books, seminars, and even a sixteen-item Authentic Leadership Questionnaire, which asks people to rate how often a leader exhibits various behaviors such as (1) soliciting views that challenge the leader's deeply held positions; (2) saying exactly what he or she means; and (3) demonstrating beliefs that are consistent with actions.[5] There are, of course, places that will train you in authentic leadership skills, such as the Authentic Leadership Institute, whose website promises to "transform" leaders and help people develop their authentic leadership.[6] The idea that one would and could be trained to become or at least appear authentic oozes with delicious irony. This is sort of like the famous quote from the late comedian George Burns: "Sincerity—if you can fake that, you've got it made."[7]

The idea of authentic leadership epitomizes almost everything that I believe characterizes the leadership industry generally, much of which does not help either science or practice: (1) a well-intentioned, values-laden (2) set of prescriptions—lots of "shoulds" and "oughts"—(3) that are mostly not representative of most people in leadership roles, and (4) are recommendations that are almost certainly not implementable and may be fundamentally misguided.

It is hard to determine exactly when the authentic leadership movement began, but in 2004 the Gallup Leadership Institute sponsored an inaugural conference at the University of Nebraska-Lincoln on authentic leadership development. That conference resulted in a volume of published papers as well as a special issue of the *Leadership Quarterly*, an academic journal focused on leadership studies. The conference and the papers provide important insights into the authentic leadership movement.

First, the motivations of the contributors to this movement are honorable and well-intentioned. The quest for authentic leadership begins with the acknowledgment of the many contemporary problems laid on the door of leadership. Leadership failures, even before the latest financial crisis, were common. Moreover, the challenges confronting a world of increasing inequality in both income and life expectancy, rapid technological change, and growing global interdependence along many dimensions (ranging from economic integration to the rapid spread of contagious diseases, such as SARS) are substantial. These failures and challenges call for better, more effective leaders, to do good and make things better.

The authentic leadership movement is not only filled with pure motives—"a renewed focus on restoring confidence, hope and optimism"—but it is also values-laden. As one example, authentic leadership derives from the positive psychology movement and also from humanistic psychologists such as Carl Rogers and Abraham Maslow.[8] The movement shares some of its intellectual leaders and many of its core ideas.

Second, the authentic leadership movement is filled with prescriptions and calls to action. For example, from an article on authentic leadership from the special issue of the *Leadership Quarterly*, "Bill George . . . succinctly states, 'We need leaders who lead with purpose, values, and integrity; leaders who build enduring organizations.'"[9] A few pages later: "Leaders must promote an inclusive organizational climate that enables themselves and followers to continually learn and grow."[10] And so it goes, with the "need," "musts," and "shoulds" omnipresent. As such, the authentic leadership literature is a good example of the lay preaching, filled with admonishments, promises of better times, and warnings about what will happen if the prescriptions aren't followed, that characterizes much of the leadership industry.

HOW COMMON IS AUTHENTIC LEADERSHIP?

One might reasonably assume that authentic leadership is relatively rare, given all the leadership problems that presumably would be solved if there were more authentic leaders and if the need for authentic leadership development had been met. If authentic leadership were common or easily achieved, less research and other efforts would presumably be required on its behalf.

What the writing and speaking about authentic leadership does *not* do is attempt to empirically estimate base rates—how frequent or pervasive authentic leadership is. It is important to estimate base rates to assess whether authentic leadership is rare or widespread, and if it is rare, why that might be so; as I've previously argued, base rates are also important to judge the effects of change and improvement efforts. Put simply, how would one know if authentic leadership development, leadership training, writing, speaking, coaching, or teaching was doing any good if there were no comparisons between the initial state of the world and what happened as a consequence of all of these activities?

Although an assumption that authentic leadership is scarce and rare seems to follow from the attention to talking about and developing it, it is virtually impossible to estimate the frequency of the occurrence of authentic leadership. A search of Google Scholar, which, as you may recall, has more than two million entries on "leadership," produces precisely zero entries for the total of the search terms "proportion of authentic leaders," "percentage of authentic leaders," "occurrence of authentic leadership," and "amount of authentic leadership." Searching Google itself produces zero results for the query "How many authentic leaders are there?" but if you remove the quotes, there are literally millions of articles and links providing advice on how to develop your authentic leadership qualities and why you might want to do so. By the way, one can, in the medical domain, find incidence rates for virtually all diseases and medical conditions, because in medicine, people seem to believe that it might be important to understand the scope, ecology, and geographic incidence of a phenomenon, none of which seems to be of concern to the leadership industry.

WHY AUTHENTIC LEADERSHIP IS NOT DESIRABLE

What is authentic leadership, anyway? If you do a search on this term and click on many of the websites that first appear, authentic leadership is apparently a seemingly endless list of positive attributes including ethics and energy and a long list of behaviors including having impact, exercising integrity, exerting influence, demonstrating initiative,[11] dreaming, taking care of yourself, exhibiting courage, building teams[12]—a set of undoubtedly positive actions that have at best a tangential relationship to any commonsense notion of authenticity as contrasted with positive or effective leadership or living in general. Consulting the scholarly literature provides a tighter and somewhat more useful definition: "individuals who are 'in tune' with their basic nature and clearly and accurately see themselves and their lives." Or, in a similar vein, "owning one's personal experiences, be they thoughts, emotions, needs, wants, preferences, or beliefs, processes captured by the injunction to 'know oneself.' "

By this definition, the former New York congressman and New York City mayoral candidate Anthony Weiner, famous for sending pictures of his private parts to various women he met on the Internet, was, if nothing else, authentic. He was certainly "owning" his thoughts, needs, and wants. As this extreme example suggests, getting along, let alone being successful in the world, often requires a large amount of inauthenticity and self-regulation. Leaders need to be and do what their followers and society require, not what the leader feels like being or doing at the moment.

A friend's daughter fell in with the wrong crowd at college and wound up with a boyfriend who was also a drug dealer. She took an overdose, fell into a coma, and eventually died several months later. The pain of this experience can hardly be imagined. My friend, a senior-level college administrator, naturally received sympathy from his colleagues while he was going through this heartbreaking experience and afterward. But the fact is, the large organization in which he had an important leadership role did not cease its operations while his personal tragedy was unfolding, and his subordinates, bosses, and peers needed him not only to do his job but also, on occasion, to provide them with the motivation and encouragement they needed. In short, as he told me, "The experience of losing a daughter is part of my soul, a sadness I will never get over. But you also have to go on doing your job for the institution and people who are counting on you, regardless of how you may feel on a particular day."

Is he inauthentic? I will let you decide. But the simple fact is that as a prescription for leadership, being true to your role, fulfilling your obligations regardless of your wants and desires, doing what will make you successful in the environment in which you are working, are behaviors likely to be much more useful than being true to yourself and your feelings at the moment. After all, what if your real self is an asshole?

Moreover, as Gary Loveman has stated, there comes a time in your career, as you move up, when critical relationships simply have to work. When you are in school, if you don't like a particular classmate, that is fine. Don't hang out with that person; don't even talk to the individual if you don't want to. But if you are both senior executives in an organization in a relationship that inevitably entails a high degree of interdependence, you cannot afford to not "like" the other person. Moreover, your personal feelings are largely irrelevant to your need to make the relationship successful. So one of the things that happens as you move up the organizational ladder, Loveman suggests, is that you lose the freedom to act on your personal beliefs, feelings, and predilections—your "authentic self"—and you have to direct your behavior according much more to what you need to do to be successful, regardless of how you feel at the moment.

Here's another problem with the prescription to be your authentic self: People change and grow all the time as a result of their work experiences. No one is born a doctor, lawyer, nurse, professional golfer, carpenter, or, for that matter, as a creature that walks and talks. We learn not only skills, but also the values and the culture that surround our particular jobs and organizations. We become what we do, in terms of not just skills but also preferences and values. One of the more robust findings in social psychology is that attitudes follow behaviors.[13] After you have been a doctor, or a tax accountant, or a professor for long enough, you probably come to like what you have to do every day, and in many respects you also become the role you have been doing.

Learning and adapting to what we do never stops. So what does it mean to be true to yourself? Is that your high school self? Your college self? Your postcollege self? Your role as a friend? A family member? An employee? A leader?

People need to figure out how to be effective, regardless of their wants, needs, upbringing, and so forth. They need to learn how to be successful in the environments they confront, or they must learn how to find different and better environments. People need to grow, develop, and change, not get stuck in their temporarily authentic selves.

BECOMING USEFULLY INAUTHENTIC

Sitting in my office is a young woman born in Taiwan and raised by parents who taught her to respect authority, to be modest and self-effacing, to avoid conflict, and to work hard in order to succeed. She has come to see me because a peer who has the same boss at her iconic Silicon Valley employer has made a move to absorb her business unit into the one he leads. Should she follow the dictates of her upbringing and what she has come to define as her fundamental persona and be modest and nice, or should she fight for herself using tactics that she might have in the past seen as inconsistent with who she is?

After about fifteen minutes of listening, I remark about how frequently she has described herself in her situation as being the youngest of her peers, the person with the least tenure in the company, and the only woman reporting directly to her boss. "I'm sure that is all true," I say, "but let me give you three other adjectives you might use to describe yourself: the smartest, the most analytically skilled, and the person among your peers who has run the project that has had the biggest financial impact." She hesitates—she was raised to be modest, of course. Then, sitting up a little straighter in her chair, she remarks that yes, I am probably correct. "So," I continue, "there are, as we now see, at least six adjectives to describe you. All of them are true and accurate. You get to pick which of the three you carry around in your head. But your choice has enormous consequences for your sense of what you deserve and what you are going to be willing to do." I am pleased to report that she largely got over herself and her upbringing and navigated the situation successfully.

This story or some variant thereof, although often without the happy ending, repeats itself endlessly and helps explain why women are underrepresented at senior levels in corporations and law firms. As we saw in the last chapter, confidence as much as competence determines success, and successful people are not bashful about promoting themselves and eschewing any feelings of modesty in the process. Sheryl Sandberg, the COO of Facebook, founded a movement, Lean In, on the basis of the insight that women are often not quite pushy enough—but that with support from others, with practice, with knowledge of the relevant social science literature, women can change their behavior and become more successful.

Does this imply that women need to become less "authentic" to be successful? Quite possibly, if women's typical behavior, such as eschewing competition, not negotiating as hard as men, not asking for promotions, and not trying to stand out, holds their careers back. One could easily read Sandberg's book *Lean In*[14] and similar books as pleas for women to do what it takes to be successful, regardless of how they feel, how they have been trained, or what seems to be comfortable in the moment. For women, and for men, being true to oneself is useful only to the extent that someone's true self has the qualities that make people successful. Otherwise, people need to put on, to assume, the qualities required to present themselves in the most favorable light.

Or to take another example, many people around the world consider the former U.S. president John F. Kennedy to have been an inspiring figure, a great speaker, and a charismatic leader. He wrote a well-regarded book about courage and overcame physical ailments to win the presidency. He gave one of the most-quoted inaugural addresses. But as a review of a book on Kennedy by the author Thurston Clarke noted:

> As Mr. Clarke points out, Kennedy was "one of the most complicated and enigmatic men ever to occupy the White House": a man who compartmentalized different aspects of his life and who frequently said and did contradictory things. His most essential quality, the literary critic Alfred Kazin is quoted as saying, was "that of the man who is always making and remaking himself."[15]

Does this make Kennedy any less of a successful leader? I don't think so. Nor is it unusual. People make and remake themselves all the time and adjust their behaviors to the situations they face.

Or consider Nelson Mandela, the highly revered father of South Africa who served more than twenty years in prison under the apartheid regime before emerging to become South Africa's first black president. Like Kennedy, Mandela was a man of contradictions, as documented by Bill Keller, the former editor of and now a columnist for the *New York Times*. Keller, who knew Mandela personally for a long time, wrote:

> First, Mandela's brief membership in the South African Communist Party, and his long-term alliance with more devout Communists, says less about his ideology than about his pragmatism. He was at various times a black nationalist and a nonracialist, an opponent of armed struggle and an advocate of violence, a hothead and the calmest man in the room, a consumer of Marxist tracts and an admirer of Western democracy, a close partner of Communists and, in his presidency, a close partner of South Africa's powerful capitalists.[16]

Does this make Nelson Mandela inauthentic? And if so, who cares?

One of the most important leadership skills is the ability to put on a show, *to act like a leader*, to act in a way that inspires confidence and garners support—even if the person doing the performance does not actually feel confident or powerful. Deborah Gruenfeld, a social psychologist, teaches a class at Stanford Business School called Acting with Power, which is designed to build these important leadership skills. The course description aptly presents why acting is such an important leadership skill, particularly for people inside hierarchical organizations:

> Many people struggle with "authority issues" that make certain hierarchical roles and positions difficult for them. This course draws on the craft of acting and the science of psychology to help students learn to use themselves to develop the characters that can play these roles effectively.

> This class is designed specifically for students who have
> trouble "playing" authoritative roles; those who find it
> difficult to act with power, status and authority.

Gruenfeld's class recognizes an essential truth that, as the sociologist Erving Goffman described decades ago, people are inevitably putting on a show as they present various facets of themselves to others during social interactions.[17] The issue is how to become more effective in this self-presentation activity.

Acting is essential to effective leadership. For the eleven years from 1986 to 1997, Harriet Rubin was not just a writer but also an editor at Currency books, an imprint of a larger publishing house. During that time Rubin both published and, more important, got to know many famous, iconic leaders very well— people like Dee Hock, who was instrumental in the founding of Visa, Andy Grove of Intel, Phil Knight of Nike, Howard Schultz of Starbucks, and Max De Pree of Herman Miller. As Rubin tried to discern what made these individuals so successful in their leadership roles, she came to discover the importance of *inauthenticity*, of being able to play a role:

> It [their success] always had to do with pretense, playing
> a role, and the theatrical arts. I was intrigued . . . by a
> story told at Intel about Grove's time as leader. Grove
> insisted that his brilliant but shy managers attend a
> seminar they called "wolf school." Attendees learned
> how to lean into a superior's face and shout out an idea
> or proposal. By dramatically showing a fierce belief in
> themselves, they would convince Intel's hard-nosed man-
> agers of the value of their idea. If they didn't feel fierce,
> they had to pretend. The message: Act powerful and you
> become powerful.

Teach your murmuring voice to howl. Oddly enough, many leaders I met seemed to be at their strongest when they were most inauthentic. If was as if their reserves of character had been created not by digging out their authentic selves, but by playing a character.[18]

Rubin argued that when people enter into leadership roles, they might not see the qualities that reside within them. Instead, she sensibly argued, people develop leadership qualities by practicing them, by acting them out and rehearsing them until they become natural and part of the individual. Harriet Rubin and the leaders she got to know came to appreciate the complexity and multidimensionality of people, and they understood how leadership positions required certain behaviors and personas, regardless of how someone felt at that moment or what his or her "true" persona was.

WHY AUTHENTIC LEADERSHIP MAY BE ALMOST IMPOSSIBLE

Not only is authentic leadership often not very useful, it may be almost impossible to do. If we have learned anything from all of the social science research over the past several decades—and actually we have learned quite a bit—it is that people's attitudes and behaviors are profoundly affected by the situations in which they are embedded. So to the extent that being true to oneself entails ignoring or resisting situational constraints, the prescriptions of authentic leadership are at variance with how people act.

A classic study demonstrated the effect of situations on people's behavior and why the idea of behaving authentically is unlikely. Seymour Lieberman of the Institute for Social Research at the University of Michigan surveyed the attitudes of nearly all the employees at a four thousand–person, unionized home appliance manufacturer in the Midwest. Then twenty-three employees became foremen and thirty-five employees became union stewards. A new survey was conducted. Not surprisingly, the people who had moved into management (who had become foremen) exhibited more favorable attitudes toward the company and its incentive system, while those who had been elected stewards showed more favorable attitudes toward the union and also changed to be more favorable to the seniority system. A control group of people did not show any change in attitudes, as would be expected. Then the U.S. entered a recession and some of the foremen became frontline employees again, as did some of the shop stewards. The people who returned to their original roles exhibited changes in attitudes back toward their original values—with the former stewards becoming less pro-union and the former foremen becoming less pro-management.[19]

The basic idea motivating this research—"a person's role will have an impact on his attitudes"—is a fundamental tenet of role theory and has been tested numerous times over the ensuing years. In one demonstration of the idea relevant to leadership, the late Gerald Salancik and I studied fifty-three supervisors in the housing office of a large state university. We found that supervisory behavior could be explained by the expectations of others with whom the individual interacted, with the expectations of subordinates more important for affecting social behaviors and the expectations of bosses more important for explaining the leaders' task-relevant behaviors.[20] All of this makes sense: Where someone stands on a variety of issues and attitudes depends on where that individual "sits" in an organization. Position affects the information people receive, the structure of the rewards and evaluations they face, the social interactions they encounter as part of their work, and their identities. So of course people are affected by job roles.

But given this effect of position on behavior, then what does it mean to say that someone is "authentic"? In the case of the Lieberman study, people who were promoted to stewards became more authentic union members; people who became foremen became more authentic company leaders—that is, until their roles changed and so did their attitudes. The idea that people are unchanged and unchanging across situations, or even that they should be, seems inconsistent with most of what we know about human psychology.

And it is not just attitudes that adjust to situations—so do fundamental dimensions of people's personality. Many people believe that personality is fixed once someone reaches adulthood or maybe sooner, but that is not the case. The sociologists Melvin Kohn and Carmi Schooler conducted numerous studies investigating the effects of someone's occupation and job conditions on such dimensions of their personality as their cognitive flexibility. They consistently found a pattern of reciprocal relationships such that personality affected the type of jobs and occupations people chose, but that once in those jobs, personality was also affected by the job and occupational conditions.[21] If something as fundamental as one's personality changes in response to job conditions, then the notion of being true to one's authentic self makes no empirical sense—because that self is changing in response to the individual's environment, including the work environment.

We have seen in this chapter that the idea of behaving authentically as a leader is almost certainly rare, because this is a concept that is at once both psychologically impossible—because of situational effects on personality and behavior—and also not very useful, because of the requirements for acting as a leader regardless of how one may feel at the moment. The fact that there are lots of prescriptions for leaders to be authentic is, however, not surprising. As many of the chapters in this book illustrate, the leadership industry is rife with prescriptions that are neither commonly adopted nor completely useful. Which, to reprise a frequent refrain, is why the leadership industry has had such a small effect on the organizational world.

CHAPTER 4

Should Leaders Tell the Truth—and Do They?

T he virtues of telling the truth are as American as the country's first president, George Washington. The apocryphal story of the six-year-old Washington being given a hatchet, chopping down a young cherry tree, and when confronted by his father, bravely crying out, "I can't tell a lie. I did cut it with my hatchet" is familiar in popular culture.

Few people know or remember that the story originated with Mason Locke Weems, sometimes called Parson Weems. His occupation was that of a book agent and author. Weems apparently developed the story in order to boost the sales of a book he wrote about Washington. The story's theme of honesty and honor fit the needs of Americans in the early 1800s for heroic figures, a need that remains a cornerstone of the leadership industry today.[1] Ironically, a tale about America's first president not lying is itself apparently a lie.[2]

Telling the truth is a foundation of religion. To take one example, "Thou shalt not bear false witness against thy neighbor," sometimes colloquially restated as "thou shalt not lie," is one of the Ten Commandments. The Bible, both the New and Old Testament, has numerous passages decrying lying and forecasting ruin for those who do. The apocryphal story of the snake deceiving Eve in the Garden of Eden presents deception as the ultimate source of evil.[3]

Many of those ubiquitous sources of leadership advice also advocate candor, honesty, and transparency.[4] The logic seems sensible, even unassailable. Leaders should be candid and open, because if leaders lie, then subordinates, the leaders' own bosses, and the leaders' peers presumably won't trust what the leaders say, and trust is important to effective leadership (a theme we will explore further in the next chapter). Moreover, if leaders lie, others around them will do the same as they model the leader's behavior. If few people in a workplace tell the truth, then almost no one will have accurate information about what is really going on. And valid information about what is happening and the results of decisions is essential to both learn from experience and to make more effective choices. And if leaders lie, they will have committed a sin, reflecting negatively on themselves and undermining their authority and credibility. Research shows that "people view duplicity as one of the gravest moral failings."[5]

There's only one problem with the admonitions in favor of truth-telling: lying is incredibly common in everyday life and rampant among leaders of all sorts of organizations, including some of the most venerated leaders and companies. It logically follows that if some specific behavior is pervasive, that behavior must confront few sanctions, or else it would be rarer. One of the reasons lying persists is that there are few adverse consequences for it; and as we will see, positive results very often come from not telling the truth.

My conclusion: if we actually want to build more truthful organizations, we need to understand some of the empirical realities about lying, including its startling pervasiveness and efficacy.

SOME LEADERS HAVE BUILT CULTURES OF TRUTH-TELLING

Of course, there are successful leaders who have sought to build cultures of truth-telling in order to enhance the effectiveness of their firms. Kent Thiry, the CEO of DaVita, a kidney dialysis provider and disease management company, helped create a culture that emphasizes "no brag, just facts." In town hall–style meetings with employees around the United States, Thiry and other senior managers encourage employees to ask anything—even about salaries—and to raise concerns and issues. When Thiry or his colleagues do not know the answer, they say they do not know. When problems that surfaced previously have not been adequately addressed, they admit their mistakes. Even in DaVita's formal measurement and reporting systems, whenever there is a crucial operational indicator that cannot be produced by the company's current systems, they put the indicator on the reports anyway, with the notation "not available"—something that encourages people to figure out how to obtain data on crucial measures of performance.

But, in most situations and in most organizations, openness and candor are not default behaviors. Part of the problem comes from the fact that the higher one rises in an organization, the more likely it is that people will tell you you're right. People will agree with powerful leaders as a strategy of ingratiation, as nothing is as flattering as others' telling you how right and how smart you are. But even if individuals don't intend to flatter the powerful, hierarchical position is often assumed to be associated with intelligence and skill. If people think an individual in a senior position is smart and successful, they will bias their evaluations of that person's behavior and decisions and overestimate their wisdom. Why? Because they assume that a person in power in a senior position must have positive qualities, as they have been successful. In short, power comes to equal omniscience.

These tendencies make building a culture of truth-telling a difficult task requiring conscious effort. Creating a culture of candor requires work, constant diligence, and difficult decisions. In part because of the effort required, in part because hearing the truth can be unpleasant, and in part because people naturally think that those who agree with them are smarter and better, Kent Thiry's leadership behavior is unusual.

Or take another case. When Gary Loveman left Harvard Business School to become the COO (and then CEO) of Harrah's Entertainment, now called Caesars, he was determined to build a culture of truthfulness, one in which people actually admit their mistakes. Loveman defines lying as saying something that you know not to be true at the moment you say it—which is different from something that you believe to be true that subsequently turns out to be false.

Loveman has often publicly bemoaned the widespread absence of truth-telling in the business world, whether it was the CEO of Bear Stearns telling the world the company's balance sheet was in great shape just days before the company collapsed and then continuing to deny culpability,[6] Lehman Brothers' CEO doing the same thing, the traders in the London office of JPMorgan Chase grossly underestimating and misinforming others about the losses on a trade gone bad,[7] or the numerous other instances of duplicity that accompanied the financial meltdown of 2007 and 2008 and what followed.

Loveman received a Ph.D. in economics from MIT and then taught at Harvard Business School before being appointed by then-CEO Phil Satre to the job of chief operating officer of Harrah's in 1998. The academic culture from which Loveman came emphasizes tolerating and even encouraging substantive disagreements with colleagues in an effort to uncover the truth. And academic culture also has a norm of being true to the data in the quest for understanding—academic values emphasize not fabricating results and even being willing to share your data with others. Loveman, in part because of his background and in part because of his own persona, believed that there is never any excuse for lying. While he and the company did not necessarily need to tell everyone everything that those others might inquire about, what they did say had to be truthful.

One example dramatically illustrates Gary Loveman's insistence on truth-telling. In one of the Harrah's properties, a manager was terminated and the individual went home and killed himself. The company's PR department wanted to put out a press release saying that the individual had died as a result of an accident, something that was untrue and known to be untrue at the time the release would be issued. Loveman refused to let the press release come out as written. He noted that the release could just say the individual died, and he also noted that the company did not have to even issue a statement, but he refused to let the company release a statement that was not truthful. He said that he received much pushback about this decision—after all, this is precisely the sort of instance in which euphemisms and small untruths occur all the time, and no one is really harmed. But Loveman believed that the road to a culture of untruthfulness began with small steps, and he was unwilling to countenance the first of such steps.[8]

Loveman also sanctioned employees who told him they knew how to fix problems when they really didn't. To him, the point of having multiple units and a corporate headquarters and staff was to be able to share knowledge with poorly performing units so they could improve. But providing help and spreading best practices required units and their leaders to admit when they did not know something or had made a mistake. Loveman himself modeled this behavior of being willing to admit areas in which he was incompetent, such as building design, and he also admitted his mistakes. In management training and other meetings, Loveman would regale his managers about the mistakes he had made, such as passing on an opportunity to purchase Steve Wynn's Macao gambling subconcession when it was offered to Harrah's and also messing up the employee health plan. Loveman believed that you could run a company successfully only if people admit what they do not know and talk about their mistakes. In that way, he believed decisions would be made on the basis of facts rather than just hopes and dreams.

BUT LEADERS LIE ALL THE TIME

Loveman, Thiry, and other exemplars of transparency and candor are notable not just for their leadership skills but also for their rarity. One of the sometimes-unnoticed ironies about our search for heroic leader behavior, illustrated in oft-told tales and case studies, is that the very fact that such behavior is heroic—which implies it is exceptional and exemplary—speaks to how unusual such behavior, such as honesty, actually is.

Even in academia, where standards of integrity and the pursuit of truth are highly valued, problems proliferate. For instance, there is the case of Fred Walumbwa, a professor at Florida International University whose area of research includes, ironically, ethical leadership. *Leadership Quarterly* retracted five of his papers because of suspected scientific fraud, including two papers on authentic leadership and one paper concerning ethical leadership. Oh well.[9]

One of the reasons leaders lie is that they seldom face serious consequences for doing so. Yes, some CEOs and for that matter football coaches have lost their jobs for lying about their credentials on their résumés. But in many instances, particularly if an individual is successful or the untruth fits what people want to believe, leaders just sail along. Here are a few examples.

In 2011 as the U.S. government moved toward a shutdown because there was no ability to reach agreement between the Democrats and Republicans on spending priorities, Jon Kyl, a Republican senator from Arizona, took to the floor of the Senate to berate the fact that the Obama budget included funding for Planned Parenthood, an organization that is the bête noire of the Republican right. During his speech, Kyl noted that "well over 90 percent" of the organization's activities are related to abortion. When numerous sources pointed out that the actual proportion of Planned Parenthood's budget devoted to providing abortion as contrasted with other women's health services was only about 3 percent, Kyl's office, facing a media firestorm including satiric segments on the television shows *The Colbert Report* and *The Daily Show with Jon Stewart*, issued a statement saying that the senator's remarks were not intended to be a factual statement.[10]

Of course, you may think that elected politicians regularly lie and apparently face few consequences for doing so. That is sort of what we expect, not only from the campaign promises soon forgotten but also as politicians distort opponents' records and even disagree with proven science. Then how about government civil servants, people who do not face the task of running for election? When the U.S. director of national intelligence, James

Clapper, was asked during a Senate hearing if the government collected data on millions or hundreds of millions of Americans, he said no. But of course this was not a truthful response, as people learned when Edward Snowden released classified information about the widespread surveillance of the telephone and Internet activities of U.S. foreign citizens and even leaders of foreign governments. Once the facts became known, Clapper later apologized before Congress for giving a "clearly erroneous" answer that he intended, at the time he gave it, to be as close to the truth as possible, given his other objectives. Clapper kept his job, of course.[11]

Some of my colleagues maintain that business leaders are certainly better than politicians or government officials. Maybe not. It's hard to overlook, for example, those tobacco industry CEOs, all testifying in front of Congress that they had no knowledge of the health effects of smoking. Subsequently, we learned that their companies had conducted lots of research showing the adverse health effects of smoking, and these CEOs knew about the studies. Or what about the various financial industry executives claiming their balance sheets were in fine shape just days before filing for bankruptcy? Or the bank executives in the United States and the United Kingdom who had to raise equity capital even when they had just said they would not have to, because they had plenty of equity compared with the level of their non-performing loans? Or the automobile industry executives, who when confronted with data showing large differences in fatalities related to the design of cars,[12] insisted that the cars were safe even when they weren't, and harassed their critics, even when the executives knew about internal documents substantiating the problems? The list is lengthy. Just pick up a newspaper or consult your favorite news source online; some reasonable fraction of news stories every day are about senior people in all sorts of organizations—our so-called leaders—not telling the truth.

It doesn't matter what industry we examine either—whether it's the financial industry, big tobacco, automobiles, or even that much-vaunted center of innovation and youthful vigor, Silicon Valley. Look no further than Lawrence J. Ellison, the cofounder and CEO of the Oracle Corporation. Ellison is one of the richest men in the world. Oracle operates in an industry, software, in which not telling the truth about product features and particularly if and when a product will be ready is so common that there is even a term for this ubiquitous prevarication: "vaporware." Ellison, particularly in the early days of the company, understood that to get and keep customers in a competitive business, one sometimes needed to misrepresent product availability. In David Kaplan's book *The Silicon Boys*, a history of the Silicon Valley, Kaplan asked a colleague of Ellison's about Larry's propensity to exaggerate product features and particularly product availability. This is what Kaplan wrote:

> More than a few authors, employees, customers, and stockholders have marveled at Ellison's ability to fudge the facts. . . . "Does Larry lie," asks Ed Oates, an Oracle cofounder who's known him for twenty-five years. "We prefer to say that Larry has a problem with tenses. For example, 'our product is available now' might mean it'll be available in a few months or that Larry was thinking about one day developing the product." . . . "Temporally challenged," another colleague calls it. "Not a lie, just a different version of the truth." . . . One man's prevaricator is another man's visionary.[13]

The software industry illustrates another principle that can help explain why lying is so common: the idea that in competitions, you must meet what your competitors are doing. In this instance, if your competitors distort the truth about product features and availability, do you really have any choice but to do the same? William F. Miller, a former president of SRI International, a former provost of Stanford University, a member of the National Academy of Engineering, and a colleague of mine, has a distinguished and exemplary biography.[14] One of his positions during his long, illustrious career was as nonexecutive chairman of Borland Software. I recall running into Bill one evening as we were both headed to our cars in the parking lot. He bemoaned the fact that Borland had competitors who were misrepresenting product features and when a product would be released—the famous vaporware problem. Miller told me that he did not want Borland to do the same, but since customers were buying the promises of others, economic survival practically dictated that Borland had to use the same tactics as its competitors. My reply was along the lines of, "Get over the ambivalence if you are going to do this, because you and your colleagues will need to be as convincing as the competition." The lesson: sometimes survival demands that you do what prevails in the ecosystem in which you are competing.

And then there's Steve Jobs, the visionary leader of Apple who transformed the company upon his return as CEO into one of the most successful and highly valued firms on the planet. People sometimes forget the phrase "reality distortion field," and how it originated. It came from a member of the Macintosh team in the 1980s, and it was used to describe Jobs's behavior, and particularly his predilection to create his own version of reality about Apple, its products, and its success. After Jobs died, an old FBI file on him became public. According to materials released by the FBI, "several individuals questioned Mr. Jobs's honesty stating that Mr. Jobs will twist the truth and distort reality in order to achieve his goals."[15]

As the foregoing suggests, leaders often lie. And no wonder. In the first place, studies of both children and college undergraduates show that the ability to create "credible, deceptive messages predicted dominance in preschool children and men but not women."[16] So lying helps people attain powerful positions. Moreover, leaders are, by definition, people in positions of great power. And research consistently demonstrates that "powerful people lie more often and with more ease." Leaders prevaricate with greater aplomb because "power, even when minimally endowed in the laboratory, mitigates the impact of stress associated with dishonesty. . . . The experience of power also brings illusory control, and their perceived control may aid the liar in the production of a convincing narrative. . . . Finally, high-power individuals are less sensitive to societal norms; e.g., norms that condemn the use of deception."[17] Thus, powerful people—leaders—are able to lie more successfully, and they do so.

LYING IN EVERYDAY LIFE

It's not just bosses who don't tell the truth. A survey conducted by *Sales and Marketing Management* magazine of 316 sales and marketing executives reported that "45 percent of managers have heard their reps lying about promised delivery times, 20 percent have overheard their members give false information about the company's service, and nearly 78 percent of managers have caught a competitor lying about their company's products or services." The article detailed numerous instances of salespeople deceiving customers, with many of the cases coming from selling Internet advertising.[18]

And it's not just about "putting a shine" on something that may or may not be quite accurate. In fact, not only executives but many people at all levels lie on their résumés. For instance, people lie by listing educational credentials they don't really have or by exaggerating their job responsibilities and accomplishments.

David Edmondson, at one time the CEO of the electronics retailer RadioShack, was forced to resign from the company when it was discovered that he had told the company he had two college degrees when in fact he had none.[19] As reported by ADP Screening and Selection Services, a subsidiary of the payroll company ADP, out of about 2.6 million screening background checks, "44 percent of applicants lied about their work histories, 41 percent lied about their education, and 23 percent falsified credentials or licenses."[20]

A senior executive at the search firm Heidrick & Struggles told me that lying on résumés has become so common that executive search firms now make it a routine part of background checking to confirm everything listed by a candidate that can be confirmed, such as degrees and job histories. Perhaps more surprising, the senior executive said this in a tone that conveyed that résumé distortion was well known and sort of expected in the executive search business. If any inaccuracies are discovered, a résumé will be corrected, but the fact of lying in itself does not disqualify the candidate from further consideration. As he noted, if such behavior eliminated people from being considered for jobs, the applicant pools would be too small.

There is also lying in negotiations. Many people do not honestly reveal what is the lowest offer they are willing to accept or, for that matter, the highest amount they would be willing to pay, or other information about their resources and preferences. One experimental economics study found that when people could obtain at least a moderate advantage from lying about their resource endowments, many did so.[21] Many individuals also misrepresent their emotional state in negotiations, feigning anger, disappointment, and surprise, for example, to achieve strategic advantage. There is a substantial literature, primarily in various law reviews but also elsewhere in the social sciences, that discusses the ethics of using deception as part of the negotiating process, as well as some limited research assessing the effectiveness and consequences of lying.[22]

The very existence of such an extensive discussion of these ethical issues suggests that misrepresentation is frequently part of the negotiating process. So apparently Mark Twain was correct when he wrote, "Truth is such a precious commodity, it should be used sparingly." And Niccolò Machiavelli demonstrated great insight when he endorsed the art of deception: "You must be a great liar . . . a deceitful man will always find plenty who are ready to be deceived."[23]

Research on lying shows that it is commonplace in everyday life. A random sample of one thousand people in the United States found that 40.1 percent of respondents admitted to telling a lie in the previous twenty-four hours.[24] One overview of the relevant social science literature noted:

> Most of us lie . . . with astounding regularity. According to a 2011 survey, people in the United States do so, on average, 1.65 times a day. And it's not just Americans—or, for that matter, humans—who deceive: recent studies of 24 other primate species found that they regularly lie to one another . . . one in 10 text messages involves a lie of some kind. . . . According to a study of online daters, a full 81 percent exaggerated their attributes on their dating profiles.[25]

Five social psychologists empirically investigated how common lying was and whether or not people who told lies were bothered by doing so. Their reasoning was that if lying was somehow counternormative and was considered deviant behavior, people would be bothered by their lying even if they were willing to admit that they lied. The study found that college students reported telling two lies a day, on average, while community members told one. The authors noted that "many of the lies of everyday life are told to avoid tension and conflict and to minimize hurt feelings and ill-will," a finding consistent with other studies.[26] Sometimes lies seem to function to smooth over difficult situations and to lubricate relationships—for instance, complimenting people on their appearance (even if it is insincere) or saying things that downplay disagreements. Because lies are so much a part of how people present themselves to appear more favorably during social interactions, and are also used to smooth over relationships, lies ought to be "of only minor cognitive or emotional significance to the people who tell them." And that is precisely what the research showed.[27]

One reason why lying is common is that the ability to lie or deceive others offers evolutionary benefits and, as a consequence, has increased over time. A second reason is that "manipulative ability is a foundation of social power and the ability to lie successfully is an important skill linked to personal and professional success."[28] Simply put, lying is useful for getting ahead. There is a reciprocal relationship between power and lying: the powerful deceive more often, and the ability to deceive effectively creates social power.

An experimental study of deception found that engaging in deception helped the individuals who deceived to present their communications in a more dominant fashion.[29] Being forceful and dominant—a form of exhibiting confidence—helps individuals to be seen as more powerful. The study found that the dominant communication styles that came from those engaging in deception enhanced the credibility of those individuals, and thus helped them in achieving their objectives. As the authors noted, "Persuasive deceivers became more dominant" . . . and

"Participants felt empowered by the act of deception itself." This study shows that deceiving others not only creates career success but also causes the person engaging in the deception to feel more powerful, which would be a desirable psychological outcome. No wonder lying is so common.

Yet another reason that lying is common is that although most people believe they can reliably discern when they are being lied to, the evidence suggests that they can't. Some analyses of people's judgments of the truthfulness of others show that, on average, people are no more accurate than the flip of a coin.[30] Even a review of multiple studies, which showed that people are better able than chance to discern lying, reported an accuracy rate of only 54 percent.[31]

If lying is common and imperfectly detected in everyday life, it should be even more common and less often detected when done by leaders. That is because power of the sort that leaders possess leads to even fewer behavioral inhibitions. And because observers, believing that the world is a just and fair place and that leaders are to be venerated rather than scrutinized, are even less likely to check on the truthfulness of what leaders say. Thus, everyone lies—the typical leader just does so more frequently and with fewer risks of detection.

THERE ARE FEW SANCTIONS FOR LYING

Leaders lie in part, as we will soon see, because there are benefits to doing so—and because the downside of being caught is so small. There are few sanctions for lying, and, by contrast, there are often punishments for those who have the temerity to call out others who engage in deception.

One study demonstrated both the importance of peers—insiders—for discovering and reporting fraud,[32] but also concluded "that the career prospects of employees who report corporate malfeasance are so dismal that it is surprising that people whistleblow at all."[33] Whistle-blowers in settings ranging from the government to private industry are shunned and often have trouble finding subsequent employment. In an experimental study, researchers found that even though some individuals are willing to report lying, when "groups can select their members, individuals who report lies are generally shunned, even by groups where lying is absent."[34] The title of the study, "Nobody Likes a Rat," says it all, and reflects that even in childhood, tattletales are more likely to confront social ostracism than to receive praise for revealing problems or bad behavior.

Numerous examples demonstrate that lying, even on financial statements or in statements made to investors, seldom brings permanent harm to its perpetrator. As the *New York Times* columnist Floyd Norris has documented, a court in Germany ruled that sometimes lies are necessary, and in the United States, the Supreme Court is "considering whether to reverse a decision . . . and make it impossible for most investors to ever recover if they fall victim to corporate lies."[35]

Oracle is scarcely the only company to ever misrepresent its financial statements by overstating revenues. On August 27, 1990, the company admitted it had seriously misrepresented its revenue for five consecutive quarters, and less than a year later it admitted to making even more mistakes. All of this resulted in an investigation and a fine by the Securities and Exchange Commission in the early 1990s. No serious consequences ensued either for Oracle or for its CEO, Larry Ellison. As reported by the *New York Times*, "Now, with its stock again soaring, Oracle's faithful fans on the Street tend to dismiss the past as a mere case of 'overaggressive' accounting."[36]

In fact, misstating revenue and engaging in other financial statement inaccuracy was reasonably common prior to the Sarbanes-Oxley reform, with one study finding almost two thousand restatements during 2006 alone.[37] That is one reason that one of the financial and corporate governance reforms that emerged from the financial crisis is to require CEOs to personally attest to the accuracy of the financial information their firms release. However, it is far from clear that this policy has significantly diminished financial statement misrepresentations or the need to subsequently restate financial results.

I recall a dinner I attended in Palo Alto with a number of executives in the semiconductor industry. One way that revenue is distorted is by keeping the books open after the end of a quarter, so that sales booked, for instance, on July 1 are credited to the quarter that supposedly ended on June 30. These individuals, who came from some of the leading semiconductor companies, not only told me that such a practice was quite common (and not just in that specific industry), but they joked that someday a company would have to cancel a quarter because it had extended the previous quarter so long to make its revenue targets. When I expressed some degree of disapproval and surprise at their openness about this practice, the people at the table looked at me as though I were crazy, naive, or maybe both.

A cycle of behavior is created. Because lying produces few to no severe sanctions, lying increases in frequency. Because lying is then common, it becomes normative, in the sense that norms describe common behavioral patterns. Because lying becomes normative, it isn't sanctioned, because it makes no sense to try to punish widespread, almost taken-for-granted behavior.

I'm certainly not saying that lying is virtuous or to be encouraged, or that a world in which not telling the truth is both reasonably common and tolerated is in any way a perfect world. I'm just saying that the evidence is quite clear that leaders (and, for that matter, other people) frequently don't tell the truth and face few to no consequences for doing so. And this fact is something worth understanding, rather than continuing to pretend that leaders are the paragons of truthfulness that they are so often portrayed to be.

THE POSITIVE CONSEQUENCES OF LYING

If lying is common, and if sanctions for lying are either mild or nonexistent, it makes sense to ask how and why lying might actually be useful and helpful, and therefore why it is more accepted and acceptable than commonly recognized. One reason people lie is to smooth over otherwise difficult situations—to make relationships and interactions proceed more smoothly. And lying often accomplishes this goal of making important social relations work better. Because people lie often for good reason, one interesting research finding is that people judge others' deceptions much more harshly than their own. As one review of part of the literature on lying noted:

> As deceivers, people are practical. They accommodate perceived needs by lying. . . . People may lie in the interest of impression management. . . . They exaggerate, minimize, and omit. . . . Regarding half-truths and self-editing as necessities of social life, deceivers see deception as similar to these sanctioned practices. . . . lies occasion little anxiety, guilt, or shame. . . . They are easy to rationalize.[38]

To take just one business-relevant example that illustrates how common prevarication is and to what ends, Marc Effron, the president of the human resources consulting firm the Talent

Strategy Group, surveyed more than two hundred companies in early 2014 about their talent management practices. He reported that "73% of companies have decided that lying to their employees about their potential to advance is the right choice."[39] In hierarchical organizations, where there are many fewer promotion opportunities than contenders, companies have apparently decided that telling people the truth about their actual promotion prospects will demotivate them. Companies also think that when people know their actual (small) likelihood of being promoted, turnover will increase and companies will lose those solid performers who make things run but who do not see much potential for further career growth. In these cases, companies that lead people to believe they have better promotion prospects than they actually do maintain more positive relationships with their employees, at least for a while. In fact, this positive relationship may last even longer because people frequently do see themselves as above average and are prone in many instances to engage in wishful thinking.

A second answer to the question of the benefits of lying comes from a series of experiments that show that individuals actually have higher levels of positive affect when they cheat, a phenomenon researchers call the "cheater's high." The studies in question eliminated some alternative explanations for why cheaters feel happier, such as the fact that they earned financial rewards or believed that their good performance made a statement about their abilities. The authors noted, "Even when prospects for self-deception about unethical behavior have been reduced, the high cheaters experience from 'getting away with it' overwhelms the negative affective consequences that people mistakenly predict they will experience after engaging in unethical behavior."[40]

Not only do lies often smooth over difficult situations, not only are people readily able to rationalize their own prevarications, and not only do people apparently feel good about engaging in deception and getting away with it, there's a fourth explanation as to why lying may be helpful and often unpunished: Lies, told often enough and convincingly enough, can become the truth—sometimes with positive effects. That is because what people say, whether truthful or not, helps construct a social reality that then becomes real.

One of the most important ideas in social and organizational psychology is that of the self-fulfilling prophecy.[41] The fundamental idea is that if people believe that some situation is real, it becomes real. Relevant to this chapter's focus on lying, the sociologist Robert Merton noted that "the self-fulfilling prophecy is, in the beginning a *false* definition of the situation evoking a new behavior which makes the originally false conception come *true*" (emphasis in original).[42]

There are numerous examples of the self-fulfilling prophecy. For instance, bank runs: if all the customers of a bank believe the bank is in danger of failing, they will withdraw their deposits and the bank will fail. Another example is analysts' expectations for stock prices: if everyone believes a stock price will go up, everyone will encourage clients to buy, and the stock price will rise.

One pertinent example of the self-fulfilling prophecy is the effect of leaders' expectations on the behavior and performance of others. Research shows that people who are expected to do well often perform at a high level because of those expectations, while those, including students in school, for whom others hold low expectations, often underperform.[43] Leaders' expectations are particularly potent in their effects, because leaders are in positions of power, which gives their beliefs greater weight.

Self-fulfilling prophecies exist in the domain of consumer purchasing behavior as well. People buy products when and to the extent they think they are cool—witness the long lines outside Apple stores when the company introduces a new phone or tablet computer. Product desirability often depends on the ancillary features and services developed by others—software in the case of computers, applications in the case of smart phones—as well as people's beliefs that the product will be around for a while, as no one wants to purchase something that then disappears, which affects a product's resale value and even its usability. Consequently, the ability to convince others of a company's future success is one of the key tasks of a CEO, and, if successful, it helps ensure a firm's future success—because others will develop ancillary products and services that create more value and because customers have more confidence in the company and its products, which will increase their likelihood of actually purchasing the good or service.

No one was better at the task of creating the perception of success and coolness than Steve Jobs. In the early 1980s, Apple Computer (as it was known then) faced an existential threat. After the Apple II's introduction, IBM had launched its own personal computer, and many people felt that IBM would crush Apple. Then came the Lisa, Apple's next product, which was not a very good—or successful—product. So when Apple was to introduce the Macintosh in 1984, people would need to be convinced that the product would be successful, so they would buy it, and developers of software needed to be convinced that Apple would sell enough computers and survive long enough to make it sensible for them to develop the software that would make the computer useful—and thereby help ensure its sales. The Macintosh was introduced to a packed auditorium with much fanfare and the famous "1984" advertisement, which ran only once on television, during the Super Bowl. Almost all industry observers and analysts were captivated, and the Macintosh was a success. Jobs's ability, honed and implemented over decades, to continually and convincingly make the case that Apple was the coolest company with the neatest products to all of the various company constituents ensured Apple's success.

Leaders also affect companies' ability to survive difficult economic circumstances. If employees believe that a company is going to fail, they will leave—and the best ones, who have the greatest chance of finding other good jobs, will leave first. As talent drains out, the odds of turning the company around are reduced. Thus, one important task of leaders is to convince their employees that success is possible. Believing in success, people will expend more effort and exhibit more confidence, and by so doing, thereby create success.

One of the most impressive accomplishments of Steve Jobs was to convince talented people that their working at Apple was the most productive use of their working time, because the company would be successful and they would have a hand in changing the world. His recruitment of John Sculley from Pepsi-Cola with the line "Would you rather sell colored water or change the world?" is only one instance of Jobs's ability to attract talent. He recruited Joel Podolny from his job as dean of the Yale School of Management by presenting the opportunities at Apple as being much more interesting than even running a university. In fact Podolny's first job at Apple—he now runs all of human resources—was to lead Apple University.

In many instances, leaders convince customers to buy their products, investors to part with their money—a particularly important task for start-ups—talented employees to join, and stay, and suppliers to work with their company by presenting the organization as more successful than it really is. By so doing, leaders enlist the resources and support that will ultimately make the organization successful. This is why I often say that the ability to misrepresent reality is a crucial—maybe the most crucial—leadership skill.

And leaders convince others to hire them and to keep them in their leadership positions, sometimes in spite of poor performance or a not-so-great track record, by their ability to articulate a compelling case for why they should hold the job. That is why, as we saw in chapter 2, exhibiting confidence is so important for career advancement. If you don't feel confident, or competent, then getting and keeping a good job entails misrepresenting your true feelings—being able to lie convincingly about your ability to do the job. But often, if people believe you can do the job, you can, because they will give you the advice and support to make you successful.

An example of this phenomenon is illustrated by the life of Frank Abagnale, which was the subject of the movie *Catch Me If You Can*. Before he was nineteen, Abagnale had convinced others that he was a Pan Am pilot, a Georgia doctor, and a Louisiana parish prosecutor. "His primary crime was check fraud," and he became so skilled "that the FBI eventually turned to him for help in catching other check forgers."[44]

This is all to say that sometimes, maybe even often, saying what is not true at the moment helps make the statement true down the road. This is because of various forces that the untruthful statement brings into play, thus making the statement become true. Whether or not this self-fulfilling process provides a sufficient justification for not telling the truth depends on one's view of the ethics and rationale for lying. But there is no question that sometimes lies become the truth for the very fact of their being told and believed—with, on occasion, positive consequences for companies and leaders.

And there is at least one additional positive consequence from not telling the truth—the ability to get things done by forestalling the opposition that might occur if people knew precisely what was going on and what an individual's intentions really were. For example, John F. Kennedy assured the American people that there were no plans to invade Cuba even as his administration was plotting the Bay of Pigs invasion, and Franklin Roosevelt assured the United States in 1940 that he had no plans to send American troops to fight in the war then breaking out in Europe. But perhaps the classic case of lying and its positive consequences in helping presidents get things done was Abraham Lincoln. Meg Mott, a professor of political theory at Marlboro College, refers to Lincoln as a skillful liar, for good effect. According to the journalist John Blake,

> Lincoln lied about whether he was negotiating with the South to end the war. . . . He also lied about where he stood on slavery. He told the American public and political allies that he didn't believe in political equality for slaves because he didn't want to get too far ahead of public opinion, Mott says.[45]

A LIE TAKES TWO PEOPLE

When Sherron Watkins, the vice president for corporate development at the Enron Corporation, went to Kenneth Lay, the CEO, to voice her concerns about the proliferation of and the accounting for all of the special-purpose entities being set up to mislead investors and artificially boost perceived profits and Enron's stock price, her reward was that Andy Fastow, the company's chief financial officer, sought to have her fired. That's not unusual. In the conflict between money and truth, bet on the money—in Enron's case, the fortunes that senior corporate executives made from running, for decades, what was essentially a massive accounting fraud.[46] No one wants to hear that the golden eggs being laid by the goose aren't actually golden, so people close their eyes, either actively or passively, to lies and distortions all the time.

A lie typically involves two parties who are in interaction with each other—the person who tells the lie and the person who signals that he or she wants to hear it. In the massive Ponzi scheme and financial fraud committed by Bernard Madoff, some people who knew that the returns and their lack of variability were too good to be true nonetheless decided not to look too closely, hoping that they were real. CEOs who receive overly optimistic sales forecasts often hope that they will come true and therefore don't ask too many probing questions. In many ways, people are complicit in their own deception. That is certainly true in the case of the leadership industry as well. People, wanting to believe the best about others and the world, not only fail to do due diligence but signal that they want to hear the myths and tales that have become so much a part and parcel of leadership lore. So that's what they get.

People are complicit in one other way as well: People have a choice once they uncover that others have told them lies—to continue associating with, doing business with, and in other ways failing to sanction the individual doing the lying, or to do the opposite. Of course, if people were doing something like associating with one another in the first place, they must have perceived some benefit, so expecting them to stop is naive. This is one reason that the lying continues; in the end, it does not matter, at least in terms of affecting people's subsequent actions.

The dynamic just described concerning individuals' reactions to leaders who lie has been extensively explored in the domain of consumer choice, in particular in an innovative study that sought to understand the "reasoning processes consumers use to generate support for public figures who have acted immorally."[47] The study identified and demonstrated empirical support for two distinct processes. One process is moral rationalization, "the process of reconstruing immoral actions as less immoral in order to maintain support for an immoral actor."[48] Fudging a little on financial statements—well, lots of people and companies do it, and it's not that bad. Promising software that doesn't exist—sort of what customers expect and no one is really harmed. You get the picture.

The second process the authors call "moral decoupling," which is "a psychological separation process by which people selectively dissociate judgments of performance from judgments of morality."[49] So the marital infidelities of golfer Tiger Woods could be argued to be irrelevant to his skills as a golfer, and Bill Clinton's dalliance with Monica Lewinsky believed to not detract from his performance in foreign affairs and stewarding the economy.

This research confirms my argument about observers' complicity in creating and perpetuating a culture of immorality or, more specifically to the subject of this chapter, lying. Our motivation to rationalize and decouple so we can continue doing what we want to do helps ensure the absence of sanctions for lying. And with positive reasons to deceive—creating a reality in which what was originally untrue becomes true—and with few to no sanctions for doing so, why would we expect most leaders or anyone else to do anything different?

Now that I'm at about the halfway point of this book, I think it will be helpful to review what I'm trying to accomplish, a task particularly important given the subject matter of this chapter. Many people instinctively recoil from the idea of deception, strategic misrepresentation, lying—call it what you will—and don't see their own misstatements in the harsh way they view those that come from others. Taught to be truthful, wanting to think of themselves as honest and upstanding, many individuals gloss over their own behavior and embrace the "shoulds," the normative aspects of what people and leaders are supposed to be and do.

But by ignoring the evidence, the social science facts about deception, or, for that matter, any other topic pertaining to leadership, by pretending that common behaviors aren't really that common, we miss the important opportunity to understand the social world as it is—the first step on the road to changing it. Admonitions to behave in ways that run counter to what many people regularly do will have no effect without understanding the psychology of *why* people's behavior is the way it is. Only by using that understanding to design social systems and interventions will things conceivably be made different.

Ignoring the frequency of lying, the fact that it is positively associated with both having and acquiring power, and the possibility that lying is a behavior that is often quite effective won't change any of these oft-documented facts. All that ignoring reality will accomplish—and that includes the form of "ignoring" that comes from finding some rare and possibly untrue exception to everyday life—is what the talks and books about leadership so often do: present a world that is notable in its discrepancy from what people see and how they often behave themselves.

CHAPTER 5

Trust: Where Did It Go, and Why?

A former student, seemingly on the way to success, is in my office. Let's call him Harold. Having founded an eco-friendly irrigation technology business, backed by some of Silicon Valley's prestigious venture capital firms, Harold, the business's CEO, has come to see me to show me a separation agreement he's been handed by his outside lawyer, while his "alumni mentor" sits across the table from him next to the lawyer. This was the very same woman who had agreed to provide advice and support as he grew his company; the very same person whom he had originally introduced to his company. And now, she was here to tell him it was time to go, to step down as CEO of the company he'd founded.

We were discussing what to do, but his options were very limited at this point.

"Were there warning signs?" I asked. "Of course," Harold replied, as he detailed many over the past few months. "Why didn't you do anything?" Because, he commented, he was ultimately being pushed out of the company by his alumni mentor. Harold hadn't paid attention to the early warning signs because he had trusted her to protect him and to have his best interests in mind. Big mistake, as it turned out.

"She was rich and successful from previous jobs in some high-profile Silicon Valley companies," he continued. "I could not believe she would be interested in messing around with such a small, new venture." I thought, If you put a chicken in a cage with a python, you know what is going to happen. You don't ask about the chicken's size—is it too small for the python to bother with—or if the chicken is organic or free-range, or its proportion of white meat, or its breed. Pythons eat chickens. This woman had become rich and successful over the course of her career by doing to others what she was now doing to this former student. Her behavior had been learned over time, had stood her in good stead, and had become, as a consequence, almost automatic. She had learned to exploit relationships to her advantage and was doing it again. Her behavior wasn't personal; it wasn't directed against Harold. It was just her modus operandi. Harold had done well in my course on power, but obviously he had not learned all the lessons yet. This recent event would cement his learning. He had trusted too much, and in the wrong person.

It is often asserted that trust is essential for effective leadership. After all, how can someone build a successful enterprise, a task that invariably requires the collaboration and cooperation of many interdependent people, if there is not trust among them? Trust is more efficient and cost-effective in coordinating and ensuring collaborative behavior than the financial incentives or contracts that, as Oliver Williamson, a Nobel prize–winning economist, first pointed out decades ago, are difficult to write in ways that cover every possible future contingency.[1]

Trust is the glue of many social relationships, and organizations are essentially all about social relationships. Research in experimental economics consistently shows that when people try to take advantage of others, they get punished by those others or observers, even if administering such punishment is costly, and even if there will be no future interactions among the people involved.[2] People expect trustworthy, honest behavior and react when they don't see or receive it.

I am a big fan of trust. I try to be trustworthy and honest in my own behavior. The social science literature certainly demonstrates that leaders who inspire trust and build workplaces in which employees trust their leaders perform better.[3] In fact, workplace trust is one of the fundamental dimensions measured by the surveys done by the Great Place to Work Institute and their international affiliates to determine the best places to work. Decades of evidence demonstrates that companies with high levels of workplace trust enjoy higher stock market returns.

But I no longer believe that trust is essential to organizational functioning or even to effective leadership. Why? Because the data suggest that trust is notable mostly by its absence. Nevertheless, organizations continue to roll along, as do their leaders who seemingly suffer few consequences for being untrustworthy.

WHAT DO WE KNOW ABOUT TRUST?

Although many commentators on leadership consider trust to be essential for social and economic organization, few contemporary leaders garner much trust. Consider some representative data. The 2013 Edelman Trust Barometer, based on surveys conducted all over the world, reported that fewer than one in five respondents believed that government or business leaders would actually tell the truth when confronted with a difficult issue.[4] The 2014 index reported that trust in CEOs remained below 50 percent worldwide.

Maritz, a company that does customer and employee research and polling, reported in 2011 that only 14 percent of Americans believed their company's leaders were ethical and honest, while just 10 percent of those polled trusted management to make the right decisions in times of uncertainty. That same poll uncovered that just 7 percent of employees believed that their senior management's actions were completely consistent with their pronouncements.[5] These are not exceptions found by lots of digging using online searches. Any search for data on trust in leadership reveals that such trust is generally lacking, and if there are trends, they are mostly in the wrong direction, down not up, except for some recovery from the nadir of the 2007–2008 financial crisis. So it cannot be true that trust is necessary for organizations to function, because numerous organizations are operating even though trust in leaders is in short supply.

Roderick Kramer, a business school professor, has studied and written about trust for decades. In an insightful article, Kramer makes the following important points: First because trust is essential for human survival, it is hardwired into us so that in many cases we are predisposed to trust too much and the wrong people. Second, we are likely to trust those who are similar to us, something that the Edelman surveys also confirm. Third, and most important, our ability to accurately discern who is taking advantage of us is remarkably poor. Kramer cites the case of Bernie Madoff and his $65 billion Ponzi scheme as just one example of the many instances in which massive frauds have been perpetrated even on seemingly sophisticated, well-connected individuals. Kramer also lists just a small but nonetheless extensive selection of the numerous business frauds perpetrated over the decades, ranging from false claims of automobile safety (including the Pinto, the Ford model with the exploding gas tank, and the Chevrolet Corvair, the subject of Ralph Nader's pathbreaking book *Unsafe at Any Speed*) to the AIG insurance group's financial collapse from uncontrolled gambling on financial derivatives.

In his article, Kramer details the reasons why people are frequently unable to spot untrustworthy people or situations. Those reasons include the tendency to see what we want or expect to see (sometimes called confirmation bias); an illusion of personal invulnerability in which we underestimate the likelihood of bad things happening to us; a related illusion of unrealistic optimism; a tendency to believe that we are above average in our abilities (the above-average effect), which also applies to our perception of being above average in our ability to figure out whom to trust; and the fact that indicators of trustworthiness can be faked, often with great success.

On the point that people are not very good at discerning whom to trust, Kramer notes that many studies have found that detecting cheaters is difficult. In his own research, he instructs students in negotiations to use their intuitive theories of how to build trust. He writes:

> Usually, they make it a point to smile a lot; to maintain strong eye contact; to occasionally touch the other person's hand or arm gently . . . They engage in cheery banter to relax the other person, and they feign openness . . . by saying things like, "Let's agree to be honest and we can probably do better at this exercise." . . . Their efforts turn out to be pretty successful.

Kramer's description sounds like the behavior of most leaders. Kramer also found that even when the negotiating partners were told that half of the people had been instructed to deceive them, they were no better at detecting the deceivers than people not so forewarned were. Kramer's excellent and insightful bottom-line recommendation: temper your trust.[6]

WHAT HAPPENS WHEN LEADERS VIOLATE TRUST?

Not only is trust unnecessary—although it may be helpful to leaders if they can foster it—but there also seems to be only limited consequences for violating trust. Think about it: if violations of trust brought severe sanctions, fewer such violations would occur, and as a consequence, trust in leaders would be higher than it is.

To that point, it's worth noting that nothing happened to Harold's alumni mentor who ousted her mentee from the company he was ostensibly running. I suspect that she engaged in this behavior because she had learned over the course of her career that violations of trust are seldom—which is not to say never, but seldom—followed by adverse consequences. In fact, if the violation of trust brings the violator money and power, there are essentially no consequences at all. That is because our desire to bask in reflected glory and our motivation to achieve status in part by associating closely with high-status others overcome any ill will toward those who violate trust but wind up with money, power, and status.

Consider, as an interesting example of this phenomenon, Bill Gates, the famous and incredibly wealthy cofounder of Microsoft. As described in David Kaplan's book on the origins of the Silicon Valley, *The Silicon Boys*, as well as in an article by Steve Hamm and Jay Greene in *BusinessWeek* [7] and in a book by Harold Evans, *They Made America*,[8] Gates and Microsoft bought the operating system that led to Microsoft's success from

Seattle Computer for $50,000—an operating system essentially copied from one developed by a computer whiz with a Ph.D. named Gary Kildall. Kildall died at fifty-two after twice being hurt by Gates.

Although there is considerable controversy over the exact details, everyone acknowledges that Kildall invented an operating system, CP/M (Control Program/Monitor), which by the late 1970s was running 500,000 machines and bringing his company, Digital Research, Inc. (DRI), substantial revenues. When IBM entered the PC business, it needed an operating system and approached Microsoft, which to that point had been building programming languages such as Basic. IBM came to Microsoft under the mistaken belief that Microsoft was the progenitor of CP/M. Gates introduced IBM to Kildall, but when DRI and IBM did not come to terms, for reasons that remain disputable, Gates sensed an opportunity, buying a similar operating system from Seattle Computer and never mentioning that he intended to resell it to IBM. Microsoft renamed the system MS-DOS for "Microsoft Disk Operating System." The operating system was quite similar to the CP/M operating system built by Kildall, but of course copyrighting or patenting software is difficult today, and pursuing claims for the appropriation of intellectual property was almost unheard of in the early 1980s. Kildall had been outmaneuvered by Gates, "who may not have had Kildall's talent for programming, but his instincts for business were a whole lot better."[9]

As Kaplan describes the turn of events:

[Kildall] couldn't imagine being knifed in the back—certainly not by Gates. The two had known each other since Gates was a thirteen-year-old hacker in Seattle and Kildall was getting his doctorate. . . . They discussed merging their young companies . . . there seemed to be a gentleman's agreement that neither would get involved in the other's business. DRI would stay away from languages, and Microsoft would leave operating systems alone.[10]

Even after this incident, Kildall continued to trust Gates, with unfortunate consequences. In the mid–1980s, Kildall became interested in CD-ROM technology and cofounded the company KnowledgeSet, which built the first interactive encyclopedia on a CD-ROM. Kaplan describes what happened next:

> Kildall took a long time to recognize how Gates did business. . . . To share his ideas and hear others, Kildall planned a conference near Pacific Grove [California]. . . . On a visit to see family in Seattle, Kildall mentioned the conference to Gates. Three months later . . . Gates called Kildall about his *own* Microsoft CD-ROM conference to be held in Seattle . . . Unlike Kildall, Microsoft didn't even have a CD-ROM on the market; yet Gates-the-imitator would be seen as a leader in the field.[11]

This tale is well known. It has appeared in books and magazines and online. More important, the software community was a small one at the time, and these incidents were widely known within the network of software programmers and company founders. If there were adverse consequences for Gates or Microsoft from these episodes, I can't see them.

Or how about some other examples? There's Martha Stewart, the lifestyle doyenne, who was recently back in court. Not for insider trading or perjury this time, but for a contract dispute. Stewart, who once peddled her wares through Kmart, had signed what was purported to be an exclusive deal with Macy's, but she subsequently set up housewares stores-within-stores at J. C. Penney that used her name as part of their branding. Macy's was not happy, having paid Stewart a tidy sum for what the company thought was the exclusive use of her services and name. Stewart was unperturbed by the whole kerfuffle:

> Martha appears completely unsentimental, willing to scrap anything . . . and start over if she hits a roadblock or thinks there may be a better way. This seems to be what's happening with the Macy's/J.C. Penney dispute. "She was married to Macy's, but she went off and had an affair, and got in bed with a direct competitor, with J.C. Penney," Pamela Danziger, a marketing expert, said on CNN.[12]

Has Stewart suffered from not honoring her agreement with Macy's? Not that anyone can see. After all, this is "a woman who emerged from federal prison after five months as, somehow, a more sympathetic figure" and whose website continues to gain visitors with a name that apparently "has never been worth more."[13]

Why are there so few sanctions for leaders who violate trust? For many reasons. As Roderick Kramer, a social psychologist, has persuasively argued, we are predisposed to trust and have an evolutionary need to do so. Therefore, people are motivated to overlook a violation of trust as a onetime thing that won't occur again, or at least won't happen to them—because they are, after all, above average in their ability to detect people who shouldn't be trusted.

Furthermore, one consequence of the just-world effect (people's tendency to believe that the world is a just and fair place in which people get what they deserve) is that when someone is taken advantage of, others engage in a "blame the victim" exercise in which they actively seek out information that demonstrates how the victim was complicit in some way in his or her own deception and therefore deserved it. In Gary Kildall's case, one version of events suggests that he missed out on the deal that made Microsoft because he was supposedly flying that day and didn't personally attend a crucial IBM meeting, and because his wife, who first met with IBM, and then he, too, refused to sign a nondisclosure agreement. The truth is more complicated as to why he missed the meeting and as to what happened next, but Kildall's account, from an unpublished autobiography he subsequently wrote, portrays his role as much more of an innocent victim than an incompetent individual.

Most important, people are frequently strategic in their interactions. This means that they consider not just what someone has done *to* them, but what that individual might be able to do *for* them in the future. Trust-breakers for the most part retain their networks and social relationships because others in their orbit haven't been harmed by their actions, so they don't feel compelled to redress the harm. Trust-breakers frequently maintain their financial resources. Martha Stewart may have jilted Macy's, but she maintained wealth, personal contacts, and cachet, which could provide benefits to other retailers. Once Microsoft became successful, at one point becoming virtually a monopoly, there was no point in taking on Bill Gates, the richest man in the world. Don Quixote is a great literary figure, but most savvy leaders understand the implication of the term "quixotic." Few people want to fight losing causes when they have a much better alternative—making peace and cozying up to the other party.

And even when publicized, or possibly particularly when publicized, trust-breakers attain notoriety. That public visibility is a valuable resource itself. The "mere exposure effect" holds that we buy, choose, and prefer what is familiar, and what is familiar is what we hear about and read about continually.[14]

The old public relations adage that there's good publicity, bad publicity, and then there's no publicity is completely consistent with the research conducted to demonstrate the positive effects of mere exposure. For example, when I wrote a case on the networking guru Keith Ferrazzi, I asked him about his experience, which at that time was as the CEO of YaYa, a company in which Michael Milken, who in 1990 had pled guilty to six felony violations of federal securities law, had served twenty-two months in prison, and paid a fine of hundreds of millions of dollars, was a major investor.[15] Ferrazzi told me that Milken's name actually opened doors, helped him secure meetings, and was useful in building relationships for the Internet marketing firm that Ferrazzi was running. Because people had heard of Milken, that familiarity helped induce them to take the call and the meeting.

THE ADVANTAGES OF DISTRUST

The advantages of not trusting too much, of harboring a good degree of skepticism and distrust in most situations and interactions, seem obvious for the gullible individuals who lose money and careers when their trust is violated. Had people not trusted the apparently staunch pillar of society Bernard Madoff, he would never have been able to run his Ponzi scheme for so long and at such a scale. Had Harold not trusted his alumni mentor, he might still be running his company—or at least have been able to negotiate a much better severance to soften his ouster.

The best advice I can offer you, based on the many similar stories I have seen and read about, is this: the best predictor of future behavior is past behavior. People who have reneged on commitments, stolen intellectual property, sued or forced out their partners, failed to fulfill promises, and moved on to greener pastures in the past will do so again. Don't blame the victims, don't think you are going to be better or smarter, and don't believe in some personal invulnerability because of your superior intelligence and social perceptiveness or because of your education or current position. It can and will happen to you. This suggests that you would be well served to get data on people's past behaviors. Try not to be too caught up in their status, money, and trappings of success, or for that matter the positive stories they (or others) tell about themselves. Instead, carefully, systematically investigate what the people you are going to entrust with important dimensions of your future well-being have actually done.

Of course we are cognitively lazy in so many ways, which, as the famed social psychologist Robert Cialdini has noted, is why we often are so readily influenced.[16] Making the effort to check people out, and doing so with a sufficient degree of skepticism, can make life uncomfortable, because if you turn over a lot of rocks, you are more likely to find some snakes. But that form of discomfort may be much less painful than losing your job, your money, your reputation, or all three, because you put too much trust in the wrong person or the wrong company. And if you, for various business reasons, believe you have to do business with people and companies that cannot be trusted, try to do things, for instance, through legal contracts, patents, copyrights, and so forth, that can protect you against those who might seek to take advantage of your lack of power in the relationship.

Consider this cautionary tale, related to me at a Stanford alumni event in October 2013 by a Los Angeles resident who has worked in the film industry for decades. In 2008, he and two senior Hollywood colleagues put together a proposal to create a new Hollywood distribution company. They thought there was an opportunity, as the major studios, fueled by the availability of easy financing, had released too many movies into the market and therefore had stopped acquiring independent films. This meant there was, at least temporarily, an opportunity to acquire quality product for not much more than the marketing costs.

The three partners put together a business plan, agreed with a major studio to handle video rights, lined up a line of credit, and set about raising equity for the venture. Although they were trying to raise money at a bad time, as the recession was in full force by then, a theater chain backed by a private equity group was interested. Their company would give the theaters another source of product. The chairman of the theater group, who was from the private equity firm, assured the three that they "were his guys."

You can guess what happened. Their presumed "investor" brought in a consultant to presumably make the deal happen. And then "the phones went dark," as my Hollywood friend wrote in an e-mail. Nine months later, the putative investor opened its own independent film distribution company, which included the consultant on its staff, effectively executing the business plan that had been presented by the three Hollywood executives who had sought to build their own business. As one of them said in an e-mail, "We didn't have the power. Life isn't fair."

Could the three partners have done a better job of protecting their legal rights in their idea so that it could not have been appropriated, or at least appropriated so easily, by others? Quite possibly. Could they have pursued parallel options to reduce their dependence on the theater chain and its private equity investor, who wound up taking advantage of them? Maybe. But in the dynamics of the moment, having identified an interesting business opportunity and having found a large strategic partner interested in backing it, having done all this in a difficult economic environment, and after getting lots of assurances that they were the people, the three industry executives trusted too much, and they trusted the wrong people. It's not really their fault. It happens all the time.

The lesson from this case and its all-too-frequent cousins:

People will frequently act in their own interests, and if those interests involve breaching commitments made to you, then you should probably kiss those commitments good-bye. And often there won't be sanctions for violating trust, the experimental research notwithstanding. In such experiments, people have the opportunity to expend modest resources to punish the norm-violating behavior of people with whom they will almost certainly have no interdependence or future interactions. In the real world, people confront business partners—suppliers, investors, distributors—whom they may need and for whom there are few alternatives, in order to run or grow a business. So people will make excuses—this is how things happen in this industry—or they will blame the victim whose own behavior or lack of foresight or mistakes caused the difficulty. Or they will think that, the past record notwithstanding, their case will be different. For instance, even though entrepreneurs in technology often know the statistics that about 80 percent of founders are forced out of their companies by their venture capital investors, I have never heard anyone tell me that this would happen to them.

In the end, most people will continue dealing with the distributors or the financiers, in the Hollywood case, or the venture capitalist's in the case of technology entrepreneurs, or Martha Stewart or Microsoft in the case of vendors and suppliers, or, more generally, whomever they think they need to deal with to advance their immediate personal interests, the past behavior of their "partners" notwithstanding.

Can Distrust Benefit Leaders and Their Companies?

The advantages of skepticism and distrust seem clear for followers or others who might thereby avoid getting caught up in the blandishments and false promises that have become all too common in contemporary organizations. But are there advantages to creating distrust for leaders and their companies? Phrased in that fashion, the answer is almost certainly no, at least most of the time. But articulated in a slightly different way, the answer can be quite different.

It's pretty clear how to build or destroy trust. Trust implies that others know that someone or some company will honor their commitments and promises. Therefore, trust requires constancy and predictability. Because building trust entails, most fundamentally, keeping one's word and honoring promises, including the promises—either explicit or implicit— that are made to employees and customers, building and maintaining trust necessitates honoring commitments and obligations. But sometimes, or maybe even frequently, leaders and their firms either require for their economic survival or can benefit from more flexibility than previous agreements and assurances may provide. Therefore, leaders, who first and foremost are responsible for ensuring their organization's well-being, sometimes have to take tough actions. Such actions can entail breaking implicit promises or even abrogating contracts, and doing things that render the leader disliked and the company distrusted.

Before Daniel Debow and David Stein founded Rypple, a human capital software company now owned by Salesforce.com, they had cofounded a workforce management company but did not have controlling interest. When that company was sold, Debow described to me at lunch what happened—a tale that is quite common in the software space. The acquirer purchased the company for its customer list and customer contracts—it was in the software-as-a-service space with multiyear agreements (although the fundamental logic holds with possibly even more force for licensed software). Buyers of such businesses sometimes do the following calculation: regardless of whether the acquired company would maintain its level of customer service or product innovation, existing customers would confront some level of inertia in moving to a new vendor and platform. Therefore, if the purchase price is right, the acquirer can earn a handsome return on its investment as it essentially slowly drives the existing customer base away, because costs will decrease more rapidly than revenues. Precisely this sort of thing happens in the enterprise software space quite regularly. The founders discovered this was occurring to their former business when customers with whom they had developed strong relationships called them to complain about the treatment at the hands of the new owners.

But it's not just in software where this happens. Before Richard Kovacevich arrived as the CEO of Wells Fargo bank and changed its culture and strategy, the bank's strategy had been to acquire banks such as Crocker and First Interstate, slash costs and service in an often messy and painful merger integration process, and then profit from the fact that banking relationships are also characterized by inertia. This inertia meant that profits would rise at least for a while because what was being offered to customers and the associated costs were falling more rapidly than the customers could defect.

Note that profits, in these situations, come from breaking "trust" with customers by not honoring the implicit obligations to provide a certain level of ongoing customer service and product evolution and innovation, which the customers had come to expect and may have even been promised by marketing programs designed to woo them in the first place. In consulting, such situations are often called "cash cows," although few consultants would advocate quite this level of turning one's back on existing customers.

A similar arbitrage opportunity exists with employees. There are many forms of deferred compensation, ranging from pensions to retiree health benefits to the oft-observed positive age-wage relationship, which labor economists such as Edward Lazear argue are used to reward long-tenured employees and thereby ensure their retention.[17] An acquirer, either from the outside or from a management buy-out, or, for that matter, a new management team altogether, can reap substantial rewards by changing the "deal"—no longer offering pensions, retiree health benefits, and, subject to discipline by laws forbidding wage discrimination, by laying off senior workers whose wages may be above their level of productivity, as a payoff for working earlier in their careers for wages that were *less* than their productivity warranted. Defined benefit pension plans have disappeared at a rapid rate, and even company contributions to defined contribution plans have been decreasing, as are the proportion of companies offering retiree health insurance and, prior to the passage of the Affordable Care Act, the proportion of employers offering health insurance to active employees. This can happen because as a labor lawyer told me, "Companies cannot take away compensation already earned or accrued, but many employers explicitly reserve the right to change the terms of their benefits practices in the future."[18]

So employees may sign on for a particular basket of wages and benefits, but there is no assurance that those benefits—or even wages—will be maintained. Much like customers, employees also confront inertia, particularly in weak labor markets, but also to the extent that they have developed organization-specific skills that make them comparatively less valuable in the broader labor market than they are to their current employer. And finding a new job takes time and effort. These circumstances present management with the opportunity to change the deal in ways that increase profits. And there is also an opportunity to clean up the balance sheet by shedding future obligations. The airline industry has been in the forefront of doing precisely this. Look at airline income statements and balance sheets after most of them in the United States went through the bankruptcy process. And consider what their financial statements would be, even with current revenues and costs, had they maintained the pensions and other obligations that they shed through the courts.

Of course there are costs to distrust, in the form of more skeptical customers and employees who want their wages up front and not deferred in the sometimes-vain hope of realizing the benefits of those promised economic returns in the distant future. Although there is controversy about how much of the profit from leveraged buyouts comes from abrogating implicit promises, there is no question that in some specific instances, breaking promises—and thereby violating trust—has been a road to riches.

I would argue that one of the reasons the Edelman Trust Barometer and other similar measures of trust in leaders are so low is because of a recession that led to numerous cuts in wages, benefits, and employment levels. And another reason is a consolidation in industry after industry, ranging from banking to airlines to retailing to consumer products, which has increased the market power of companies vis-à-vis customers and therefore has made it easier, and more profitable, for those companies to renege on commitments implicitly made to the buyers of their offerings.

The simple fact is that maintaining trust requires honoring commitments, but commitments constrain. To take yet one more context in which this dynamic plays out, consider vendor-supplier relations. Every day companies turn their backs on alliance partners and become direct competitors. Jason Calacanis, an Internet entrepreneur (he sold Weblogs to AOL in 2005), a blogger, and an organizer of technology conferences, well understands how companies turn on their presumed partners. In an e-mail blog posting, his advice for building a start-up inside some other, larger company's ecosystem (like that of LinkedIn or Facebook or YouTube) is simply, don't. Once you develop and prove a business idea or application, he continues, the larger company is going to do its own version, almost certainly not by purchasing your start-up at some enormous price but by doing it better themselves.

Lenovo, one of the largest manufacturers of personal computers under its own label, was once a contract manufacturer for some of the big players. Ditto for most of the well-known Korean electronics companies that began making appliances and other electronics for others before moving in on those markets themselves. A company's partner today may be its competitor tomorrow. And what holds for companies is also true for the individuals inside them. Alliances are fluid for a reason—changed circumstances often result in changed networks of support and opposition.

Commitments constrain, and this holds true for personal relationships as well. That's why every day inside companies, people eliminate their supposed onetime friends and allies. Ask John Reed, who was forced out of Citigroup after its merger with Travelers by Sandy Weill, his co-leader and presumed partner. Ask Jamie Dimon, Weill's right-hand man for decades, fired by Weill when Dimon got into a dust-up with Weill's daughter. Ask Gil Amelio, ousted as Apple's CEO after he bought Steve Jobs's company Next Computer and brought Jobs back into the company, where Jobs forgot to thank him for the favor. Or the senior executives who lost internal battles at Discover, Morgan Stanley, or decades ago at Lehman Brothers. There are scores if not hundreds of examples in companies big and small of individuals often losing political battles and getting deposed in coups by the very same people they had themselves promoted, brought into the company, or thought of as partners.

Sort of like Frankenstein, leaders frequently create monsters. Through hiring and promotions, these new senior executives rather than showing loyalty, become participants in ousting their onetime sponsors. People—famous people, rich people, some people who regularly appear on most-admired lists and give talks at leading business schools—turn their backs on commitments when it suits their interests all the time. If you don't believe this, you are really not keeping up with the news.

To be clear, leaders go back on their word not because they are necessarily venal or evil, but because keeping commitments, a fundamental basis of trust, constrains their behavior. When circumstances change, so do people's behaviors, objectives, and needs. Leaders shed commitments all the time. Just ask the former employees of the city of Detroit as they watch a bankruptcy process unfold that will tell them how much of their promised pensions and other benefits they will actually receive.

We Expect Contract Violations by Companies

The behaviors described in this chapter are reasonably common in everyday life. That fact suggests two things: first, that violations of obligations must not be perceived as that serious, and second, that people, to avoid being perpetually unhappy and dissatisfied, will figure out ways of coming to terms psychologically with the reality of breaches of trust. Both processes probably operate.

There is empirical evidence consistent with the argument that breaches of contract done by companies are perceived as being not as serious or morally repugnant as when such breaches are done by individuals. Uriel Haran, a management professor, studied what happened when people saw contracts breached. He found that breaches of contract by individuals are seen as moral transgressions. Breaches of contracts by businesses, however, are viewed more as reflecting a business necessity (or reality), and therefore are seen more as legitimate business decisions with less of a moral transgression aspect.[19]

Haran's research results are completely consistent with the idea that breaches of trust—and contracts are certainly a form of binding agreement that one would expect to be honored—can and often are seen as business necessities and therefore do not provoke much moral outrage. Although Haran looked at differences in the moral outrage between breaches by individuals and companies, there may be many other factors that affect how seriously people take breaches of trust. One such factor should be how many times people have personally seen agreements violated. People become habituated. In a world such as that described in this chapter, one in which individuals and companies pursue their interests and will renege on promises to do so, moral outrage has to become attenuated, or most people, not just a relatively small slice of the population, would be more angry more of the time. That doesn't mean that people will trust contracts or other agreements to be honored—people see the world and are not stupid. But it does mean that there will be less affect, less moral outrage, less anger over what has become business as usual.

So there is a dynamic process in play. Because commitments constrain, people and companies break them, and they do so reasonably regularly. Because there are few sanctions, such trust-violating behavior becomes more frequent. Because the breaking of promises becomes more frequent, it becomes more "normative," in the sense that more entities do it. And as a more normative way of behaving, it provokes less moral outrage and comes to be seen as how business is done or how people make their way in political battles inside organizations. And the absence of moral outrage then leads to more breaches of agreements and promises, and the cycle continues.

So yes, trust is a quality widely touted as being helpful, indeed essential, for good leadership. There's only one problem: it is largely missing in most leaders and in most work organizations. You need to understand why, so you don't get fooled again.

CHAPTER 6

Why Leaders "Eat" First

In the U.S. military, officers eat after the enlisted men do, at least according to the leadership writer and speaker Simon Sinek.[1] This practice reflects the increasingly widespread recommendation that the best leaders first look out for the interests of others, particularly those who work with and for them, before those leaders take care of themselves. Simply stated, leaders who want to build engaged, high-performing workplaces look after those for whom they are responsible, and by so doing, they display the admirable qualities of generosity and unselfishness. There is even a term that describes at least some dimensions of this style of leadership, "servant leadership." To be clear, servant leadership sometimes entails more than just putting the interests of one's employees and others before one's own. Reviews of the servant leadership concept define and distinguish it by its heavy focus on the well-being of followers in contrast to the typical emphasis given to organizational well-being.[2] In that sense, the idea gives primacy not so much to followers over leaders as to putting the interests of employees over organizational performance.

The underlying logic is that by focusing on people and their needs, including the needs for interesting work and for being treated like adults and therefore for being permitted to make decisions and have some control over what they do, leaders can produce great teams and develop superior company performance *as a consequence* of the effort to put people and their well-being first.[3] Servant leadership is characterized by trust, the appreciation of others, and providing empowerment[4]—letting followers make more decisions—something that is good for both people's learning and development and also their sense of personal efficacy.

The growing emphasis on and attention to the idea of servant leadership has led to the founding of numerous centers, including the Greenleaf Center for Servant Leadership and the Spears Center for Servant Leadership, as well as servant leadership centers at some colleges and universities. Naturally, the idea of servant leadership has spawned numerous books and conferences on the topic.

Much like other forms of leadership that have attracted attention, such as authentic leadership, the idea of putting others first and taking care of and being responsible for those working for and with a leader appeals to most people's values as well as their intuitions about what leaders *should* do. Leaders, who by definition have relatively more power than others, including the power to profoundly affect the lives of others, would also seem to have greater responsibility *because* of that power, so the logic goes. With power comes responsibility, and with greater power presumably comes even greater responsibility.

Putting employees first and taking care of those for whom the leader is responsible makes ethical sense. Most religions have mandates to be generous and concerned with the welfare of others, whether through the requirement to tithe a percentage of one's income or admonitions about taking care of the poor and less fortunate.

The evidence suggests that taking care of employees also makes business sense. Consider just a few examples. Vineet Nayar became the CEO of HCL Technologies and made this Indian outsourcer incredibly successful, growing its revenues, profits, and market capitalization 600 percent in just eight years. Nayar attributes his and HCL's success to the decision, in 2005, to put employees first, even above customers.[5]

Richard Branson, the entrepreneur and founder of Virgin Atlantic Airways, advocates putting the employees first, the customers second, and the shareholders third, as did Herb Kelleher, who during his tenure at the helm of Southwest Airlines made that company not just a great place to work but also financially successful. Jim Goodnight, the cofounder and CEO of SAS Institute, the largest privately owned software company in the world, has always emphasized employee well-being and takes the company's ranking on the best-places-to-work lists very seriously. So, too, does Kip Tindell, the CEO and founder of the incredibly successful business The Container Store.

There is obvious logic to this prioritization: when companies look after the well-being of their workforce, the workforce turns over less and is more engaged, thereby reducing turnover expenses; employees, in turn, do a better job of looking after the customers and of innovating. And when the customers fare better, so do the shareholders, as research by Claes Fornell of the American Customer Satisfaction Index demonstrates.[6]

DO LEADERS PUT OTHERS' INTERESTS FIRST?

It might be great if leaders looked after employee well-being and "ate last," but, to continue the metaphor, if I were in a food line and I was very hungry, I would not count on most leaders to care much about how much food I had on my plate. As with many of the prescriptions about leadership, it is virtually impossible to assess the frequency or even the growth of servant leadership, or the extent to which leaders put the interests of others in their organizations first.

But even without comprehensive data, we can use other indicators of the extent to which leaders put their own interests ahead of the well-being of their people. First, if leaders regularly prioritized their employees, then such instances should not be particularly noteworthy, as they would occur all the time. Conversely, if leaders mostly put themselves first, those leaders who don't behave in a very self-interested way should attract a lot of notice because such behavior is so unusual even as it is also desirable. Second, the very fact that there are numerous writings addressing the difficulty of implementing servant leadership suggests that it is tough to do—which implies unselfish leadership is rare.

Perhaps a more direct way to assess whether the idea of taking care of others is gaining prominence is to ask some reasonably straightforward questions. First, how are organizational resources divided? Do leaders, like officers in the military, partake of what is left after their people are cared for, or do they cut to the front of the line and scoop up as much as they can? And when a work organization encounters difficulties and faces reduced resources, including jobs and money, how does the reduction, the economic stringency, get apportioned between leaders and others?

Stop the snickering. There are actually some places where sacrifices fall more heavily on the higher-level leaders, who in some sense are probably both more responsible for the organization's problems and also undoubtedly better able to cope financially with reduced wages and hours. At the Japanese power company Tokyo Electric Power (TEPCO), an incident put the company's very existence at risk after the Fukushima nuclear plant disaster, which followed the earthquake and tsunami, and there were widespread pay cuts. But the cuts were distributed so that the higher someone's organizational rank, the greater the percentage of a cut in pay that employee experienced. Of course, this took place in Japan, where cultural norms concerning employees are different from those in the United States, and where honor and behaving honorably are more central to leaders' identities.

The TEPCO example is clearly an exception. Power is positively correlated with hierarchical rank, and senior people mostly use their power to protect both their jobs and their salaries and perquisites. Take the case of jobs. A while ago, the organizational sociologists John Freeman and Michael Hannan asked why the size of the administrative component—administrative overhead—seems to rise inexorably in organizations. Their answer, empirically tested in a study of school districts, is simple: when times are good, the number of administrators (and probably everybody else) expands, but when times are bad, administrators, closer to the locus of decision-making and with more power, protect their jobs disproportionately, with the loss of jobs concentrated among the frontline people with less influence over the decisions about where and what to cut. Therefore, as this cycle repeats itself over time, the percentage of people in administration inexorably increases.[7] Their study speaks directly to how power leads to job protection for those in power—for the leaders, but not the led.

Income protection may be even more prevalent than protecting administrative positions. Here the sad fact is that when leaders mess up, they typically leave with lavish severance packages while regular employees suffer job losses and wage cuts. Consider, among the multitude of possible examples, Hewlett-Packard, which forced out three executives, Carly Fiorina, Mark Hurd, and Léo Apotheker, in a relatively brief period of time.

Even Apotheker, who was in the CEO job for only about eighteen months, and who did the worst financially by the company, left with many millions. After all, Fiorina, who engineered the ill-fated Compaq merger, which cemented HP's position in the dying, low-margin personal computer industry, left with a package north of $50 million.

Robert Nardelli, after coming from GE to Home Depot, which under his tenure lost market share to Lowe's and saw its stock price decline almost 20 percent, left with about $210 million when he was forced out by his board. Rick Wagoner, at the time the CEO of General Motors, was shamed into forgoing a $1 million bonus at the very moment he and his senior management colleagues were asking GM's unionized workforce for wage givebacks. GM eventually went into bankruptcy and was bailed out by the government. Wagoner, however, still got out with about $23 million.

The airline industry presents a depressingly similar picture of constant wage concessions and benefit cuts for employees ranging from pilots to flight attendants while senior leaders continued to prosper even as the companies failed—at least, if you define failure as going into bankruptcy. And then there are the retailers. In 2012, Don Thompson, the CEO of McDonald's, earned about $14 million in compensation even as the company published helpful hints for its employees, which instructed them on ways to survive on their low wages, including how to access various forms of public assistance and how to economize on various expenses.[8]

And there's the stark data on CEO pay. CEO pay is well known as being untethered from what happens to regular employees, a fact that explains why the multiple between CEO pay and that of the average worker continues to widen to nosebleed levels. As one analysis of growing CEO income noted:

Management has always been overrepresented among top earners, of course. What has changed is what they are paid. About 70 percent of the increase in income going to the top 0.1 percent from 1979 to 2005 comes from increasing pay for executives and financial services professionals. . . . One study by the Economic Policy Institute . . . found that compensation for chief executives swelled about 725 percent in real terms from 1978 to 2011. At the same time, worker compensation increased just 5.7 percent.[9]

As a consequence, the gap between CEO pay and average employee pay has increased on average from about 20 times in 1965 to more than 200 times some forty years later,[10] with other estimates indicating that a typical CEO of a large company makes more than 330 times what the average worker makes in that same company.[11] The gap between average employee and CEO pay is largest in the financial industry and smallest in technology.[12]

And it is not the case that the rise in pay comes from vast increases in corporate performance. "The growth of earnings for executives has outpaced growth in the stock market or in corporate earnings, by a wide margin."[13] Indeed, much research suggests that CEO pay is reasonably unaffected by corporate performance. One meta-analysis summarizing the results of numerous studies concluded that company size accounts for about 40 percent of the variation in CEO pay while performance explains a trivially small 5 percent.[14]

To be sure, there are exceptions, such as the ice cream maker Ben & Jerry's, the office furniture manufacturer Herman Miller, and the grocery retailer Whole Foods Market, all of which have articulated company policies limiting CEO pay to some reasonably low multiple of average employee salaries. But again, these are the few exceptions in a landscape in which leaders mostly take care of themselves. Or as a former student told me one evening at a dinner accompanied by a little too much wine, "We live in an era of shared sacrifice. The employees sacrifice, and I share in the money they give up."

The various examples of taking bonuses and other large payments while asking for wage and job cuts from the rank and file, the growing disparity between CEO and average employee pay, and CEO and senior leader economic security often obtained at the expense of the workforce—all these factors belie any widespread empirical evidence that senior leaders are taking care of others first. For the most part, leaders just take care of themselves, regardless of what they *should* do either to adhere to moral strictures or to make their organizations perform better.

WHY LEADERS DON'T LOOK OUT FOR OTHERS

Remedying self-aggrandizing leader behavior requires, first of all, understanding *why* such behavior occurs. Many well-understood, potent psychological processes help explain why leaders seldom look out for others, notwithstanding the benefits from doing so and the numerous normative exhortations for leaders to care for their subordinates' well-being. Once we understand why leaders typically eat first, we can develop recommendations that, if implemented, have a much greater chance of changing behavior than do all the inspirational speeches and stories that accomplish so little.

If you happen to strike up a conversation with a fellow passenger on a plane or a stranger at a cocktail party, one of the first things you will probably do is to see what you have in common with that other person, and similarly that individual will do the same in talking with you. That's because shared experiences and social identities—where you went to school, worked, common interests—bind people together in a unit relationship. Possibly for evolutionary reasons—those who were best able to identify relatives or others who shared similar genetic traits and then help those similar others had a higher chance of perpetuating their characteristics over generations—people are very attuned to quickly identifying and reacting to similarity and dissimilarity.

Research shows that people are more likely to help those who are similar to them, even in trivial, unimportant, and random ways—a finding that suggests identifying and helping similar others is an almost automatic, mindless behavior. Some studies show that sharing even incidental and irrelevant similarities, such as birthdates, fingerprint patterns, or initials, increases the likelihood of an individual's acceding to a request from another for help.[15] Furthermore, people are attracted to others who are similar—in fact, similarity in attitudes and other dimensions is one of the most important, fundamental bases of interpersonal attraction[16]—and prefer those with whom they share some commonality, including similarities in speech patterns, pace, and tone of voice.[17]

In short, because we prefer things that remind us of ourselves—an idea sometimes called implicit egotism—people are more likely than chance to live in states that remind them of their own names and are also more likely to choose occupations whose names remind them of their own.[18]

What this means for leaders taking care of others is this: in many work organizations, leaders share little or nothing in common with those they lead. I recall visiting a large forest-products and paper company in a relatively small town. In the company headquarters building, the executive floor was accessible only through locked doors, to which typical employees did not have unfettered access. Leaders often travel on private planes, and they have staff who attend to their wishes with such diligence that leaders need to be careful about the casual remarks they make, as others may not take them casually and implement offhanded comments. Some companies still have executive dining rooms and reserved parking based on rank. All of these practices reduce not only shared experiences but also even incidental contact.

Particularly with the growing frequency of outside succession into leadership, including the CEO position, leaders share few experiences with the people they are leading. The new bosses may be from outside the industry and as a result share little common history or experience with the rank and file. Leaders appointed from the outside are, in fact, often strangers when they take on the leadership role, except possibly to the board members who hired them. Therefore, why should leaders, sharing little in common with those they lead—indeed, in many cases hardly knowing or having contact with the led—be expected to feel close to their employees or look out for their interests? Much psychological research and theory suggest they will not.

Because of the importance of contact and similarity in creating relationships, leaders who *do* seek to be responsible for and to others try to reduce interaction barriers and thereby increase contact with the people who work in their organizations. For example, one of the things Sergio Nacach did when he took over the Andean region of Kimberly-Clark, headquartered at the time in Lima, Peru, was to remove the physical barriers that precluded access to the executive offices. Nacach wanted to build a team environment and was very much someone who appreciated all employees. But Nacach is an exception. Such barriers that separate executives from employees are common in headquarters, particularly in parts of the world that emphasize hierarchy and social distance, such as parts of Asia and South America.

Second, leaders are highly motivated to protect their self-esteem and their sense of competence, as, of course, are most human beings. One manifestation of the desire to think well of oneself would be to not blame oneself or one's close colleagues for organizational problems but instead to "externalize" such problems by coming to think the issues are because of the actions and interests of others. This mental dynamic means that leaders almost invariably distance themselves from feeling personally culpable and instead blame problems on others. So, for years Rick Wagoner and other leaders of General Motors blamed GM's economic woes on the high benefits paid to union workers, many of whom were former employees. These benefits included retiree health care and pensions, and pay for people laid off and awaiting recall. The thought that GM's problems might derive from the fact that the company produced cars that customers didn't value as highly as they did competitors' vehicles—in 2004, Toyota received an average of 30 percent more per vehicle sold—would hit too close to home. And the idea that GM's cost problems were the result of excessive management rather than worker salaries would definitely hit much too close to home.

Similarly, airline industry leaders frequently attribute economic problems to overpaid, unionized employees rather than a strategy of providing quality customer service, or a lack thereof, that has driven people away from flying. Or they attribute operational issues such as delayed flights to airport congestion, even though in the hub airports that are often dominated by one airline, the airline itself has done the flight scheduling that has created the peak loads on facilities. Once leaders use other groups such as employees, or, for that matter, other departments, as scapegoats for performance problems, expecting those leaders to then care for or about those others is just foolish.

Research shows that leaders take credit for good company performance and attribute poor performance to environmental factors over which they have no control, to predecessors, to macroeconomic issues, or sometimes to other organizational interests, particularly frontline employees.[19] So when senior leaders complain about the competitiveness problems stemming from high labor costs and excessive staffing, they are mostly referring to the costs of frontline salaries and the number of people actually doing the work.

I saw this phenomenon in action when an enormously wealthy and powerful figure in the world of finance commented at a conference I attended at UCLA that the United States was finally getting on the road back to competitiveness because autoworkers' salaries—at least for new employees—had come down to a level where they were even lower than comparable positions in Mexico. His statement so shocked me that I turned to the man sitting next to me, the labor historian Sanford Jacoby, to be sure I had heard correctly. I had. On that particular occasion I refrained from asking what executive salaries were in his firm or in finance more generally, and if the United States would be more competitive if those salaries were reduced.

Leaders who have come up through the ranks and have done many if not most of the organization's jobs are much more likely to look out for the interests of those they lead because they have been there themselves. That is one plausible explanation for why, in general, leadership in the military is not just better but why senior military officers typically show a higher level of concern for the well-being of their people than do leaders in many companies. Military leaders come up through the ranks, so they once were in the positions of the people they lead, and therefore have much more empathy for and understanding of their subordinates. Outside succession, and particularly succession by industry outsiders with limited frontline experience, exacerbates the tendency for leaders to not give the interests and well-being of others much priority.

INDUCING LEADERS TO TAKE CARE OF OTHERS

As will be explored further in the next chapter, selfish and self-interested leaders are not necessarily the biggest problem in workplaces—the problem is expecting relatively rare behavior to be common and then acting on the basis of that expectation. Expecting reciprocity, generosity, and selflessness is a wonderful sentiment but will almost certainly produce disappointment in many if not most organizational situations. That does not mean, however, that there is nothing that might be done to induce leaders to be more concerned with the well-being of those they lead.

In the first place, the field of leadership should learn something from economics and agency theory. Agency theory is a formal, analytical exploration of a pervasive, important, and profound problem: Owners delegate operational control to managers and managers delegate responsibility in turn to lower-level managers. But owners and leaders at all levels often have difficulty monitoring and therefore controlling or even evaluating what the people to whom they have delegated power are doing. Consequently, the problem that agency theory addresses is how to align incentives and develop contracting arrangements, including optimal compensation schemes, so that in the course of pursuing their own narrow interests, agents, the people to whom power has been delegated, will also wind up serving the interests of the principals who have delegated that decision-making authority to them.[20]

The point of agency theory is that with the right measurements and incentives, many of the problems entailed in aligning otherwise conflicting interests can be solved. Without going quite that far, there is nonetheless much that might be done in the case of leaders looking out for the welfare of others. As noted earlier, before Hewlett-Packard got carried away with a series of unfortunate outside CEOs, the company at one point based manager reviews in part on survey results from people working in the managers' units. That measurement provided managers with some real incentive to look out for their people. SAS Institute evaluates leaders on their ability to attract and retain talent. In that very strong culture organization, leaders who do not take care of those they lead, even while setting high performance expectations and meeting business objectives, do not last very long in the company.

If leaders are expected to take care of and develop their people, then it is essential to measure whether or not they do, and then hold them accountable for those measurements. For instance, at DaVita, the kidney dialysis company, measurement is ubiquitous and important, including measurements of leader behaviors oriented toward the people they lead.

DaVita has a senior management internal development program called the Redwoods program. Many of DaVita's frontline facility leaders are nurses, but more recently the company has begun to hire MBAs to enrich its talent pool. The person in charge of the management development program, himself an MBA, naturally enough favored people like him. So he disproportionately selected other MBAs to participate in the program. But because the company measured who actually was selected for this program, the outcome of his bias was visible, and when it persisted, the individual was fired. The new person knew to treat nurses as fairly as any other group in getting them ready for promotion.

Measurement and incentives won't solve everything, but they might solve quite a bit. When leaders' own jobs and salaries depend on how well they look after others, they will do so. Until then, relying on leaders' generosity of spirit or the exhortations of the leadership literature is an ineffective and risky way to ensure that leaders take care of anyone other than themselves. If we really want leaders to look out for others, companies and maybe even the larger society need to give them some pretty concrete reasons to do so.

Also, if part of the problem is the psychological distance between leaders and rank-and-file employees and their work, there are ways to diminish that separation. One is the simple management-by-walking-around practice that has been discussed and advocated for decades.[21] Another useful practice is to ensure that leaders understand what the frontline people actually do. At DaVita, a program called Reality 101 requires that people who ascend to the rank of vice president, either by internal promotion or outside hire, spend a week in a dialysis center—not observing, but doing real work. Southwest Airlines used to have its senior leadership spend a day in the field once a quarter doing a frontline job (one that each individual was qualified to do—no flying planes if you were not a pilot!). At the online retailer Zappos, all new hires, regardless of their level, undergo customer service training at one of the company's warehouses.

A related practice is to spend greater attention to promoting people from within, something strong-culture organizations invariably seek to do as a way of ensuring that the culture is maintained by those who understand it best. Promotion from within has other favorable results, such as signaling to those inside the organization that they are as valued and as valuable as unknown outsiders—which will serve to both motivate and retain internal talent.

And another useful policy is making sure that the people who are promoted have had exposure to the core of the organization's activities, whatever those are, at some point in their careers. That way, the leaders would both better understand and appreciate the work of the frontline people who design and build the products and provide the customers with service.

Exhortations for leaders to be concerned with others may work to increase such behavior for people otherwise already inclined in that direction. But ensuring more psychological identification with and contact between leaders and those they lead, and using measurements and incentives to both assess and reward the desired and desirable behaviors of leaders that demonstrate actual taking care of others, are much more reliable ways to ensure that at least a few more leaders "eat last."

CHAPTER 7

Take Care of Yourself

A tenured professor at a leading business school met with his associate dean for a performance review and to discuss the following year's increase in salary. Now, to be clear, universities are not the most cutthroat, short-term-performance oriented places, particularly compared with most businesses. Plus, the money sloshing around the richest, most prestigious universities reduces the politics and interpersonal competition even further.

Their discussion focused on why, given this individual's consistently high ratings on teaching and research performance, his raise was so small. The answer: business schools, including this one, pay higher salaries than most other university departments, and to preserve some semblance of compensation equity across the campus, business school budgets earmarked for salary increases are constrained by the central university administration. Translation: raise dollars are scarce. The associate dean then explained that the business school needed to use those scarce salary resources to retain the people who were going to be the most crucial to the *future* leadership and well-being of the school. The message, stated almost but not quite this bluntly: regardless of your outstanding record and past contributions, you are, because of your age and career stage, the past, not the future. Like most workplaces, this one, too, needed to invest in the future, and therefore it intended to allocate scarce raise dollars accordingly.

You may think your employer owes you something for your past contributions and good work—but most employers don't agree. Whether it is paltry raises, painful rounds of layoffs, or cost-cutting moves to open-office plans, companies, and, for that matter, nonprofits and government agencies, look after themselves and their own interests to ensure their survival and prosperity. So a senior editor of a major publisher was laid off without warning, even though he had built the business over many years and made millions or maybe tens or hundreds of millions of dollars for his employer. No matter. As we saw in the last chapter, nice speeches and noble sentiments notwithstanding, leaders mostly take care of themselves first—and maybe second and third, also—regardless of what they are *supposed* to do. The obvious conclusion: you should do the same.

If you hold the expectation that your hard work and good efforts are invariably going to be appreciated, acknowledged, and rewarded by your employer in perpetuity, it's time to get over yourself. If you believe that there is some implicit contract of, on the one hand, your doing good work and being loyal in return for reward and recognition or even a *job* from your employer—an implicit bargain or contract—don't expect such implicit contracts to be honored. Data show that companies violate implicit contracts with their employees all the time. For instance, one study of 128 alumni from a graduate management program asked people at graduation and then two years later about whether or not their employers fulfilled the reciprocal obligations of the employment relationship. Some 55 percent of the respondents reported that the implicit promises made during recruitment and thereafter as they joined their employers had been breached.[1]

Nor is this emphasis on "what can you do for me in the future?" and the breaching of implicit understandings confined to the relationship between employers and their employees. When Kyle Hardrick, a basketball player for the University of Oklahoma, injured his knee, not only were he and his family stuck with medical bills, but he also had to find the money to pay for his college tuition, because his Oklahoma scholarship was not renewed.[2] This sort of thing happens all the time. According to the National Collegiate Athletic Association (NCAA), while schools cannot revoke a scholarship *because* of illness or injury, "many have players on one-year, renewable scholarships that the schools can opt not to renew." And most schools do, in fact, drop financial support for athletes should those individuals become unable to play, regardless of those individuals' past contributions to the schools' athletic programs or whether the injury was incurred helping the school's team.[3] Colleges, just like employers, spend their scarce resources on those individuals who can help them succeed in the future—and those are certainly *not* people too injured to play again. And, of course, teams in professional sports drop or trade people all the time if these folks are no longer perceived to be worth the cost—again, regardless of what the players may have done for the team in the past.

The logical conclusion from systematic data and countless cases in multiple environments, ranging from college and professional athletics to corporations to universities: relying on the good behavior and positive sentiments of work organizations for your career well-being is singularly foolish.

This should not be news to any sentient person. For more than forty years, companies in the United States have been telling their employees that the company owes its people (at most) interesting and challenging work that will help those individuals hone their skills and make or keep them marketable; companies should help employees become better skilled and ready to compete in the labor market. But both human resource departments and senior management constantly reprise the refrain, often found in formal written policies and employee handbooks, that individuals are employed "at will" and can be fired for any or no cause.[4] The company does not owe its individual employees a job, regardless of their job performance or, for that matter, any consideration for their past loyalty and service.

There are, of course, a few small exceptions to this pattern. If you happen to be one of the small minority of people covered by a union collective bargaining agreement, you will have greater employment security and, more important, access to greater levels of due process should your employer decide to get rid of you or in other ways treat you inequitably. If you are employed in some countries in Europe that have yet to follow the United States completely in its labor market regulations, or lack thereof, you will have some job protections. And protection against arbitrary dismissal varies by state, with California providing somewhat more protection than other states, for instance. Some companies have voluntarily installed internal systems to ensure fair and equitable treatment of their employees. The military tends to recognize those who have served with honor and, in many cases, have made substantial sacrifices. But to be clear, the military's honoring of past contributions arises in part because not to do so would be to discourage others from joining and staying and making similar contributions to the common good. And all that being said, even the military does reductions in force, its version of layoffs, that leave career service members scrambling for new jobs.

For the typical work organization, or for the typical individual in a social relationship, the question posed by the counterparty is typically not "What have you done for me in the past that de-serves repayment?" but rather, "What can you do for me in the future that warrants spending any time or resources on keeping you happy or keeping you at all?"

This state of affairs is sensible and inevitable for the most part. Organizations, both for-profit and nonprofit, do—and probably *should* do—what is required to ensure their continuity and success. That includes shedding employees at the drop of a hat to maintain their solvency, or sometimes simply to increase their stock price or to keep investment analysts happy.[5] Work-places are mostly—and there are obviously notable exceptions—not what many people apparently seek from them: communal settings in which people take care of each other, provide eco-nomic security and social support, and possibly even provide meaning and purpose from the work people do. Of course a few organizations—the best-places-to-work lists are a good source for many of them—do all these things. But don't count on your place of employment being one of them. Unfortunately, most people are understandably reluctant to heed this message.

RECIPROCITY: MISSING FROM THE WORKPLACE

On the phone, a former student of mine is on the verge of, and then in, tears. She needs to work for the money and is about to be fired by her current employer. Her sin? Communicating too directly and mostly not being subservient enough, obsequious enough, with her new boss.

Yes, there is a new boss. The person who hired her for her marketing acumen and appreciated her work was, as they say, "re-orged" out of his role and is now in an "individual contribu-tor" position, which means he can no longer be of much help to her. My question to her (which I albeit put much more politely than I do here): "What were you thinking? If you need to work to support yourself, you need to (a) always, and I mean always, be looking for new jobs both within your current employer and ones on the outside so you have options available to you at all times, and (b) be constantly working on your relationship with your new boss. No one can count on stability in companies these days, so you need to be prepared." Her reply was that her intelligence, conscientiousness, and her great marketing analysis and insight, qualities that had earned her positive feedback particularly from the person who had hired her, would permit her to keep her job. Her job performance would protect her from the many vicissitudes visited upon employees by jealous and insecure leaders. Bad bet.

For the most part, the leadership industry either presumes the existence of or advocates for benevolence. Leaders are expected to be virtuous and responsible, so that organizational members can trust and rely on those leaders to take care of them and to look out for their interests, so long as those employees do their jobs well. But few leaders, and few organizations, fill these prescriptions. We need to understand why.

What Happened to the Norm of Reciprocity?

At this point, you might be confused. On the one hand, a lot of evidence confirms that companies and universities do not repay the hard work and long service of their employees or, for that matter, their athletes. But on the other, there is this norm of reciprocity, a moral obligation to repay a past favor, a norm argued to be universal across societies.[6] Because reciprocity norms help solve the universal problem of ensuring cooperation among people, some scholars argue that there are evolutionary advantages that help explain reciprocity's emergence and humankind's almost mindless adherence to it.[7] What gives?

What gives is actually pretty simple. When people are in an organizational as contrasted with an interpersonal setting, they feel less obligation to repay favors and, in fact, are less likely to do so. Peter Belmi and I did a series of experiments demonstrating this effect.[8] Two of the studies involved scenarios in which people imagined that another individual had done something nice and unsolicited for them—in one instance in a personal context, and in the second in an organizational setting. The study's participants were then queried about how obligated they felt to repay the favor. So in one study, people imagined they had been invited to dinner and another person had paid for their dinner. In the second study, people imagined they were coming back from a trip and someone from work (or, alternatively, just a friend) volunteered to pick them up at the airport. In both cases, people felt less strongly motivated to reciprocate the favor when that favor had occurred in an organizational rather than a personal context.

Of course these are only hypothetical scenarios. What about actual behavior? When we conducted a study in which someone else in the experiment gave the study's participants lottery tickets for a drawing in which they could win a prize, we observed that the participants reciprocated with fewer lottery tickets when the favor was done in an organizational setting than when the identical situation unfolded under a personal context condition. In organizational settings, people feel less obligated to reciprocate favors. And that is what we found in yet another setting, one in which people were paid more than they had expected to receive, a payment described explicitly as a favor, and then asked if they would volunteer to do some additional work. Once again, people were less likely to reciprocate in organizational settings than they were in more personal, informal settings.

There are many differences between personal and organizational or work settings that help account for why the norm of reciprocity operates with less force in the workplace and, as a consequence, implicit agreements are more readily and frequently breached. First of all, the norm of reciprocity speaks to the moral obligation to repay *favors* done for you by others. It is far from clear, as the social psychologist Robert Cialdini mentioned in a conversation, that the employment relationship engenders similar moral obligations. Yes, employees may have worked hard for their employers, investing their careers for years in helping to build the organization's success. But the employees got paid for that work, and so it would seem that the act of being paid for one's labor means that the employer owes its people nothing else. There was an exchange—money for labor. In a presumably free, competitive labor market in which both sides of the transaction have choices, the fact that the transaction was consummated means that both sides felt the deal was fair. In other words, it was a fair exchange, but not one pregnant with ongoing moral obligation.

Second, organizational contexts promote both a more future-oriented and also a more instrumental, calculative, and transactional orientation on the part of people. In everyday social relationships, people expect fair treatment and favors to be reciprocated. But in work settings, things become a lot more calculative. Specifically, people make more evaluations of whether or not coworkers and superiors could be useful in the future; likewise, people show more concern with the future than with repaying past kindnesses.

These studies reinforce what commonsense observation suggests: workplaces are primarily instrumental, calculative settings largely free of moral sentiments and even normative constraints. In a nutshell, companies will treat you well as long as you seem as though you are going to be useful in the future, and companies will probably be less inclined to treat you well or to repay past contributions the minute you are perceived as being less useful in future endeavors.

WHY PEOPLE PUT THEIR FAITH IN LEADERS

Notwithstanding the foregoing, people nonetheless often seem to put their faith in their employers and their leaders. Which leads to the question: Why?

One answer comes from the classic 1941 book *Escape from Freedom* by the Frankfurt-born psychologist Erich Fromm.[9] Fromm sought to understand why people *voluntarily* embrace authoritarian regimes such as Hitler's Germany. Fromm argued that when people are freed from the restrictions placed on them by institutions or other individuals, not everyone experiences this freedom as a positive thing; in fact, many do not enjoy it and find the absence of constraint uncomfortable. Fromm suggested that some of the ways that individuals seek to minimize the negative feelings associated with freedom include engaging in conformity, destructiveness, and authoritarianism.

Jean Lipman-Blumen, a professor at Claremont Graduate University, developed and expanded much of this analysis in her insightful book on toxic leaders.[10] She wanted to understand a seeming paradox: On the one hand, numerous toxic leaders in all walks of life who led their organizations to calamity, while, on the other hand, followers who eagerly went along, sublimating themselves and subordinating their judgment to the most out-landish of follies, ranging from the catastrophe at Enron to the WorldCom financial fraud and meltdown, orchestrated by Ber-nard Ebbers, an individual with a degree in physical education who went from running a chain of motels to putting together what was presumably one of the largest telecommunication companies in the world—except, of course, that it was built on financial chicanery.

Lipman-Blumen's analysis of why people follow toxic leaders provides important insight into why people seek leaders in their lives at all, hoping, of course, that they get a good one rather than one from the more toxic, harmful variety. One such motivation is the need for security. Autonomy seems great until you have it, and then many people want the reassurance and even guidance that comes from belonging to a larger entity like a workplace that will provide at least some minimal sense of security. Lipman-Blumen, echoing Freudian analysis, notes that as children we are used to being cared for and taken care of. As adults, we may miss that quasi-parental caregiving and therefore decide to seek care from other, nonparental authority figures such as bosses.

Leaders fill other needs as well, as Lipman-Blumen discusses. People are social creatures, which is why one of the first things done to break prisoners of war—or for that matter, prisoners in general—is to isolate them from social contact. We are afraid of being ostracized, of being excluded from the group—something that accounts for a lot of teenage behavior, including teen bullying. We can seemingly avoid ostracism by joining a group with a strong leader that includes and incorporates us.

Lipman-Blumen also notes that people respond particularly well to leaders who make them feel special, part of an elite, distinguished, unusual group. Certainly that was a theme at Enron—the phrase "the smartest people in the room" stands out—but it also characterizes other workplaces as well. People love to feel good about themselves—the self-enhancement motive—and if a leader feeds their individual or collective egos, people may not ask too many questions about the leader's own behaviors and motives as they bask in the warm glow of feeling special.

Finally, people are motivated to avoid cognitive dissonance—having two discrepant, inconsistent ideas in their minds at the same time. They can do so by cognitively reevaluating one or possibly both ideas to make them more congruent. Cognitive dissonance runs rampant inside workplaces. The idea that I have joined and voluntarily remain in a place, and the idea that the place I am in is run by some incompetent, venal, mean individual, are two highly discordant thoughts. It is often difficult to change the reality of my joining and remaining in my present place of employment. It is much easier to change my perception of the leader and my workplace, deciding that they are actually wonderful and special, which is why it was so sensible for me to join and remain in the first place.

The many ways in which people conspire in their own deception, including deceiving themselves about their leaders and the organizations in which they work, would require a book in itself to do justice to this vitally important topic. Suffice it to say that all of the dynamics described here provide a good beginning for understanding why people trust and put their faith in leaders without much critical thought and are often unlikely to look too closely at what sort of leaders they actually have.

THE RISKS OF RELYING ON LEADER BENEFICENCE

On Saturday, June 22, 2013, an Anchorage newspaper reported that "local employees of a men's clothing chain store put all sales on hold . . . in protest of the abrupt firing of the store's founder and executive chairman." Yes, employees at the Anchorage, Alaska, Men's Wearhouse store walked off the job to express their displeasure with the board's removal of George Zimmer from his role as chairman of the board. The employees stopped picketing and went home when the new management threatened to call the police.[11] " 'We're avid supporters of George . . . he's been there for all of us,' said Tiffany Karling, Assistant Manager . . . 'He's given us a family feeling . . . and he's made a big impact on me for sure, personally.' "[12]

It is hardly surprising that these employees appreciated Zimmer and the culture he had created. After all, they worked in retail, a typically low-wage industry. In 2014, retail clerks and sales associates earned just 60 percent of the median hourly wage. Moreover, retail is filled with part-timers whose work hours (and therefore pay) are at the whim of scheduling software algorithms that ensure that there aren't too many people in the store for the anticipated customer traffic and also that people don't get enough hours to qualify for benefits. Retail employees struggle to earn a living wage even if they manage to work full-time, and they are people on whose behalf various advocacy groups such as Fast Food Forward push for improved job conditions. The Men's Wearhouse paid higher wages, used fewer part-timers, and offered more training and internal promotion opportunities, than other retail chains, and in turn its employees quit less frequently, often because they understood and appreciated the unique retail work environment they enjoyed.

Soon after Zimmer's departure, the organization's culture began to change in ways that signaled it would not be "employees first" as it had been in the past. With little warning and no consultation, the world of the fifteen thousand Men's Wearhouse employees changed—and not for the better. Once again, we have an example of why there is no assurance that the person in charge will remain in charge, and certainly no assurance that this individual will be replaced by another with the same values and qualities.

There is no shortage of similar examples. For instance, when the family-owned business Fel-Pro of Skokie, Illinois, was purchased by Federal-Mogul Corporation for $720 million,

employees went from working for a beneficent employer concerned about employee well-being to working for a rapidly growing company concerned about margins and share price. The
culture changed in a hurry. The sale of the *Wall Street Journal* by
the Bancroft family to Rupert Murdoch's News Corporation rad-
ically altered the work environment, as evidenced by the exodus
of longtime *Journal* employees.

The realities of estate taxes, liquidity events, private equity
ownership, going public, and so forth all conspire to ensure that
except in the case of companies that are completely or majority employee-owned, even if employees enjoy a wonderful leader
for a while, continuity in that leadership and culture is far from
assured. Stuff happens, as they say. Companies sell out, leaders
retire or die, and the new people in charge aren't the same as the
old, particularly in how they relate to and treat employees. SAS
Institute has resisted going public because Jim Goodnight, the
CEO, is concerned about the effects of public ownership on its
employee-centric, family-oriented culture. So long as he holds all
the cards, his workers' loyalty is probably justified, but only so
much as they can be certain that he'll be in charge forever. Which
they can't. Which none of us can.

And even if there aren't new owners, even the old, wonderful owners aren't wonderful and charitable 100 percent of the
time—this is business, after all, and there are economic realities.
Howard Behar, the former president of Starbucks International
and a longtime board member of the company, told me when we
talked at a Conscious Capitalism conference on April 6, 2013, in
San Francisco, why he left the board of a company where he had
worked for decades. During the financial crisis of 2007 and the
years following, Starbucks's sales declined. Although the company remained profitable, its profits declined. So the company, in
an effort to maintain its margins and presumably its share price,

laid off thousands of employees. Not because it *had* to, in the sense of maintaining its economic viability, but because it sought to preserve its economic performance, at the cost of the jobs of many of its employees. Behar did not agree with that decision or its signal about the real values of Starbucks, and so he resigned.

At a panel discussion at the same conference, Chip Conley, the founder of the amazingly successful boutique hotel chain Joie de Vivre Hotels, described why he had sold the chain and left its active management after the recovery from the same economic recession. Because of the chain's size, during the economic downturn it was impossible to fully insulate the company's operations from the financial stringency—it was simply too large to hide in some protected niche. Therefore, Joie de Vivre had done a large number of layoffs. Doing the layoffs was hard for Conley, who understood the emotional and financial costs inflicted on the people who lost their jobs. As he noted, there will be other economic cycles, and he did not want to go through the experience of doing layoffs again. Hence, the sale and his exit from day-to-day hotel operations.

The point is that even in the best cultures, with the most well-intentioned leaders, the working circumstances, including economic security, are not invariably perfect or permanent. So trusting in the kindness of organizational leaders with their own agendas, points of view, and interests is inherently perilous, even if many people do precisely that.

CREATING LESS LEADER-DEPENDENT SYSTEMS

If leaders are, as everyone I know would admit, inevitably imperfect and impermanent, there are two possible solutions for the problems this fact causes for those who work for such leaders. The first solution is an approach advocated by many leadership-development practitioners and teachers: do a better job of developing, training, educating, and selecting leaders so we change the distribution of the leaders we have in the talent pool from selfish versus selfless, competent versus incompetent, egotistical versus modest, trustworthy versus untrustworthy—you get the picture.

This is a nice sentiment, and one that animates the leadership industry and its many practitioners, but one that, for all of the psychological and social psychological reasons already covered in this book, is not very likely to work, at least on a consistent basis. There is, however, a second approach worth considering, one that grew out of the quality movement; it's an approach that helps explain why flying in an airplane has become so incredibly safe.

Whenever there is an airplane accident, or for that matter, a number of near-accidents or other problems, the customary response is to try to redesign the plane to make such problems less likely to occur in the future. This may entail changing the controls or the guidance systems, or increasing mechanical or other system redundancies—in short, doing things that make it easier for the people flying and servicing the plane to do the right thing and more difficult for them to screw up. Such an approach is completely consistent with the principles of the quality movement, which promotes fixing the system rather than relying on the skills of individuals—to produce, in other words, an environment in which ordinary, albeit conscientious, people can reliably produce desirable results.

The lesson of W. Edwards Deming and his peers in the quality movement is that relying on individual motivation and acts of great competence is a singularly unreliable way to produce consistently high levels of system performance. Deming argued that if there are performance problems and quality defects, one needs to understand how those problems arise almost naturally as a consequence of how a system has been designed—and then fix those design flaws. Put simply, attack the problems by fixing the system, not scapegoating the necessarily fallible human beings working in and operating that system—whether or not they deserved it.

Inside organizations of all kinds, there are many ways to redesign governance that would reduce the dependence of employee well-being on the vagaries of people's doing a better job of selecting and training all-powerful leaders. Such solutions mostly entail building work systems that are less leader-dependent, and instead devolve more power to a wider set of organizational constituents, particularly employees. Such systems include employee ownership; building in formalized countervailing power, such as that provided by works councils in some European countries or unions in other places; building employment systems with more distributed power by having people elect their leaders, as occurs in some partnerships; and so forth. With more distributed and balanced power, the ability of a single individual to do remarkably good—or remarkably harmful—things becomes diminished. Interestingly, these approaches seldom get much attention. Instead, we hear more pleas for better leaders—pleas that have produced little improvement in any aspect of workplaces or leader tenure in the past fifty-plus years. But never mind, maybe the future will be better.

In the absence of any sustained movement to create better management and organizational governance systems that rely more on the "wisdom of crowds"[13] and less on the hope that one's leader is better than average and not overly self-interested, it seems sensible to look out for oneself. And as I argue next, systems based on people looking out for themselves have performance advantages, at least in some circumstances, not only for the people working in them but for the system itself.

SELF-INTEREST AS A GUIDING PRINCIPLE

If leaders can be and often are toxic, primarily taking care of themselves, and even if leaders are beneficent and well-intentioned, if they are frequently unreliable or impermanent as economic circumstances change, if companies don't promise much anymore and nonetheless break their implicit bargains, then what are we to do? My answer: try doing precisely what companies have told you to do for decades, and what the fundamental principle of economics has advocated since the time of Adam Smith.

Take care of yourself and assiduously look out for your own interests in your life inside work organizations.

As the social psychologist Dale Miller documented years ago, there is a norm of self-interest—sort of like the norm of reciprocity, but possibly even stronger and more reliable.[14] Miller noted that the norm of self-interest has substantial explanatory power, in part because people assume self-interest is operating and thereby take actions that make the norm of self-interest self-fulfilling through their very behaviors.

We know something is a norm because when the norm is violated, there are sanctions, and this is precisely the case for self-interested behavior. For example, in a series of four experimental studies, Miller and his colleague Rebecca Ratner found that people expected to be evaluated negatively if they supported a cause in which they had no stake (i.e., had no self-interest), that people reacted with surprise and anger when they observed others taking action inconsistent with those others' interests, and that individuals were more comfortable taking action on behalf of some issue if that issue was described as being self-relevant.[15] While it is of theoretical and intellectual interest to understand whether self-interested behavior arises from innate proclivities or conformity to social norms, the practical advice that emerges from the copious amounts of research on self-interested behavior is the same: presume that others are acting on the basis of their self-interest, and you will be better equipped to forecast and understand their actions.

I'm sure some of you must be thinking that surely not *everyone* behaves in a self-interested way, and of course that is true. In fact, throughout this book and in life, virtually nothing about social behavior is true all the time. There are, as I have frequently noted, good bosses who look out for the welfare of others, and humane workplaces filled with engaged and trusting employees. The question is the relative proportions and, to the point of this exposition, how to *change* those proportions—which requires recognizing the facts and understanding why they are as they are.

With respect to self-interest, as Adam Grant noted in his bestselling book *Give and Take*, people who are "givers," those who are generous with their time and with their help of others, are often the most successful in building networks of support and therefore in their careers.[16] But Grant also summarized research, including his own, that found that givers were not only among the most successful individuals, they were also among the least successful, and he provided advice about how to be generous without being a patsy. But even more to the point, Grant noted that "in the workplace, givers are a relatively rare breed."[17] Therefore you should not expect to be surrounded by such people. Moreover, research suggests that cooperative cultures are quite fragile, as are cooperation and trust in prisoner's dilemma games. Once individualistic values come to dominate,[18] or once people defect in prisoner's dilemma situations,[19] trust and cooperation are difficult if not impossible to rebuild.

Thus far I have offered what are essentially self-protective reasons for taking care of yourself—acting on the basis of your own self-interest—and assuming that others will probably do so as well. But there are normative reasons that also favor taking care of oneself as an effective paradigm for organizing the workplace and many other social settings. Let me offer three such rationales.

Most people, certainly those in Western societies, favor democracy as a form of government. The United States has spent a fortune promoting democracy around the globe, often unsuccessfully, as in much of the Middle East. Yes, democracy is messy, sometimes slow and inefficient, and prone to, and indeed a progenitor of, electoral politics in all of the good and bad that such a phrase implies. But as Winston Churchill commented, "It has been said that democracy is the worst form of government except all the others that have been tried from time to time."[20] Democracy fundamentally entails people choosing their own leaders—governing by the consent of the governed. Dictatorship is the opposite of democracy, and although history provides examples of enlightened autocrats who produced great social and economic progress for their societies, gambling on getting Singapore's Lee Kuan Yew rather than Zimbabwe's Robert Mugabe seems like a risky bet. Most important, much of the discipline of political economics argues that voters and their preferences are governed by calculations of rational self-interest.

Democracy as a form of governance is venerated in governments but not in work organizations, where not only is there precious little governing with the consent of the governed, the employees, but there is also little governing with the consent of the company's owners, its shareholders, except under relatively rare circumstances. Law firms, accounting firms, management consulting firms, and other partnerships can and sometimes do elect their leaders, as do some worker cooperatives such as Mondragon in Spain and the John Lewis Partnership in the United Kingdom, both substantial economic entities. But such arrangements are rare.

The presumption seems to be that an appointed leadership is more to be trusted with the company's well-being than any form of democratic or semidemocratic process for selecting and even removing leaders. It is interesting, to say the least, that while many people and much social science theory presumes that individual voters, acting at least partly out of their own self-interest, can produce better electoral outcomes than any other system, inside economic entities, which in some cases dwarf the size of at least some governments, a different calculus is advocated. But just maybe self-interest is as sensible a motive inside companies, which are, after all, in many respects political entities, as it is in electoral politics.

In economics as well as politics, self-interest reigns supreme as a normative principle for system design. It was the Scottish moral philosopher Adam Smith who articulated a principle often repeated to the present time: "It is not from the benevolence of the butcher, the brewer, or the baker that we expect our dinner, but from their regard to their own interest." Much of the "mechanics" of economic analysis demonstrates precisely how it is that when all economic actors seek what is best for each of them individually, production costs are minimized, the right quantities of goods and services are produced, and prices, including the wages earned by labor, are determined fairly. Competitive markets require only that there may be many participants in the market and that each participant vigorously pursues its own interests. In such a system, the best possible outcomes occur, as much economic analysis demonstrates.

Competition, not just in economics but in many domains of life, in which individuals each seek their own success, is celebrated and put on a pedestal. Typical of the multitude of approving sentiments is that offered by the steel industrialist Andrew Carnegie: "And while the law of competition may be sometimes hard for the individual, it is best for the race, because it ensures the survival of the fittest in every department."

Societies generally seem to celebrate competition as individuals seek their own advantage. That is, once again, until we consider the internal workings of organizations. So once inside a company, people are not only expected to collaborate rather than to compete with each other but, more important, to cooperate with their leaders (or bosses, to use a less noble term), to voluntarily subordinate themselves to their leaders' interests and commands. That would be fine if leaders were invariably concerned about the welfare of those individuals or even the well-being of the collective. But as we have seen throughout this book, leaders often pursue their own interests. Consequently, it makes little logical sense for individuals not to do precisely the same thing, and take care of themselves, too.

But perhaps most important, beyond the better decisions and more efficient results in political and economic systems produced by self-interest seeking, there is a third benefit: encouraging individuals to be responsible for their own well-being helps them come to think of themselves as fully functioning adult human beings. Encouraging people to seek and then to follow benevolent leaders—to put their trust and faith in these individuals who, because they are human, will nevertheless be invariably flawed— strikes me as seeking to in some measure infantilize otherwise competent working adults.

As we've seen, plenty of people actively conspire in their own subordination as they seek the affiliation, self-enhancement, and security that can come from subjugating themselves to and believing in larger-than-life leadership figures. But the fact that many people apparently seek to "escape from freedom" does not mean that such a path is in any way beneficial to them or to the larger social structures, including workplaces, in which they participate.

The bottom line: If you have a beneficent environment and a leader who actually cares about you, enjoy and treasure the moment, but don't expect it to be replicated elsewhere or to even persist indefinitely where you are. The world is often not a just or fair place, our hopes and desires notwithstanding. Get over it. Take care of yourself and watch out for your interests. If others do as well, all the better. To the extent you develop self-reliance and cease relying on leadership myths and stories, you will be much better off, and substantially less likely to confront disappointment and the career consequences that devolve from relying on the unreliable.

CHAPTER 8

Fixing Leadership Failures: You *Can* Handle the Truth

t's September 2013, and I am giving a talk to alumni and other executives on some of the material covered in this book. About forty people are gathered at the newly opened Vlerick Business School facility in Brussels, Belgium. A hand goes up and an experienced senior executive comments, "I have seen everything you have described and can vouch for its accuracy. But this is depressing, even if it is true."

In my reply, I acknowledge that what one finds depressing is a relative concept, and that while this individual may find my description of the work world quite sobering, a sentiment I can certainly understand, I don't. Instead, I say, "I find it even more depressing that talented, earnest, young, and for that matter, not-so-young entrepreneurs and leaders in all types of organizations all over the world lose their jobs and their companies at unacceptably high rates."

I continue, "I find it depressing that after decades of books, lectures, leadership-development programs, and all the other components of the large leadership industry, virtually every shred of evidence shows most workplaces filled with distrustful, disengaged, dissatisfied, despairing employees. And," I conclude, forgoing any pretense of political correctness, "I find it depressing that we would want to discuss the state of leadership in organizations from the perspective of what feels good and uplifting, rather than what the evidence shows to be true."

This executive's comment is not all that unusual. After a talk about this book to an academic audience in Spain, I get a similar response—the material is provocative and probably true, but not "uplifting."

The difference between management science and medical science is telling. "Depressing" may be an emotion felt by medical researchers and by practitioners confronted on a daily basis by the inevitable limitations of current treatments, and certainly people would love to be "uplifted." But "depressing" or, conversely, "uplifting" are almost certainly not how doctors and other medical researchers evaluate evidence or figure out how to make progress in treatment. Averting our eyes from the facts may provide solace, but it does so at the price of progress. There is no theory or evidence that suggests that improvement comes from ignoring bad news, paying inordinate attention to rare, exceptional cases, or from failing to measure base rates for how often something occurs. No wonder medical science has made significant strides in treating many diseases while leadership as it is practiced daily all over the world has continued to produce a lot of disengaged, dissatisfied, and disaffected employees.

So we end where we began, with the pragmatic question of whether all the inspiration and feel-good stories produced over the decades have done any good. This is not a question about competence, motive, purpose, intentions, sincerity, or even hypocrisy (which there is in abundance). It is a simple question about the state of the world of work and leadership after the expenditure of so much time, effort, and money with so few results. Yes, some people would argue that things might even be worse without all these efforts. But holding aside the impossibility of empirically demonstrating the truth of that counterfactual argument, it is a tough argument to accept, given the dismal data on employee engagement, job dissatisfaction, trust in leaders, and career catastrophes.

The discussions about leadership often seem sort of like being under the effect of nitrous oxide (laughing gas) or other forms of mild anesthesia. By leaving people feeling good while somewhat uninformed about reality, the leadership enterprise helps produce people happily oblivious to many important truths about organizational life in the real world. In this zoned-out, semiconscious, blissful state, people are insufficiently prepared for what they will encounter at work and, most important, insufficiently energized to accurately diagnose and change that world of work. That's because people think everything is just peachy fine, or soon will be. But if the world of work in a few more decades is to look any different—or better—than the one today, people need to understand the world not as we might want it to be, but as it is. To get from one place to another, you need to know as best as you can where you are, where you want to go, and, most important, the obstacles and barriers you will likely encounter en route.

Moreover, as Jim Collins pointed out in *Good to Great,* unrealistic optimism and a failure to see the situation as it is can be not only unhelpful—it can be fatal. He called this the Stockdale paradox, after James Stockdale, a U.S. military officer held captive for eight years during the Vietnam war. Stockdale was tortured numerous times and had little reason to believe he would live to see his wife again. Although Stockdale understood his predicament, he also never lost hope that he might endure it and not only survive his ordeal but use it as a defining experience in his life. And here is the paradox:

> While Stockdale had remarkable faith in the unknow-able, he noted that it was always the most optimistic of his prisonmates who failed to make it out of there alive. "They were the ones who said, 'We're going to be out by Christmas.' And Christmas would come, and Christmas would go. Then they'd say, 'We're going to be out by Easter.' And Easter would come, and Easter would go. And then Thanksgiving, and then it would be Christmas again. And they died of a broken heart." What the optimists failed to do was confront the reality of their situation. They preferred the ostrich approach, sticking their heads in the sand and hoping for the difficulties to go away. That self-delusion might have made it easier on them in the short-term, but when they were eventually forced to face reality, it had become too much and they couldn't handle it.[1]

And, of course, such unfounded optimism often precluded taking action to deal with the situation as best one could, which is precisely what Stockdale did.

ACTUAL LEADERS VERSUS THE PRESCRIPTIONS

As detailed throughout this book, many of the most powerful and economically successful leaders in organizations of all types demonstrate little to no correspondence with the prescriptions for what leaders are supposed to do. No wonder there is so much cynicism in the workforce.

So there's Carly Fiorina, the former president of Lucent's $19 billion global service-provider business and the former CEO of Hewlett-Packard—the first woman to ever run a Dow 30 company—who has been described as someone with "a silver tongue and an iron will."[2] Fiorina was not one to brook opposition to her decisions, the frequent prescriptions for consensus-based decision-making notwithstanding. And it did not matter whether the disagreement came from inside her management team, where you didn't stay if you opposed her ideas too frequently, or from the son of cofounder William Hewlett, who fought with her mightily over the Compaq acquisition.

There's Rebekah Brooks, a former editor at the U.K.-based News International, part of Rupert Murdoch's News Corporation. Brooks was recently on trial for overseeing people who engaged in the phone-hacking of journalists and, for that matter, the hacking of a teenage murder victim's cell phone—hacking and spying on potential news targets using private detectives that occurred on a massive scale. Her success in swiftly climbing News Corporation's ranks, according to many accounts, came from Brooks's "clear-eyed ruthlessness" and unceasing and skillful networking with the rich and powerful in the establishment, including both former and current prime ministers. And of course, her success came from her ability to build a close relationship with her ultimate boss, Rupert Murdoch, who came to think of her as one of his daughters.[3]

Lyndon Johnson, the youngest Senate majority leader in the history of the United States and considered by many to be one of the most successful and productive U.S. presidents, verbally abused and berated his aides throughout his long career. He was notorious for calling them into the bathroom while he was on the toilet to give them dictation and instructions.[4] Johnson's former press secretary, Bill Moyers, commented that Johnson "possessed an animal sense of weakness in other men."[5]

Henry Kissinger, the Nobel Peace Prize–winning former secretary of state and national security adviser, wiretapped his subordinates. He did this not just to uncover national security leaks
but to monitor their loyalty—to him, not to the president or the
government. He was demeaning and even cruel to the people
who worked for him.[6]

Roger Ailes is a former political consultant and a conservative
political icon who became the head of Fox News. Fox News is
incredibly profitable, earning an estimated $816 million in 2010,
nearly a fifth of the earnings of the entire News Corporation.
Ailes is clearly one of the most powerful figures in television history. But he does not fit the typically advocated leadership profile. According to one source Ailes is a "tyrant"; he has said, "I
only understand friendship or scorched earth." The culture at
Fox News is one of intimidation: " 'It's like the Soviet Union or
China: People are always looking over their shoulders," says a
former executive with News Corp, who was quoted in a *Rolling
Stone* article.[7]

Linda Wachner rose rapidly from the position of buyer to
become the CEO of the clothing manufacturer Warnaco; she was
one of the first female CEOs in the clothing industry. Between
1993 and 1999 she earned $158 million from salary, bonuses,
options, and dividends. Although Warnaco filed for bankruptcy
in 2000, a result of too-rapid expansion, Wachner walked away
with $3.5 million in stock in the reorganized company as well
as $200,000 cash. Wachner's management approach, something
that got her to the top and kept her there for a while as she amassed
a pot of money: swearing at and publicly berating her subordinates (which drove away key talent), exhibiting colossal ego, and
showing an "abrasive and abusive" style of management.[8]

J. Edgar Hoover ruled the Federal Bureau of Investigation
with an iron hand, virtually personifying the FBI for decades. He

intimidated everyone from presidents to members of Congress. But the evidence is clear that Hoover engaged in illegal wiretapping and surveillance, blackmailed his bosses in the Department of Justice, and got rid of subordinates who in any way challenged either his power or his vision for how the bureau should operate and what its priorities should be.[9]

To work for Steve Jobs of Apple was to face the risk of at any moment being "Steved" as it came to be called, berated and fired—with such firings sometimes being rescinded on the same day. When my Stanford colleague Robert Sutton decided to add a chapter on the virtues of being an asshole to his book *The No Asshole Rule*, he did some casual research to see whom to include. Sutton did a Google search pairing the term with the names of some prominent CEOs who might fit the description. Steve Jobs came out on top, far surpassing Oracle's Larry Ellison, who came in second place.

And speaking of Larry Ellison, he has patterned his management approach after medieval samurai warriors. Ellison's outbursts in meetings with his staff are famous not just for his use of invective but for their length—sometimes going on as long as an hour.[10]

Jeff Bezos, the founder and CEO of Amazon is also famous for his outbursts of temper and his put-downs of employees, including the line, "We are going to have to supply some human intelligence to this problem."[11]

Paul Allen, who cofounded Microsoft along with Bill Gates, wrote that working with Gates was like "being in hell."[12]

Tina Brown, for more than three decades a leading figure in the world of magazine publishing, inspired fear among those who might criticize her. She was known for churning and changing magazines up until the last minute, keeping her subordinates on edge.[13]

This list of leaders who, on the one hand, earned vast sums and retained power for decades while, on the other hand, being in almost every way contradictory to the customary bromides about modesty, serving others, and being truthful is almost endless, and it's a list that grows longer all the time.

One response I sometimes get to this or similar lists is that many of these people weren't really all that successful. Fiorina and Wachner got fired, Martha Stewart is lonely, Steve Jobs at one point could hardly get anyone to attend a birthday celebration, Johnson was perpetually insecure and forced from his office by Vietnam, Hoover lived a closeted life and had few real friends, Brown's last couple of publishing ventures failed, and so forth. I have several responses. First, in the real world, almost no one lives a perfect life, perfectly happy with everything going perfectly all the time. Second and more importantly, although one can debate how truly successful these leaders were, there is no denying one fact: that each of them and the multitude of others who do not fit the leadership models so often proffered reached great heights and positions of power in the first place. So instead of attempting to reconstruct perceptions to make reality fit your view of a just and fair world, it might be more helpful to understand *why* and *how* people who don't fit the visions of what leadership should entail reached such powerful positions. Such understanding is the fundamental prerequisite for altering the dynamics that produced these people, whether you like them or not.

Moreover, it's not just that there are numerous successful leaders who don't fit the prescriptions for honesty, modesty, trustworthiness, taking care of others, authenticity, and the many other positive attributes we ascribe to leaders. It's worse. As we saw in chapter 1 and as you can see every day in the news, many of the leaders who do appear to fit the aspirational models we hear about often do so mostly because people believe the leaders' own hype and haven't looked too closely at what these leaders actually did and what it was really like to work with them. Wanting to believe in fairy tales, people avert their gaze and often actively avoid evidence that challenges their worldview.

So what we have are prescribed models of behavior that are notable by their absence in most companies or, for that matter, public agencies. And in many instances, as I have argued, the advice people receive about what to do to be successful in their careers is inconsistent with what we know about human behavior. Why do such fables persist?

If you search for the phrase "You can't handle the truth" on your favorite search engine, the first thing that will probably come up is the scene from the movie *A Few Good Men*, in which a lawyer, Daniel Kaffee, played by Tom Cruise, is interrogating Marine Colonel Nathan Jessup, played by Jack Nicholson, about whether the colonel had ordered a hazing (called a Code Red) of a soldier in his command, an act that had resulted in the soldier's death. Jessup, provoked and enraged, snarls, "You want answers?" Kaffee replies, "I want the truth." Jessup then goes into a tirade about the realities of what is required to protect the United States and its interests, beginning with the phrase "You can't handle the truth."

That sentiment, that people can't handle the truth, pervades much of the social world and governs how people behave inside and outside organizations, and for good reason. Research shows that people who deliver bad news often suffer adverse consequences[14]—hence the admonition "Don't blame the messenger." The evidence demonstrates that people actively try to avoid confronting distressing information.[15] Because they seek to avoid uncomfortable truths, individuals sometimes avoid seeking medical help in the presence of symptoms that concern them, not wanting to hear a dire diagnosis. Of course, such behavior often makes the situation worse, as real medical problems frequently become more dangerous and difficult the longer they are left untreated. Many people prefer happy movies, or at least movies with happy endings, in which good triumphs over evil, right over might, justice over injustice.

And people who want to be successful—to become or to remain insiders—avoid telling the truth if such truth could be perceived as a criticism of other insiders, people, or companies with power. As Massachusetts senator Elizabeth Warren wrote in her book *A Fighting Chance*,[16] she received precisely such advice to avoid criticizing powerful others from Lawrence Summers, a former president of Harvard University and U.S. treasury secretary:

> I had a choice. I could be an insider or I could be an outsider. Outsiders can say whatever they want. But people on the inside don't listen to them. Insiders, however, get lots of access and a chance to push their ideas. . . . But insiders also understand one unbreakable rule: *They don't criticize other insiders.*[17]

This preference for good news and uplifting stories, this reluctance to criticize powerful leaders or organizations, this unwillingness to face the problems besetting so many workplaces, pervades the world of leadership, where people make a living telling happy tales about leaders who are authentic, honest, modest, and interested in the welfare of others. But the spinners of yarns don't bother to tell the other stories, about the leaders who were the opposite. And there is little indication of the relative prevalence of the two types of leaders, and precious little attention is paid to the career consequences enjoyed by them.

Simply put, in a world where people can't handle the truth, they don't get the truth—and they suffer in numerous ways as a result. One of the most important outcomes of the happy talk is, as I indicated at the beginning of this book, a lot of horrific work environments filled with bad bosses—environments that do not change and won't change until we confront the facts about what actually is going on and why. Another consequence is career setbacks for people who fail to understand the full range of organizational dynamics.

HOW TO FACE THE REALITY OF ORGANIZATIONAL LIFE

If we want to change the world of work and leadership conduct in many workplaces, we need to act on what we know rather than what we wish and hope for. It is also imperative that we understand why we are stuck where we are. I will thus conclude by summarizing some of the various suggestions made in the earlier chapters, as well as summarizing some fundamental principles for fixing what ails the numerous set of activities devoted to educating and developing leaders, based on what we know about leaders, leadership, and the social science that helps us understand individual behavior in social and organizational contexts.

Stop Confusing the Normative with the Descriptive, and Focus More on What Is

In part because the leadership industry is in the business of educating future leaders and furthering the development of people who are currently in leadership roles, many people in the industry believe that it is important to primarily if not exclusively present models of what *should be* rather than what *is*. This belief in emphasizing what ought to be also produces recommendations to study and talk about positive models rather than the entire range of leaders, to emphasize success stories, and to avoid asking the tough questions of how many good versus bad bosses there are and why there are so many bad bosses after so many years of giving people sound advice on how to be better leaders.

For example, two colleagues who teach classes on leadership often tell me that I write about scorpions or spiders or, sometimes, cockroaches. Holding aside the prevalence and survival capacity of cockroaches and spiders, I'd like to note that my colleagues' well-intentioned message is that the job of teachers is to present positive role models and to tell people, including students at all levels, what they *should do* and how they *should be* to live more purposeful, more effective lives and create workplaces that bring out the best in everyone. In short, these colleagues believe that the job of teachers is to inspire those being educated, and to lift their aspirations and their spirits.

If you believe that this advice and the profusion of other, similar advice will create a different and better organizational world, you need to go back and reread the introduction and chapter 1. For decades, scores, maybe hundreds, possibly thousands, of leadership writers, speakers, and coaches have done exactly what so many recommend: write hagiographies of corporate leaders that bear little relationship to a more complex, nuanced reality, and, even more problematically, study truly rare and unique individuals in the hope that by describing these exceptional people, others will be both inspired by and able to learn from them.

There is not a scintilla of evidence that this approach works, as demonstrated by the numerous declining measures of workplace well-being, the declining length of job tenure for leaders and others, and the increasingly frequent career derailments and leadership failures. Nor is there much if any theoretical logic that supports the effectiveness of such an approach as a recipe for organizational change. There are certainly leaders who are truthful, trustworthy, concerned for the welfare of others, and modest. We should honor and celebrate such people. But by failing to acknowledge their rarity, we underestimate and misunderstand our challenge if we really do want to create the world that now exists mostly just on the pages of leadership books.

Watch Actions, Not Words

I am a fan of David Kelley, the founder, chairman, and managing partner of the much-awarded and highly acclaimed product design firm IDEO, and a founder of the Hasso Plattner Institute of Design (also known as the D.school) at Stanford. Kelley has created a collaborative, innovative, and, most important, healthy culture at IDEO, as evidenced by the fact that talented people stay at the firm even when they could earn more, possibly much more, elsewhere. But what I most admire is his and his colleagues' ability to instill design thinking into clients and students. One fundamental aspect of design thinking is to get people to "observe people as they deal with life's messy problems,"[18] to have them watch people work in order to design better, more helpful tools, and to observe people interacting with products in order to create more user-oriented designs.

The relevance for the leadership industry, and for you, is clear. About forty years ago, Henry Mintzberg, a business school professor at McGill University, published a book based on his observations of what managers actually do.[19] That type of observational study remains rare. Instead of intently, objectively, and clinically watching how leaders operate, we listen to what leaders *say* about what they do, how they talk about their values, the lovely sentiments they express. This is a reasonable fallback position because in many instances sensible leaders do not permit sustained, close observation of their real behavior. But when people observe what successful managers do, the results often don't conform to the typical leadership bromides. For example, one study of fifty-two managers in three very different organizations found that "two activities were significantly related to managerial success: interaction with outsiders and socializing/politicking."[20]

As the clichéd phrase "walking the talk" makes clear, there is often some degree of disconnection between leaders' pronouncements and what is written about them, and what leaders actually do and their success doing it, a fact we have seen throughout this book. So there's the late Warren Bennis, an iconic figure in the leadership industry and a well-known author, speaker, and authority on leadership, who had the temerity to take on the task of being president of the University of Cincinnati for six years in the 1970s after serving as the academic vice president and acting executive vice president at the University at Buffalo. Bennis's tenure at Cincinnati was not entirely successful, but the important point is that people who were there at the time or knew those who were will tell you that the Warren Bennis who was president and the Warren Bennis who wrote books about transparency and trust were not quite the same people.

Bennis's behavior, somewhat inconsistent with his espoused beliefs, was undoubtedly provoked by the aggravations and frustrations he confronted in trying to do his job, as a university presidency is a highly political position charged with pleasing or at least coping with multiple constituencies with often incompatible demands. In a book that, among other things, draws on his own experience, Bennis bemoaned the unconscious conspiracy that kept visionary leaders like himself from being successful in their jobs: "I had become the victim of a vast, amorphous, unwitting, unconscious conspiracy to prevent me from doing anything whatever to change the university's status quo."[21] He got buried under a mountain of trivial decision-making,[22] in part because Bennis, like many people, was much more skilled at advocating decentralization than he was in practicing it.

The implication for you: Pay attention to what is *really* going on and to people's real behavior and performance. Become a skilled and unbiased observer, and, to the extent you can, eliminate hopes and expectations from your observations. Everyone has to navigate a number of organizations, each with its own leader and culture. You would be well served to pay attention to what you see and not to what people are saying and the lovely values and sentiments they are expressing. Rhetoric and reality are often decoupled in social life, and in leadership it is almost the norm.

Sometimes You Have to Behave Badly to Do Good

The leadership industry mostly advocates behavior consistent with how good parents raise their children and congruent with universal religious and human values. Seldom considered is the possibility that the reason such values and behaviors aren't more common is that they are at times quite ineffective. Simply put, there are occasions when you have to do bad things to achieve good results.

Most of the drugs currently used to treat cancer are toxic poisons. Radiation, also used to treat cancer, kills if the dose is too high. Many therapeutic advances entail trying to get the chemical substances or the radiation focused more precisely on the cancerous cells, sparing the healthy tissue, in the recognition that you need the poison but want to focus it as much as possible to avoid dangerous side effects. Surgery to treat and possibly cure disease involves first cutting into people. The point is that sometimes to do good, you have to have the courage and wisdom to perform harmful, painful, actions. In his book *Complications: A Surgeon's Notes on an Imperfect Science* about his journey into medicine, the author and physician Atul Gawande relates that to become a doctor, medical students need to learn to take action, even if the action will possibly entail error, and even if the action is, at least at first, uncomfortable for the doctor, an action like making an incision or putting in a stitch.[23] Although medical students practice cutting cadavers, the first cut or stitch into a live, real human being remains challenging.

Leadership is no different. Making change, improving situations, getting things done, winning in very competitive environments, often requires being willing and able to engage in behaviors and exhibit qualities that some people might find repugnant. Maybe that's why there is such a leadership shortage and why the leadership industry, with its failure to acknowledge this fundamental truth, continues to fail.

For example, as the United States prepared to compete in the World Cup in 2014, an article about the team and its coach raised a provocative question: "Are the Americans bad at playacting? And if so, should they try to get better?"[24] For those not versed in soccer arcana, playacting refers to the practice of falling to the ground and feigning significant injury to draw a penalty against the opposing team and player, even if only gently bumped, nudged, or barely touched. The analysis concluded, "The best attackers in the world . . . regularly fall to the ground, particularly if they feel that they are going to lose possession. And why not? If it works, they get a free kick. If it doesn't, they were going to give up the ball anyway."[25] This practice runs counter to American ideals—but it also put the team at a disadvantage. Sometimes, maybe even often, the choice comes down to playing the game, whatever that game is, the way others do or losing.

In the fall of 2013, the world celebrated the five-hundred-year anniversary, more or less, of the appearance of Machiavelli's *The Prince*. One commentary on this important and still-relevant work noted:

Machiavelli teaches that in a world where so many are not good, you must learn to be able to not be good. The virtues taught in our secular and religious schools are incompatible with the virtues one must practice to safeguard those same institutions. . . . Machiavelli has long been called a teacher of evil. The author of "The Prince" never urged evil for evil's sake. The proper aim of a leader is to maintain his state (and, not incidentally, his job). Politics is an arena where following virtue often leads to the ruin of a state, whereas pursuing what appears to be vice results in security and well-being. In short, there are never easy choices, and prudence consists of knowing how to recognize . . . the hard decisions you face and choosing the less bad as what is the most good.[26]

Abraham Lincoln, the U.S. president credited with saving the Union and freeing the slaves, was not above using deception to get his way. As he struggled to get the Thirteenth Amendment to the Constitution passed, he dissembled about where a Southern negotiating delegation, sent to hammer out the terms that would end the war, actually was. He offered government positions and other emoluments to representatives whose votes he needed, in effect selling votes for government jobs. In many instances during the Civil War, Lincoln overstepped his formal powers, risking impeachment, in his efforts to protect and preserve the United States. Lincoln's political maneuverings, nicely described in Doris Kearns Goodwin's book *Team of Rivals* and illustrated in Steven Spielberg's movie *Lincoln* illustrate the truth of Machiavelli—that often to do good things, even great things, people need to be willing to take whatever actions are required, and to not shy away from tough fights, unpopularity, and, yes, even decisions that skirt the edge of illegality.[27]

Another essay, reviewing books about Machiavelli, not only reinforced the message that "politics is a dirty business, requiring leaders to do things their private conscience might abhor," but also made an important point about the actual source of bad leader behavior:

> A leader guided by public necessity is less likely to be cruel and vicious than one guided by religious moralizing. . . . After all, someone who believes he has God on his side is capable of anything.[28]

Unless and until the leadership industry both acknowledges and embraces that wisdom, progress in fixing the reality of organizational life will remain imperceptible.

Advice to Leaders Depends on the Ecosystem in Which They Are Operating

Everyone wants advice, which is why the "how-to" industry, covering topics from losing weight to getting your finances under control to being a better leader, is so large. The advice business is also largely impervious as to whether or not the advice actually gets implemented, since the profit comes from selling the advice. In fact, to the extent that people heed the advice and solve their problems, future profit opportunities from addressing the same issue yet again disappear.

In the case of leadership, much of the advice has been largely noncontingent—leaders should be authentic, truthful, caring for others, inspiring of trust, and so forth, attributes put forward as universal qualities and behaviors to be developed. But the problem is that if you are not a scorpion or a spider in a forest of them, your survival chances may be quite low. A process of differential selection, attraction, and retention, along with the criteria used to determine who advances up a hierarchy, together tend to ensure that workplaces are filled with people who are largely consistent in their leadership style with each other, particularly at the higher ranks. Consistency in behavior also comes from the process of social learning, in which people figure out what to do by looking at what others in their immediate environment are doing and what the results are.

This fact means that answering the question "What should I do to be a better leader?" depends not just on what your personal objectives are and how you define "better," although those are obviously crucial considerations. The answer to how to be a better leader also depends on knowing the environment you are in, its norms, and, most important, what behaviors will be seen as demonstrating weakness and incompetence and what actions will signal strength, confidence, and skill. To be a better leader you must, at a minimum, display the attributes required to get you into the position in the first place and then be able to hold on to it.

Although there are large regularities in the answers to these questions, it is nonetheless the case that environments do differ. The leadership qualities required to succeed—or maybe even to survive—in the software company Oracle, with its competitive culture, frequent firings of senior executives, and workplace with high levels of turnover, are undoubtedly quite different from those required in the food retailer Trader Joe's, the former president of which is a leading figure in the Conscious Capitalism movement, an ideology that emphasizes the idea of serving multiple stakeholders and taking customer and employee well-being seriously.

Stop the Either-Or Thinking

One of the wonderful things about movies is their obvious symbolism. In the Star Wars movies, Luke Skywalker wears white and Darth Vader, black. That's how we think about things—good or evil, heaven or hell, honest or dishonest, effective or ineffective. But this cognitive reductionism oversimplifies a much more nuanced reality. While it may provide some emotional comfort that comes from feelings of false certainty about how things are, thinking of things as black or white makes it much more difficult to deal with the real world and its many complications. A quick perusal of the scholarly literature reveals the many demonstrable downsides that derive from oversimplification, ranging from harmful diet recommendations based on simplistic ideas about what foods are good or bad for you to overtreatment of various cancers under the assumption that people either have cancer or they don't.[29] The fact that complexity in evaluation and analysis can be helpful may be one reason that a study of decision-making found that higher-status individuals engaged in more complex thinking.[30]

Stopping the good-bad, oversimplified stories we tell is going to be tough, as they seem to be what most people, even intelligent, well-educated people, seemingly prefer. The Soviet dissident Alexander Solzhenitsyn offered some important wisdom on this topic:

> If only there were evil people somewhere insidiously
> committing evil deeds, and it were necessary only to
> separate them from the rest of us and destroy them. But
> the line dividing good and evil cuts through the heart of
> every human being. And who is willing to destroy a piece
> of his own heart?[31]

In their book *Built to Last,* Jim Collins and Jerry Porras decried either-or thinking, the belief that things have to be one way or their opposite.[32] Take their advice on this issue, even when, and maybe particularly when, analyzing and understanding leaders and leadership. If we acknowledge and even celebrate the complexity, multidimensionality, and multifaceted truth about everyone, including leaders and ourselves, and if we recognize the strengths and the weaknesses that all individuals have, we will possibly develop a more accurate understanding of social dynamics and a more veridical and therefore helpful map of the organizational landscapes we seek to navigate.

Forgive, but Remember

This phrase is my adaptation of a similar sentiment from Charles Bosk's well-regarded book about surgeons in training, *Forgive and Remember.*[33] Forgiving while remembering is a value espoused in medical practice and in medical education for good reasons. Forgive, so that people will be more inclined to admit their mistakes, but remember, so that they and their peers will be less likely to make the same mistakes again.

Virtually all religious traditions advocate forgiveness, if for no other reason than that holding grudges harms the holder of the ill will, not the target. People do deserve second, and maybe third, fourth, and fifth, chances. But not to recognize that the past often predicts the future, and therefore, not to remember people's histories in their leadership roles and not to use that history in making decisions, and instead somehow presuming better behavior in the future than was exhibited in the past, is just asking for trouble.

There are many examples in business of ignoring past leader behavior, producing decisions that people come later to regret.

To work for George Steinbrenner, the owner of the New York Yankees baseball team, was, as a player or a manager, to experience a micromanager who was prone to vituperative tirades and who regularly fired people—in the case of manager Billy Martin, several times. Nonetheless, players and coaches would join the organization somehow hoping it wouldn't happen to them or they wouldn't mind.

No one should have been surprised when the board of Sunbeam fired CEO Al Dunlap on June 15, 1998. The company's stock price was plummeting because Sunbeam, a manufacturer of outdoor grills and kitchen appliances, had juiced the apparent sales results by stuffing the distribution chain of wholesalers with product. Before coming to Sunbeam just two years prior, Dunlap had sold Scott Paper to Kimberly-Clark, increasing its value mostly if not exclusively by laying off employees and cutting costs, something that had earned him the nickname "Chainsaw." As the business journalist John Byrne wrote, "Scott became the sixth consecutive company that was sold or dismembered by Dunlap since 1983."[34] Downsizers and cost-cutters do what they do, and a CEO well-known for his temper, hubris, and poor treatment of subordinates isn't likely to change.

And there are literally hundreds of examples in sports, particularly college sports, where schools will apparently overlook past peccadillos if a coach won, only to have troublesome elements of past behavior create "new" problems—actually just the same old behavior occurring yet again.

Consider the case of Mike Rice, the Rutgers basketball coach fired in 2013 when, according to an article in the *New York Times Magazine*, "ESPN aired footage of him screaming at and demeaning his players, yanking them by their jerseys, shoving them, kicking them; throwing balls at their heads and groins; taunting them with homophobic slurs."[35] Rutgers had hired Rice from Robert Morris University. He had been the same person there: "Rice might not have crossed the line at Robert Morris, but he also wasn't a completely different person there from the one he would become at Rutgers. . . . All of the words people [used] to describe him at Robert Morris . . . [were] not that far from 'out of control'. . . . Rice [developed] a reputation for his success, but also for his temper."[36]

The most fundamental principle of learning theory is that behavior is a function of its consequences. When behavior is rewarded, that behavior gets repeated with even greater frequency. When behavior is ignored or punished, the frequency of the behavior diminishes.[37] In the world of leadership, and particularly the world of senior leadership, what seems striking is how few consequences there are for all varieties of bad behavior, ranging from underperforming in one's job role to serious ethical lapses to treating employees badly. Consequently, even as leaders aren't trusted and workplaces remain toxic, not much changes, because often leaders are able to get away with doing a great deal of harm.

Craig Dubow was Gannett's CEO at a time when the company's stock price went from $75 to $10 a share and twenty thousand employees lost their jobs. Not only did Dubow retire (rather than be fired), he left with a package worth about $37 million in health, retirement, and disability benefits, as well as having a salary income of about $16 million in the preceding two years.[38]

Or consider the case of Stan O'Neal, the CEO of Merrill Lynch who loaded the company up with debt and oversaw the firm's precipitous decline. As Merrill was sinking into the financial abyss, the company was taken over by Bank of America after O'Neal's ouster in 2007. No big problem for O'Neal, who left with an enormous severance package estimated at over $150 million. The aluminum giant Alcoa appointed O'Neal to its board of directors in 2008. According to someone at Alcoa, it was

O'Neal's knowledge of financial markets and impending financial problems that made him valuable to Alcoa. I suppose that, having helped cause a financial crisis, he could credibly claim to be an expert on them.[39]

Charles O. Prince, who formerly led Citigroup until 2007 and the financial crisis that caused the bank huge losses and devastated its stock price, remained on the boards of Xerox and Johnson and Johnson after leaving Citi. In another example of this, "Andrea Jung, who . . . stepped down as the chief executive of Avon amid a bribery investigation and financial struggles . . . is still a director of Apple."[40] And Marshall Cohen, a director of American International Group, the insurance company brought low by its derivative bets and bailed out by the government during the 2007–2009 recession, was *subsequently* put on the board of a New York investment bank. That same bank also appointed as a director Henry S. Bienen, who had been on the board of Bear Stearns between 2004 and when the company was rescued from collapse by JPMorgan Chase.[41]

Systematic research supports the message of these cases. As noted in an article in the *New York Times*, "even in the most extreme circumstances—like the financial crisis—directors bore little consequence for their poor decisions."[42] A study found that director turnover increased less than 1 percent in financial institutions during the financial crisis, and there was little difference in director turnover between good and poorly performing banks, even those that received government bailouts. Nor were things different for the nonfinancial companies in the S&P 1500. The chance of being forced out as a director because of the company's poor performance was less than 1 percent.[43]

Steven L. Rattner, a former vice chairman of investment bank Lazard and cofounder of the private equity firm the Quadrangle Group, provides another lesson in the pervasive tendency to not hold leaders very accountable for their behaviors—a practice that virtually ensures that leader behavior will remain unchanged and that, through a process of social learning, other leaders will learn that how one behaves does not matter that much. Rattner, the White House overseer of the automobile industry during the 2007–2009 recession, got into trouble because of his business practices and ethics, or lack thereof:

> He was accused of using "pay to play" practices while raising money from a New York state pension fund. . . . In 2010, he paid more than $16 million to Andrew M. Cuomo, who was then New York's attorney general, and the Securities and Exchange Commission to settle the civil cases. . . . He was "banned from appearing in any capacity before any public pension fund within the State of New York for five years" . . . he stepped down from his position in the Obama administration.[44]

But as the *New York Times* writer Andrew Ross Sorkin makes clear, Rattner's fall from grace and power was quite temporary; two years later, he was managing the fortune of New York's mayor Michael Bloomberg, serving as a pundit on major cable news channels, writing op-eds for the *Times*, and even getting back into the Obama administration's good graces, campaigning for the president's reelection in 2012. Obama needed to win Ohio, the home of many automobile parts suppliers, who appreciated Rattner's help to the industry during the recession.

For sure, Rattner's subsequent success demonstrates the importance of persistence and resilience, but it also shows something else: "His re-emergence may also be a telling commentary about the way the nation's elite flock to people with power—and those with powerful friends."[45] The elite glom on to powerful people partly because they forgive past transgressions and partly because of the "fear of alienating themselves from other people" who associate with those with power. This continued association occurs almost regardless of what people have done, are doing, or, for that matter, are likely to do in the future.

CONNECTIONS AND DISCONNECTIONS

The problem with leadership is at its core a story of disconnections:

- the disconnect between what leaders say and what they do;
- the disconnect between the leadership industry's prescriptions and the reality of many leaders' behaviors and traits;
- the disconnect between the multidimensional nature of leadership performance and the simple, noncontingent answers so many people seek;
- the disconnect between how the leadership industry is evaluated (happy sheets that tap inspiration and satisfaction) and the actual consequences of leader failures (miserable workplaces and career derailments);
- the disconnect between leader performance and behavior and the consequences those leaders face;
- the disconnect between what most people seem to want (good news, nice stories, emotional uplift) and what they need (the truth);
- the disconnect between what would make workplaces better and organizations more effective, and the base rate with which such prescriptions get implemented.

And there are even more disconnects—such as the disconnect between the leadership industry and the leaders whom that industry serves, and the disconnect between the people who bear the consequences of leader behavior and the leadership industry's manifest and many failings.

Framed in this way, the remedy for the many leadership failures seems simple, and it is: to restore the broken connections, the linkages between behavior and its consequences, words and actions, prescriptions and reality.

But this task will not be easy. The disconnections serve many powerful interests, and they serve those interests extremely well. The leadership industry rolls along, profiting from the disconnect between its prescriptions and what gets done, a disconnection that means not only problems remain but also the business opportunities from speaking, writing, blogging, and so forth about those problems. Leaders love the disconnect that leaves them unaccountable for the workplaces they mess up and their poor performance and bad behavior. And worst of all, lots of people are complicit in the disconnect between the reality that exists and what they would prefer to believe and the stories they want to and often pay to hear.

It is possible to restore at least some of these connections, some of the time. One way to begin might be to reconnect with the real world. One of the important but troubling phenomena that occur in organizations of all types is that the higher you rise, the more that people will tell you how smart and right you are, and the less connection you will have to the realities of organizational life. So good leaders seek to keep themselves grounded in the realities of what they are doing and, more important, why they are doing it.

When Rudy Crew was in the process of being forced from his position as chancellor of New York City's schools by that other Rudy, Rudy Giuliani—who, no surprise, has also written a book on leadership—Crew decided he needed to reconnect with the essential reality of why he was doing what he was doing, a reality embodied in the one million children in New York's schools, many of whom could not read at grade level. These children looked like a young version of himself and represented the reason Rudy Crew went into education in the first place. So Crew decided to go to a school.

As Crew told the story to a class I taught, he went into a classroom, maybe it was second or third grade, and there was an African American child working on a math problem. He was not having a lot of success, as after he did the problem, the eraser would come out and the kid would rub out the answer and start over. Crew came up to the boy and asked him what he was doing and how it was going. The child replied that he was doing math and having trouble doing it. "Keep at it, you'll get it," said Crew.

As Crew and those accompanying him were preparing to leave that classroom a while later, the child came up to Crew and asked, "Mister, who are you?" Crew replied that he was the chancellor, the person in charge of all of the city's schools. "Wow," said the boy, "you're the man." And then, in the way that only small children can, with complete openness and lack of malice, the kid asked Crew, "Are you any good at your job?" "Some days I think I am," Crew replied, "and some days I'm not so sure." The pupil looked up at Crew, smiled, and said, "Well, just keep at it. You'll get it."

I am not sure what will make a difference in the leadership crises that cost leaders their careers and provide too many employees with enervating work environments. But I am quite sure what will *not* work: more of the same inspiring sentiments based neither in the social science research about human behavior nor in the facts about the state of play in the leadership industry. In the end, people can handle the truth, and the sooner they confront those truths, the better off everyone will be. And until then, everyone, not just leaders, but everyone, will have to keep working away, until we get it.

Acknowledgments

I never forget how much that appears under my name alone owes its existence to the many people who provide the examples, ideas, challenges, colleagueship, encouragement, and friendship that make what I do so enjoyable and, indeed, possible. This holds particularly true for this book.

Stanford's Graduate School of Business furnishes much more than a salary and research support. It tolerates all of my many idiosyncrasies and affords me probably the only job from which I would not have been fired. I never for a minute take my work environment for granted. I deeply appreciate and acknowledge the opportunity to be at Stanford, surrounded by such remarkably amazing colleagues and students.

This book was inspired in part by my interactions with Rajiv Pant. It was Rajiv who first used the phrase "feel-good leadership literature." It was Rajiv who provided some of the stories and examples incorporated in this book. But mostly it was Rajiv Pant who helped me see how much damage was occurring because of the current incarnation of the leadership industry. Rajiv's support and friendship mean a great deal, not only for this book but in my life.

Hearty thanks go to Robert Gandossy not only for reading an early version of the manuscript and providing lots of moral support, but also for sending me numerous e-mails with attachments containing relevant material. Bob helped me understand the importance of this project and why I had to see it through. I have known Bob for decades, and my admiration for him only grows.

Plentiful thanks also to Rich Moran. Rich also read an early version of the manuscript and offered his invariably wise and helpful counsel on how to make the book better, more readable, and more marketable. Kathryn Clubb, another longtime friend, adviser, and consultant extraordinaire, provided encouragement concerning how it was "about time" that someone took on this topic. And this book in many ways began—at the time I wasn't even conscious of it—on long walks along Sawyer Camp Trail in San Mateo County with the incomparable Peter Sims. Regardless of whether we agreed or disagreed or were somewhere in the middle, the discussions with Pete have shaped my thinking in profound ways.

My interactions with the amazing Bob Sutton shaped not only my thinking but even the questions I began to ask. Watching Bob, and learning from him, has been an important part of my journey and was instrumental to the development of this manuscript. Bob is an amazingly wonderful friend. I hope to continue learning from him and debating ideas for many years to come.

There are so many generous and wonderful people who have shared their research, stories, and insights and provided advice on everything from titles to marketing—and in so doing, provided a big impetus for me to take on this topic, as well as helping me with their perspectives on the issues addressed. Big thanks go to Roderick Kramer, Beth Benjamin, Charlie Bresler, Bruce Cozadd, Fabrizio Ferraro, Gary Loveman, Christine Hung, Mary Ellen Player, Marcelo Noll Barboza, Jose Salibi Neto, Sutha Kamal, Seema Kumar, Yohei Iwasaki, Alex Tauber,

Ivy Millman, Howard Behar, Chip Conley, George Zimmer, Peter Fabian, Jean Lipman-Blumen, Rudy Crew, and Christine Whiteman Janhunen, and the many others I have almost certainly inadvertently forgotten to mention.

If I had a dollar for every minute I have debated and discussed leadership generally and the ideas in this book more specifically with Charles O'Reilly, I would be wealthy. But come to think of it, I am already wealthy beyond compare from my friendship with O'Reilly. Charles provided not only leads on relevant literature and, of course, his own research, but encouragement and support that is valuable beyond measure or even comprehension. I have known Charles O'Reilly now for more than forty years, and knowing him and having the benefit of his wisdom and support is something I treasure every day.

Great thanks go to my amazing agents. Don Lamm is a dear friend I have known for fifteen years, since we met at the Center for Advanced Study in the Behavioral Sciences. Truth be told, I don't think Don wanted me to do this particular book in this particular way—although he now vigorously disputes this fact. Regardless of his original view, like the great person and true friend he is, he read an early draft, and throughout the book preparation process he supplied detailed comments and his inestimable wisdom about content and the publishing process, along with unwavering support. Christy Fletcher of the Fletcher Agency has been a great and enthusiastic advocate for this project, a confidante, and an adviser who employed her truly remarkable skills to find this book the best possible home—and then to find the book yet another home when my first editor was laid off and the company's business book publishing operation closed. Working with Hollis and Don is a privilege—they are the best.

A very special thanks to my editor, Hollis Heimbouch. I have known Hollis since her days at Harvard Business School Press.

Hollis was the boss of the editor on my last book on power. When *Leadership BS* needed a new publisher on short notice, she did not use our panic against us but instead held to her original offer and graciously stepped in to bring the manuscript to life. But even more important than publishing the book, Hollis understood and supported what I was trying to do in a deep and profound way. Throughout the publication process, she has offered such fantastically helpful and constructive developmental advice.

And then, of course, there is Kathleen. Her most common remark on the fact that we have been together now for more than twenty-nine years is "I can't believe it." Neither can I. Sometimes you hit the jackpot. And then sometimes you hit the jackpot more frequently—by the time this book comes out, much more than 10,585 times (for those who are curious, that's 29 years times the 365 days in each year). In ways that only she and I know, I literally owe her my life. Kathleen has been, is, and always will be the center of my world.

Notes

Preface

1. See, for instance, Thomas P. Duffy, "The Flexner Report—100 Years Later," *Yale Journal of Biology and Medicine* 84, no. 3 (September 2011): 269–76.

Introduction: Things Are Bad—Here's Why

1. See, for instance, Jerry Hirsch and Jim Puzzanghera, "Lawmaker: GM Response to Ignition Switch Issue 'Smacks of Cover-Up,'" *Los Angeles Times*, June 18, 2014.
2. Zlati Meyer, "This Week in Michigan History: GM's President Says Sorry to Ralph Nader for Harassment," *Detroit Free Press*, March 18, 2012, www.freep.com/article/20120318/NEWS01/203180469.
3. Robert B. Kaiser and Gordy Curphy, "Leadership Development: The Failure of an Industry and the Opportunity for Consulting Psychologists," *Consulting Psychology Journal: Practice and Research* 65, no. 4 (December 2013): 294–302.
4. Barbara Kellerman, *Hard Times: Leadership in America* (Stanford, CA: Stanford University Press, 2015).
5. See, for instance, Stanley Lieberson and James F. O'Connor, "Leadership and Organizational Performance: A Study of Large Corporations," *American Sociological Review*, 37, no. 2 (April 1972): 117–30; and Gerald R. Salancik and Jeffrey Pfeffer, "Constraints on Administrative Discretion:

The Limited Influence of Mayors on City Budgets," *Urban Affairs Quarterly* 12, no. 2 (June 1977): 475–98.

6. James R. Meindl, Sanford B. Ehrlich, and Janet M. Dukerich, "The Romance of Leadership," *Administrative Science Quarterly* 30, no. 1 (March 1985): 78.

7. Pierre Gurdjian, Thomas Halbeisen, and Kevin Lane, "Why Leadership-Development Programs Fail," *McKinsey Quarterly*, January 2014, www.mckinsey.com/insights/leading_in_the_21st_century/why_leadership-development_programs_fail.

8. Barbara Kellerman, *The End of Leadership* (New York: HarperCollins, 2012), 154.

9. ASTD Staff, "$156 Billion Spent on Training and Development," December 6, 2012, www.astd.org/publications/Blogs/ASTD-Blog02012/12/.

10. Gurdjian, Halbeisen, and Lane, "Why Leadership-Development Programs Fail"; Kaiser and Curphy, "Leadership Development," 294.

11. Robert I. Sutton, *The No Asshole Rule: Building a Civilized Workplace and Surviving One That Isn't* (New York: Business Plus, 2007).

12. Charlotte Rayner, "The Incidence of Workplace Bullying," *Journal of Community and Applied Social Psychology* 7, no. 3 (June 1997): 199–208.

13. Lyn Quine, "Workplace Bullying in NHS Community Trust: Staff Questionnaire Survey," *British Medical Journal* 318, no. 7178 (January 1999): 228–32.

14. Lyn Quine, "Workplace Bullying in Nurses," *Journal of Health Psychology* 6, no. 1 (January 2001): 73–84.

15. Christine M. Pearson and Christine L. Porath, "On the Nature, Consequences, and Remedies of Workplace Incivility: No Time for 'Nice'? Think Again," *The Academy of Management Executive* 19, no. 1 (February 2005): 7–18.

16. Ibid., 7.

17. Susan Adams, "Americans Are Starting to Hate Their Jobs Less, Study Shows," *Forbes*, June 28, 2012, www.forbes.com/sites/susanadams/2012/06/28/americans-are-starting-to-hate-their-jobs-less-study-shows/.

18. Susan Adams, "New Survey: Majority of Employees Dissatisfied," *Forbes*, May 18, 2012, www.forbes.com/sites/susanadams/2012/05/18/new-survey-majority-of-employees-dissatisfied.

19. *State of the American Workplace: Employee Engagement Insights for U.S. Business Leaders* (Lincoln, NE: Gallup, 2012).

20. Steve Crabtree, "Worldwide, 13% of Employees Are Engaged at

Work," Gallup, October 8, 2013, www.gallup.com/pol/165269/world
wide-employees-engaged-at-work/.

21. Cited in Mark Crowley, "Gallup's Workplace Jedi on How to Fix Our
    Employee Engagement Problem," *Fast Company*, June 4, 2013.

22. Xu Jia-ni, Yu De-hua, and Li Jian-gang, "The Mediating Effects of Psy-
    chological Empowerment on Leadership Style and Employee Satisfaction
    in Hospitals," in *2012 International Conference on Management Sci-
    ence and Engineering, 19th Annual Conference Proceedings* (September
    20–22, 2012, Dallas, Texas), 1215.

23. S-C Chou, D. P. Boldy, and A. H. Lee, "Measuring Job Satisfaction in
    Residential Aged Care," *International Journal for Quality in Health Care*
    14, no. 1 (February 2002): 49–54.

24. Stina Fransson Sellgren, Goran Ekvall, and Goran Tomson, "Leadership
    Behaviour of Nurse Managers in Relations to Job Satisfaction and Work
    Climate," *Journal of Nursing Management* 16, no. 5 (July 2008): 579.

25. *CEO Succession Practices: 2012 Edition*, report #R-1492-12-RR (New
    York: Conference Board, 2012).

26. Ken Favaro, Per-Ola Karlsson, and Gary Neilson, *CEO Succession
    Report: 12th Annual Global CEO Succession Study* (New York: Booz
    and Company, 2012).

27. Bill Gentry, "Derailment: How Successful Leaders Avoid It," in *The ASTD
    Leadership Handbook*, ed. Elaine Biech (Washington, DC: ASTD Press,
    2010), 312.

28. Robert Hogan and Joyce Hogan, "Assessing Leadership: A View from the
    Dark Side," *International Journal of Selection and Assessment* 9, no. 1/2
    (March–June 2001): 41.

29. Ronald J. Burke, "Why Leaders Fail: Exploring the Darkside," *Interna-
    tional Journal of Manpower* 27, no. 1 (2006): 91–100.

30. Gurdjian, Halbeisen, and Lane, "Why Leadership-Development Programs
    Fail."

31. These figures come from Brad Hall, "Today's Leadership Development
    Approach Does Not Work," *The Street*, April 14, 2014, www.thestreet
    .com/story/12668089/1/todays-leadership-development-approach-does
    -not-work.html.

32. Institute for Corporate Productivity, *The Top 10 Critical Human Capital
    Issues: Enabling Sustained Growth through Talent Transparency*, 2014.

33. Kaiser and Curphy, "Leadership Development," 295.

34. S. A. Rosenthal, *National Leadership Index 2012: A National Study of*

Confidence in Leadership (Cambridge, MA: Center for Public Leadership, Harvard Kennedy School, Harvard University, 2012).

35. Kaiser and Curphy, "Leadership Development," 295.

36. Donald A. Palmer, "The New Perspective on Organizational Wrongdoing," *California Management Review* 56, no. 1 (Fall 2013): 8.

37. Pete Weaver and Simon Mitchell, *Lessons for Leaders from the People Who Matter: How Employees Around the World View Their Leaders* (Pittsburgh: DDI International, 2012).

38. D. S. Wilson and E. O. Wilson, "Rethinking the Theoretical Foundations of Sociobiology," *The Quarterly Review of Biology* 82, no. 4 (December 2007): 328.

39. See, for instance, Jon K. Maner and Nicole L. Mead, "The Essential Tension between Leadership and Power: When Leaders Sacrifice Group Goals for the Sake of Self-Interest," *Journal of Personality and Social Psychology* 99, no. 3 (September 2010): 482–97.

40. This story was widely covered in the media that covers the Silicon Valley. See, for example, M. G. Siegler, "Dick Costolo: Mission Accomplished," *TechCrunch*, October 4, 2010, www.techcrunch.com/2010/10/04/dick -costolo/; see also the links in that article.

41. Supriya Kurane and Gerry Shih, "Twitter Chief Operating Officer Resigns as Growth Lags," Reuters, June 12, 2014, www.reuters.com/article/2014/06/12/ us-twitter-managementchanges-idUSKBNOEN07420140612.

42. This story is widely told and known. See, for instance, "Dr. Semmelweis' Biography," Semmelweis Society International, 2009, http://semmelweis .org/about/dr-semmelweis-biogrpahy/.

43. www.cdc.gov/mmwr/preview/mmwrhtml/rr5116a1.htm.

44. Boas Hamir, Robert J. House, and Michael B. Arthur, "The Motivational Effects of Charismatic Leadership: A Self-Concept Based Theory," *Organization Science* 4, no. 4 (November 1993): 577–94.

45. J. A. Conger, R. N. Kanungo, and S. T. Menon, "Charismatic Leadership and Follower Effects," *Journal of Organizational Behavior* 21 (2000), 747–67.

46. Daan van Knippenberg and Sim B. Sitkin, "A Critical Assessment of Charismatic-Transformational Leadership Research: Back to the Drawing Board?," *Academy of Management Annals* 7 (2013): 1–60.

47. Institute for Corporate Productivity, *Next Practices for Global-Minded Organizations*, 2013, www.i4cp.com.

48. Dennis E. Clayson, "Student Evaluations of Teaching: Are They Related

to What Students Learn? A Meta-Analysis and Review of the Literature," *Journal of Marketing Education* 31, no. 1 (April 2009): 16.

49. J. Scott Armstrong, "Are Student Ratings of Instruction Useful?" *American Psychologist* 53, no. 11 (November 1998): 1223.

50. Ibid.

51. Ibid.

52. Institute for Corporate Productivity.

53. Gurdjian, Halbeisen, and Lane, "Why Leadership-Development Programs Fail."

Chapter 1: Why Inspiration and Fables Cause Problems and Fix Nothing

1. Rosabeth M. Kanter, "Power Failure in Management Circuits," *Harvard Business Review* 57 (July–August 1979): 65–75.

2. Review of *Power: Why Some People Have It—and Others Don't*, by Jeffrey Pfeffer, *Publishers Weekly*, June 21, 2010, www.publishersweekly.com/978-0-06-178908-3.

3. Vlerick's website is www.vlerick.com/en; I accessed it on December 28, 2013.

4. AGSM's website is www.business.unsw.edu.au/agsm/about/why-agsm; I accessed it on January 14, 2015.

5. Bill George and Peter Sims, *True North: Discover Your Authentic Leadership* (San Francisco: Jossey-Bass, 2007).

6. Thomas F. O'Boyle, *At Any Cost: Jack Welch, General Electric, and the Pursuit of Profit* (New York: Knopf, 1998).

7. Jonathon D. Brown, "Evaluations of Self and Others: Self-Enhancement Biases in Social Judgments," *Social Cognition* 4, no. 4 (December 1986): 353–76.

8. See, for instance, Frederic D. Woocher, "Did Your Eyes Deceive You? Expert Psychological Testimony on the Unreliability of Eyewitness Identification," *Stanford Law Review* 29, no. 5 (May 1977): 969–1030.

9. Ben Dolnick, "Star-Struck," *New York Times Magazine*, August 4, 2013, p. 50.

10. William von Hippel and Robert Trivers, "The Evolution and Psychology of Self-Deception," *Behavioral and Brain Sciences* 34, no. 1 (February 2011): 1–16.

11. Melvin J. Lerner, *The Belief in a Just World: A Fundamental Delusion* (New York: Plenum, 1980).

12. Chip Heath and Dan Heath, *Made to Stick: Why Some Ideas Survive and Others Die* (New York: Random House, 2007).

13. Sigmund Freud, *The Future of an Illusion*, trans. W. D. Robson Scott (Mansfield Center, CT: Martino Publishing, 2011 [1927]).

14. Jeffrey Pfeffer and Robert I. Sutton, *Hard Facts, Dangerous Half-Truths, and Total Nonsense: Profiting from Evidence-Based Management* (Boston: Harvard Business School Press, 2006).

15. Vernge G. Kopytoff and Claire Cain Miller, "Yahoo Board Fires Chief Executive," *New York Times*, September 6, 2011.

16. Michael Eric Dyson, "A Useful Hero," *New York Times Magazine*, January 16, 2000, p. 14.

17. Rick Lyman, "To Call Mandela a Saint Is to Dishonour His Memory," *Daily Maverick*, December 6, 2013, http://www.dailymaverick.co.za/opinionista/2013-12-06-to-call-mandela-a-saint-is-to-dishonour-his-memory/#.VNpK2fnF98E.

18. John Storey and Elizabeth Barnett, "Knowledge Management Initiatives: Learning from Failure," *Journal of Knowledge Management* 4, no. 2 (2000): 145–56.

19. A. C. Edmondson, "Learning from Failure in Health Care: Frequent Opportunities, Pervasive Barriers," *Quality and Safety in Health Care* 13, suppl. 2 (December 2004): ii3.

20. Philip R. P. Coelho and James E. McClure, "Learning from Failure," *American Journal of Business* 20, no. 1 (2005): 1.

21. Jerker Denrell and Chengwei Liu, "Top Performers Are Not the Most Impressive When Extreme Performance Indicates Unreliability," *Proceedings of the National Academy of Sciences of the United States of America* 109, no. 24 (June 12, 2012): 9331–36.

22. Jonah Berger, Marc Meredith, and S. Christian Wheeler, "Contextual Priming: Where People Vote Affects How They Vote," *Proceedings of the National Academy of Sciences* 105, no. 26 (July 1, 2008): 8846–49.

23. Chen-Bo Zhong and Sanford E. DeVoe, "You Are How You Eat: Fast Food and Impatience," *Psychological Science* 21, no. 5 (2010): 619–22.

24. Francesca Gino, Michael I. Norton, and Dan Ariely, "The Counterfeit Self: The Deceptive Costs of Faking It," *Psychological Science* 21, no. 5 (2010): 712–20.

25. Chen-Bo Zhong, Vanessa K, Bohns, and Francesca Gino, "Good Lamps Are the Best Police: Darkness Increases Dishonesty and Self-Interested Behavior," *Psychological Science* 21, no. 3 (2010): 311–14.

26. Brian Wansink, *Mindless Eating* (New York: Bantam Books, 2006).

27. Lisa L. Shu, Francesca Gino, and Max H. Bazerman, "Dishonest Deed, Clear Conscience: When Cheating Leads to Moral Disengagement and Motivated Forgetting," *Personality and Social Psychology Bulletin* 37, no. 3 (March 2011): 330–49.

28. Nicholas A. Christakis and James H. Fowler, "The Spread of Obesity in a Large Social Network over 32 Years," *New England Journal of Medicine* 357, no. 4 (July 26, 2007): 370–79.

29. Lee Ann Kaskutas, Jason Bond, and Keith Humphreys, "Social Networks as Mediators of the Effect of Alcoholics Anonymous," *Addiction* 97, no. 7 (July 2002): 891–900.

30. Keith Ferrazzi, "Managing Change, One Day at a Time," *Harvard Business Review* 92 (July–August 2014): 23–25.

31. Ibid., 24.

32. See, for instance, Edwin A. Locke and Gary P. Latham, "Building a Practically Useful Theory of Goal Setting and Task Motivation: A 35-Year Odyssey," *American Psychologist* 57, no. 9 (September 2002): 705–17.

33. Benoit Monin and Dale Miller, "Moral Credentials and the Expression of Prejudice," *Journal of Personality and Social Psychology* 81, no. 1 (July 2001): 33–43.

34. Daylian M. Cain, George Loewenstein, and Don A. Moore, "The Dirt on Coming Clean: Perverse Effects of Disclosing Conflicts of Interest," *Journal of Legal Studies* 34, no. 1 (January 2005): 1–25.

35. Sonya Sachdeva, Rumen Iliev, and Douglas L Medin, "Sinning Saints and Saintly Sinners: The Paradox of Moral Self-Regulation," *Psychological Science* 20, no. 4 (April 2009): 523–28.

36. Anna C. Merritt, Daniel A. Effron, and Benoit Monin, "Moral Self-Licensing: When Being Good Frees Us to Be Bad," *Social and Personality Psychology Compass* 4, no. 5 (May 2010): 344.

37. Jeffrey Pfeffer and Robert I. Sutton, *The Knowing-Doing Gap: How Smart Companies Turn Knowledge into Action* (Boston: Harvard Business School Press, 1999).

Chapter 2: Modesty: Why Leaders Aren't

1. "Bill Bradley Qutoes," ThinkExist.com, http://thinkexist.com/quotes/bill_bradley, accessed January 21, 2015.

2. Beth Belton, "Chicago Mayor Blasts New Trump Sign," *USA Today,* June 13, 2014.

3. Keith Morrison, "'Apprentice' Lessons for Business Students?,"

NBCnews.com, April 17, 2004, www.nbcnews.com/id/4757288/ns/dateline_nbc/t/apprentice-lessons-business-students.

4. "Donald Trump: The Genius of Self-Promotion," ABCnews.com, September 16, 2004, http://abcnews.go.com/Primetime/story?id=132337.

5. Jim Collins, "Level 5 Leadership: The Triumph of Humility and Fierce Resolve," *Harvard Business Review* 83 (July 2005): 136–46.

6. See, for instance, Ralph M. Stogdill, "Personal Factors Associated with Leadership: A Survey of the Literature," *The Journal of Psychology: Interdisciplinary and Applied* 25 (1948): 35–71.

7. Silke Astrid Eisenbeiss, "Re-thinking Ethical Leadership: An Interdisciplinary Integrative Approach," *The Leadership Quarterly* 23, no. 5 (October 2012): 791–808.

8. Colette Hoption, Julian Barling, and Nick Turner, " 'It's Not You, It's Me': Transformational Leadership and Self-Deprecating Humor," *Leadership and Organization Development Journal* 34, no. 1 (2013): 4–19.

9. Brett W. Pelham, Mauricio Carvallo, and John T. Jones, "Implicit Egotism," *Current Directions in Psychological Science* 14, no. 2 (2005): 106–10.

10. Jack L. Knetsch, "The Endowment Effect and Evidence of Nonreversible Indifference Curves," *American Economic Review* 79, no. 5 (December 1989): 1277–84.

11. Ibid.

12. Christian J. Resick, Daniel S. Whitman, Steven M. Weingarden, and Nathan J. Hiller, "The Bright-Side and the Dark-Side of CEO Personality: Examining Core Self-Evaluations, Narcissism, Transformational Leadership, and Strategic Influence," *Journal of Applied Psychology* 94, no. 6 (November 2009): 1365–81.

13. C. Wortman and J. Linsenmeier, "Interpersonal Attraction and Techniques of Ingratiation," in *New Directions in Organizational Behavior*, eds. B. M. Staw and G. R. Salancik (Chicago: St. Clair Pess, 1977), 133–78.

14. D. R. Forsythe, R. Berger, and T. Mitchell, "The Effects of Self-Serving vs. Other-Serving Claims of Responsibility on Attraction and Attribution in Groups," *Social Psychology Quarterly* 44, no. 1 (March 1981): 59–64.

15. W. Wosinska, A. J. Dabul, R. Whetstone-Dion, and R. B. Cialdini, "Self-Presentational Responses to Success in the Organization: The Costs and Benefits of Modesty," *Basic and Applied Social Psychology* 18, no. 2 (1996): 229–42.

16. Michael Maccoby, *The Productive Narcissist: The Promise and Peril of Visionary Leadership* (New York: Broadway Books, 2003).
17. Seth A. Rosenthal and Todd L. Pittinsky, "Narcissistic Leadership," *The Leadership Quarterly* 17, no. 6 (December 2006): 617–33.
18. Ibid.
19. R. Raskin and C. S. Hall, "The Narcissistic Personality Inventory: Alternate Form Reliability and Further Evidence of Construct Validity," *Journal of Personality and Social Psychology* 45, no. 2 (1981): 159–62.
20. Arijit Chatterjee and Donald C. Hambrick, "It's All about Me: Narcissistic Chief Executive Officers and Their Effects on Company Strategy and Performance," *Administrative Science Quarterly* 52, no. 3 (September 2007): 351–86.
21. J. M. Twenge, S. Konrath, J. D. Foster, W. K. Campbell, and B. J. Bushman, "Egos Inflating over Time: A Cross-Temporal Meta-analysis of the Narcissistic Personality Inventory," *Journal of Personality* 76, no. 4 (August 2008): 875–901.
22. J. D. Foster, W. K. Campbell, and J. M. Twenge, "Individual Differences in Narcissism: Inflated Self-Views across the Lifespan and around the World," *Journal of Research in Personality* 37, no. 6 (December 2003): 469–86.
23. James W. Westerman, Jacqueline Z. Bergman, Shawn M. Bergman, and Joseph P. Daly, "Are Universities Creating Millennial Narcissistic Employees? An Empirical Examination of Narcissism in Business Students and Its Implications," *Journal of Management Education* 36, no. 1 (2012): 5–32.
24. Raymond B. Nickerson, "Confirmation Bias: A Ubiquitous Phenomenon in Many Guises," *Review of General Psychology* 2, no. 2 (June 1998): 175–220.
25. Robert B. Zajonc, "Attitudinal Effects of Mere Exposure," *Journal of Personality and Social Psychology Monograph Supplement* 9, no. 2 (June 1968): 1–27.
26. Karin Proost, Karel De Witte, Bert Schreurs, and Eva Derous, "Ingratiation and Self-Promotion in the Selection Interview: The Effects of Using Single Tactics or a Combination of Tactics on Interviewer Judgments," *Journal of Applied Social Psychology* 40, no. 9 (September 2010): 2155–69.
27. For a review of this literature, see ibid.
28. C. Anderson, S. Brion, D. A. Moore, and J. A. Kennedy, "A Status-Enhancement Account of Overconfidence," *Journal of Personality and Social Psychology* 103, no. 4 (October 2012): 718–35.

29. Jessica A. Kennedy, Cameron Anderson, and Don A. Moore, "When Overconfidence Is Revealed to Others: Testing the Status-Enhancement Theory of Overconfidence," *Organizational Behavior and Human Decision Processes* 122, no. 2 (November 2013): 275.

30. Rosenthal and Pittinsky, "Narcissistic Leadership," 623.

31. Discussed in Charles A. O'Reilly III, Bernadette Doer, David F. Caldwell, and Jennifer A. Chatman, "Narcissistic CEOs and Executive Compensation," *The Leadership Quarterly*, 25, no. 2 (April 2014): 218–31.

32. Amy B. Brunell, William A. Gentry, W. Keith Campbell, Brian J. Hoffman, Karl W. Kuhnert, and Kenneth G. DeMarree, "Leader Emergence: The Case of the Narcissistic Leader," *Personality and Social Psychology Bulletin* 34, no. 12 (2008): 1663–76.

33. Barbara Nevicka, Annebel H. De Hoogh, Annelies E. Van Vianen, Bianca Beersma, and Doris McIlwain, "All I Need Is a Stage to Shine: Narcissists' Leader Emergence and Performance," *Leadership Quarterly* 22, no. 5 (October 2011): 910–25.

34. Malcolm Gladwell, "The Talent Myth," *The New Yorker,* July 22, 2002.

35. Jacqueline Z. Bergman, James W. Westerman, and Joseph P. Daly, "Narcissism in Management Education," *Academy of Management Learning and Education* 9 (2010): 119–31.

36. This research is summarized in Jacqueline Z. Bergman, James W. Westerman, and Joseph P. Daly, "Narcissism in Management Education," *Academy of Management Learning and Education* 9, no. 1 (March 2010): 119–31.

37. Barbora Nevicka, Femke S. Ten Velden, Annebel H. B. De Hoogh, and Annelies E. M. Van Vianen, "Reality at Odds with Perceptions: Narcissistic Leaders and Group Performance," *Psychological Science* 22, no. 10 (October 2011): 1259.

38. Val Singh, Savita Kumra, and Susan Vinnicombe, "Gender and Impression Management: Playing the Promotion Game," *Journal of Business Ethics* 37, no. 1 (April 2002): 79.

39. Sylvia Ann Hewlett and Ripa Rashid, *Asians in America: Unleashing the Potential of the "Model Minority"* (New York: Center for Work Life Policy), 20–21.

40. Ibid., 21–22.

41. P. Babiak, C. S. Neumann, and R. D. Hare, "Corporate Psychopathy: Talking the Walk," *Behavioral Sciences and the Law* 28, no. 2 (March/April 2010): 174–93.

42. P. C. Patel and D. Cooper, "The Harder They Fall, the Faster They Rise: Approach and Avoidance Focus in Narcissistic CEOS," *Strategic Management Journal*, 35, no. 10 (October 2014): 1528–40.

43. Scott O. Lilienfeld, Irwin D. Waldman, Drisitn Landfield, Steven Rubenzer, Ashley L. Watts, and Thomas R. Faschingbauer, "Fearless Dominance and the U.S. Presidency: Implications of Psychopathic Personality Traits for Successful and Unsuccessful Political Leadership," *Journal of Personality and Social Psychology* 103, no. 3 (September 2012): 489.

44. Ashley L. Watts, Scott O. Lilienfeld, Sarah Francis Smith, Joshua D. Miller, W. Keith Campbell, Irwin D. Waldman, Steven J. Rubenzer, and Thomas J. Faschingbauer, "The Double-Edged Sword of Grandiose Narcissism: Implications for Successful and Unsuccessful Leadership among U.S. Presidents," *Psychological Science* 24, no. 12 (December 2013): 2379–89.

45. O'Reilly et al., "Narcissistic CEOs and Executive Compensation," 17.

46. Ibid., 21.

Chapter 3: Authenticity: Misunderstood and Overrated

1. http://michiganross.umich.edu/about/dean-alison-davis-blake.

2. "What's Magical about Working for Disney? I'd Rather Go to Afghanistan," *Daily Mail* (London), October 27, 2010, www.dailymail.co.uk/news/article-1324098/work-Disney-id-fight-Taliban-Afghanistan.html.

3. Arlie Russell Hochschild, *The Managed Heart: Commercialization of Human Feeling* (Berkeley, CA: University of California Press, 1983).

4. Arlie Russell Hochschild, "Emotion Work, Feeling Rules, and Social Structure," *American Journal of Sociology* 85, no. 3 (November 1979): 551.

5. F. O. Walumbwa, B. J. Aviolio, W. L. Gardner, T. S. Wernsing, and S. J. Peterson, "Authentic Leadership: Development and Analysis of a Multidimensional Theory-Based Measure," *Journal of Management* 34, no. 1 (February 2008): 89–126.

6. See the institute's website at www.authenticleadership.com.

7. The origins of this quote are unclear, although it is indisputable that George Burns used a version of it in his comedy routine and in a memoir. See http://quoteinvestigator.com/2011/12/05/fake-honesty/.

8. This description of authentic leadership is drawn from the chapter that introduced the special issue of the *Leadership Quarterly*, Bruce J. Avolio and William L. Gardner, "Authentic Leadership Development: Getting to the Root of Positive Forms of Leadership," *The Leadership Quarterly* 16, no. 3 (June 2005): 315–38.

9. Ibid., 316.

10. Ibid., 327.

11. Michael Hyatt, "The 5 Marks of Authentic Leadership," July 3, 2012, http://michaelhyatt.com/the-five-marks-of-authentic-leadership.html.

12. "10 Things Authentic Leaders Do," Holden Leadership Center, University of Oregon, http://leadership.uoregon.edu/resources/exercises_tips/leadership_reflections/10_things_authentic_leaders_do.

13. Gerald R. Salancik and Mary Conway, "Attitude Inferences from Salient and Relevant Cognitive Content About Behavior," *Journal of Personality and Social Psychology* 32, no. 5 (November 1975): 829–40.

14. Sheryl Sandberg, *Lean In: Women, Work, and the Will to Lead* (New York: Knopf, 2013).

15. Michiko Kakutani, "Kennedy, and What Might Have Been," *New York Times*, August 12, 2013.

16. Bill Keller, "Nelson Mandela, Communist," *New York Times*, December 7, 2013.

17. Erving Goffman, *The Presentation of Self in Everyday Life* (New York: Anchor Books, 1959).

18. Harriet Rubin, "Shall I Compare Thee to an Andy Grove?," *Strategy+Business*, Winter 2007.

19. Seymour Lieberman, "The Effects of Changes in Roles on the Attitudes of Role Occupants," *Human Relations* 9, no. 4 (November 1956): 385–402.

20. Jeffrey Pfeffer and Gerald R. Salancik, "Determinants of Supervisory Behavior: A Role Set Analysis," *Human Relations* 28 , no. 2 (March 1975): 139–54.

21. See, for instance, Melvin L. Kohn and Carmi Schooler, "Occupational Experience and Psychological Functioning: An Assessment of Reciprocal Effects," *American Sociological Review* 38, no. 1 (February 1973): 97–118; and Melvin L. Kohn and Carmi Schooler, "Job Conditions and Personality: A Longitudinal Assessment of Their Reciprocal Effects," *American Journal of Sociology* 87, no. 6 (May 1982): 1257–86.

Chapter 4: Should Leaders Tell the Truth—and Do They?

1. See, for instance, *Wikipedia*, s.v. "Parson Weems," January 1, 2015, 18:32, http://en.wikipedia.org/wiki/Parson_Weems.

2. John Blake, "Of Course Presidents Lie," CNN.com, November 24, 2013, www.cnn.com/2013/11/24/politics/presidents-lie/.

3. Charles F. Bond, Jr., and Bella M. DePaulo, "Accuracy of Deception

Judgments," *Personality and Social Psychology Review* 10, no. 3 (2006): 214–34.

4. See, for instance, Warren Bennis, Daniel Goleman, and James O'Toole, *Transparency: Creating a Culture of Candor* (San Francisco: Jossey-Bass, 2008).

5. Bond and DePaulo, "Accuracy of Deception Judgments," 216.

6. Andrew Clark, "Former Bear Stearns Boss Jimmy Cayne Blames Conspiracy for Bank's Collapse, *Guardian* (U.K.), May 5, 2010, www.the guardian .com/business/2010/may/05/bear-stearns-boss-denies-blame.

7. Patricia Hurtado, "The London Whale," Bloombergview.com, January 9, 2015, www.bloomberg.com/quicktake/the-london-whale.

8. This example and many of Loveman's other statements that I have quoted can be seen on video from a presentation in my class, "Gary Loveman, January 30, 2009," available for purchase through the Graduate School of Business, Stanford University.

9. "Leadership Journal to Retract Five Papers from FIU Scholar," *Retraction Watch* (blog), February 7, 2014, http://retractionwatch.com/2014/02/07/ leadership-journal-to-retract-five-papers-from-FIU-scholar.

10. There are numerous sources concerning this episode. See, for instance, Eyder Peralta, "Sen. Jon Kyl Corrects Erroneous Statement on Planned Parenthood," *The Two-Way* (blog), NPR.org, April 22, 2011, www.npr .org/blogs/thetwo-way/2011/04/22/135641326.

11. Again there are literally scores of sources for this well-publicized gaffe. See, for instance, Abby D. Phillip, "James Clapper Apologizes to Congress for 'Clearly Erroneous' Testimony," ABCNews.com, July 2, 2013, http:// abcnews.go.com/blogs/politics/2013/07/james-clapper-apologizes-to -congress-for-clearly-erroneous-testimony/.

12. Ralph Nader, *Unsafe at Any Speed: The Designed-In Dangers of the American Automobile* (New York: Grossman, 1965).

13. David A. Kaplan, *The Silicon Boys and Their Valley of Dreams* (New York: William Morrow, 1999), 122–23.

14. See Miller's faculty biography on the Standford website at www.gsb .stanford.edu/faculty-research/faculty/william-f-miller.

15. Adam Satariano and Karen Gullo, "Steve Jobs's FBI File Notes Past Drug Use, Tendency to 'Distort Reality,'" Bloomberg News, February 9, 2012.

16. Caroline F. Keating and Karen R. Heltman, "Dominance and Deception in Children and Adults: Are Leaders the Best Misleaders?," *Personality and Social Psychology Bulletin* 20, no. 3 (June 1994): 312.

17. D. R. Carney et al., "The Deception Equilibrium: The Powerful Are Better

Liars but the Powerless Are Better Lie-Detectors" (unpublished manuscript, 2014), 2.

18. Erin Strout, "To Tell the Truth," *Sales and Marketing Management*, July 2002, 42.

19. Floyd Norris, "RadioShack Chief Resigns after Lying," *New York Times*, February 21, 2006.

20. Pamela Babcock, "Spotting Lies," http://www.shrm.org/publications/hrmagazine/editorialcontent/pages/1003babcock.aspx.

21. Uri Gneezy, "Deception: The Role of Consequences," *American Economic Review* 95, no. 1 (March 2005): 384–94.

22. For a good overview of the relevant literature, see Ingrid Smithey Fulmer, Bruce Barry, and D. Adam Long, "Lying and Smiling: Informational and Emotional Deception in Negotiation," *Journal of Business Ethics* 88, no. 4 (September 2009): 691–709.

23. These quotes are taken from Peter Reilly, "Was Machiavelli Right? Lying in Negotiation and the Art of Defensive Self-Help," *Ohio State Journal on Dispute Resolution* 24, no. 3 (2009): 481.

24. Kim B. Serota, Timothy R. Levine, and Franklin J. Boster, "The Prevalence of Lying in America: Three Studies of Self-Reported Lies," *Human Communication Research* 36, no. 1 (January 2010): 2–25.

25. Megan Garber, "The Way We Lie Now," *The Atlantic*, September 2013, 15–16.

26. See, for instance, Jill Doner Kagle, "Are We Lying to Ourselves about Deception," *Social Service Review* 72, no. 2 (June 1998): 234–50.

27. Bella M. DePaulo et al., "Lying in Everyday Life," *Journal of Personality and Social Psychology* 70, no. 5 (May 1996): 979–95.

28. Lisa L. Masssi Lindsey, Norah E. Dunbar, and Jessica C. Russell, "Risky Business or Managed Event? Perceptions of Power and Deception in the Workplace," *Journal of Organizational Culture, Communications and Conflict* 15, no. 1 (2011): 55.

29. Norah E. Dunbar et al., "Empowered by Persuasive Deception: The Effects of Power and Deception on Dominance, Credibility, and Decision Making," *Communication Research* 41, no. 6 (August 2014): 852–76.

30. Paul Ekman and Maureen O'Sullivan, "Who Can Catch a Liar?," *American Psychologist* 46, no. 9 (September 1991): 913–20.

31. C. F. Bond and B. M. DePaulo, "Accuracy of Deception Judgments," *Personality and Social Psychology Review* 10, no. 3 (2006): 214–34.

32. Alexander Dyck, Adair Morse, and Luigi Zingales, "Who Blows the

Whistle on Corporate Fraud?," *The Journal of Finance* 65, no. 1 (February 2010): 2213–53.

33. Ernesto Reuben and Matt Stephenson, "Nobody Likes a Rat: On the Willingness to Report Lies and the Consequences Thereof," *Journal of Economic Behavior and Organization* 93 (September 2013): 385.

34. Ibid., 384.

35. Floyd Norris, "Corporate Lies Are Increasingly Immune to Investor Complaints," *New York Times*, March 20, 2014.

36. Diana B. Henriques, "Oracle Agrees to a Fine over Accounting Moves," *New York Times*, September 25, 1993, www.nytimes.com/1993/09/25/business/company-news-oracle-agrees-to-a-fine-over-accounting-moves.html.

37. Michael Cohn, "Study Finds Financial Restatements Declined after Sarbanes-Oxley," *Accounting Today*, July 24, 2014, www.accountingtoday.com/news/sarbanes-oxley/study-finds-financial-restatements-declined-Sarbanes-Oxley-71444-1.html.

38. Bond and DePaulo, "Accuracy of Deception Judgments," 216.

39. Marc Effron, "Calculating the Optimal Length of Time to Lie to Your Employees," *Talent Quarterly* 1, no. 1 (2014): 14.

40. Nicole Reudy, Celia Moore, Francesca Gino, and Maurice E. Schweitzer, "The Cheater's High: The Unexpected Affective Benefits of Unethical Behavior" (unpublished manuscript, July 18, 2012), available at SSRN: http://dx.doi.org/10.2139/ssrn.2112614.

41. Robert K. Merton, "The Self-Fulfilling Prophecy," *The Antioch Review* 8, no. 2 (Summer 1948): 193–210.

42. Ibid., 195.

43. See, for instance, Dov Eden, "Self-Fulfilling Prophecy as a Management Tool: Harnessing Pygmalion," *Academy of Management Review* 9, no. 1 (January 1984): 64–73.

44. *Wikipedia*, s.v. "Catch Me If You Can," January 29, 2015, 15:09, http://en.wikipedia.org/wiki/Catch_Me_If_You_Can.

45. John Blake, "Of Course Presidents Lie," CNN.com, November 24, 2013, www.cnn.com/2013/11/24/politics/presidents-lie/.

46. Bethany McLean and Peter Elkind, *The Smartest Guys in the Room: The Amazing Rise and Scandalous Fall of Enron* (New York: Portfolio, 2003).

47. Amit Bhattacharjee, Jonathan Z. Berman, and Americus Reed II, "Tip of the Hat, Wag of the Finger: How Moral Decoupling Enables Consumers to Admire and Admonish," *Journal of Consumer Research* 39, no. 6 (April 2013): 1167.

48. Ibid., 1168.
49. Ibid., 1169.

Chapter 5: Trust: Where Did It Go, and Why?

1. Oliver E. Williamson, *Markets and Hierarchies* (New York: Free Press, 1975).
2. The literature on this point is extensive. See, for instance, Ernst Fehr and Simon Gachter, "Fairness and Retaliation: The Economics of Reciprocity," *The Journal of Economic Perspectives* 14 (2000): 159–81.
3. See, as only two of numerous examples, John O. Whitney, *The Trust Factor: Liberating Profits & Restoring Corporate Vitality* (New York: McGraw-Hill, 1994); Robert Sharkie, "Trust in Leadership Is Vital for Employee Performance," *Management Research News* 32, no. 5 (2009): 491–98.
4. "2013 Edelman Trust Barometer Finds a Crisis in Leadership," http://www.edelman.com/news/2013-edeloman-trust-barometer-finds-a-crisis-in-leadership
5. "Americans Still Lack Trust in Company Management Post-Recession," http://www.martiz.com/Press-Releases/2011/Americans-Still-Lack-Trust-in-Company-Management-Post-Recession.
6. Roderick M. Kramer, "Rethinking Trust," *Harvard Business Review*, June 2009, 69–77.
7. Steve Hamm and Jay Greene, "The Man Who Could Have Been Bill Gates," *BusinessWeek*, October 24, 2004, www.bloomberg.com/bw/stories/2004-10-24/the-man-who-could-have-been-bill-gates.
8. Harold Evans, with Gail Buckland and David Lefer, *They Made America: Two Centuries of Innovators from the Steam Engine to the Search Engine* (Boston: Little, Brown, 1984).
9. David A. Kaplan, *The Silicon Boys and Their Valley of Dreams* (New York: William Morrow, 1999), 112.
10. Ibid., 113.
11. Ibid., 115–16.
12. Ann Friedman, "Martha Stewart's Best Lesson: Don't Give a Damn," *New York*, March, 14, 2013.
13. Ibid.
14. There is an enormous literature on this important phenomenon. See, for instance, Robert B. Zajonc, "Attitudinal Effects of Mere Exposure," *Journal of Personality and Social Psychology* 9, no. 2 (June 1968): 1–27; Robert F. Bornstein and Paul R. D'Agostino, "Stimulus Recognition and

the Mere Exposure Effect," *Journal of Personality and Social Psychology* 63, no. 4 (October 1992): 545–52.

15. Nick Baumann, "Apparently We've Forgotten Who the Milkens Are," *Mother Jones*, August 18, 2011, www.motherjones.com/2011/08/lowell-milken-institute-ucla.

16. Robert B. Cialdini, *Influence: Science and Practice*, 3rd ed. (New York: HarperCollins, 1993).

17. For example, see Edward P. Lazear and Robert L. Moore, "Incentives, Productivity, and Labor Contracts," *Quarterly Journal of Economics* 99, no. 2 (May 1984): 275–96.

18. Jeffrey Pfeffer, *What Were They Thinking? Unconventional Wisdom about Management* (Boston: Harvard Business School Press, 2007), 82.

19. Uriel Haran, "A Person-Organization Discontinuity in Contract Perception: Why Corporations Can Get Away with Breaking Contracts but Individuals Cannot," *Management Science* 59, no. 12 (December 2013): 2837–53.

Chapter 6: Why Leaders "Eat" First

1. Simon Sinek, *Leaders Eat Last: Why Some Teams Pull Together and Others Don't* (New York: Portfolio, 2014).

2. A. Gregory Stone, Robert F. Russell, and Kathleen Patterson, "Transformational versus Servant Leadership: A Difference in Leader Focus," *Leadership & Organization Development Journal* 25, no. 4 (2004): 349–61.

3. Jeffrey Pfeffer, *The Human Equation: Building Profits by Putting People First* (Boston: Harvard Business School Press, 1998).

4. Robert F. Russell, "The Role of Values in Servant Leadership," *Leadership & Organization Development Journal* 22 (2001): 76–84.

5. Steve Denning, "Valuing Employees (Really!): Lessons from India," *Forbes*, October 5, 2011, www.forbes.com/sites/stevedenning/2011/10/05/valuing-employees-really-lessons-from-india/.

6. See, for instance, Eugene W. Anderson, Claes Fornell, and Donald R. Lehmann, "Customer Satisfaction, Market Share, and Profitability: Findings from Sweden," *Journal of Marketing* 58, no. 3 (July 1994): 53–66; and Eugene W. Anderson, Claes Fornell, and Sanal K. Mazvancheryl, "Customer Satisfaction and Shareholder Value," *Journal of Marketing* 68, no. 4 (October 2004): 172–85.

7. John Freeman and Michael T. Hannan, "Growth and Decline Processes in Organizations," *American Sociological Review* 40, no. 2 (April 1975): 215–28.

8. This example is cited in Sam Polk, "For the Love of Money," *New York Times*, January 18, 2014.

9. Annie Lowrey, "Even among the Richest of the Rich, Fortunes Diverge," *New York Times*, February 11, 2014.

10. Ibid.

11. "The Whys and Wherefores of Executive Pay," *Harvard Business Review*, July 2014, 32–33.

12. Elliot Blair Smith and Phil Kuntz, "Disclosed: The Pay Gap between CEOs and Employees," *Bloomberg Businessweek*, May 2, 2013.

13. Lowrey, "Even among the Richest."

14. Henry L. Tosi, Steve Werner, Jeffrey P. Katz, and Luis R. Gomez-Mejia, "How Much Does Performance Matter? A Meta-Analysis of CEO Pay Studies," *Journal of Management* 26, no. 2 (April 2000): 301–39.

15. See, for example, Jerry M. Burger, Nicole Messian, Shebani Patel, Alicia del Prado, and Carmen Anderson, "What a Coincidence! The Effects of Incidental Similarity on Compliance," *Personality and Social Psychology Bulletin* 30, no. 1 (January 2004): 35–43.

16. Donn Erwin Byrne, *The Attraction Paradigm* (New York: Academic Press, 1971).

17. Benedict Carey, "You Remind Me of Me," *New York Times*, February 12, 2008.

18. Brett W. Pelham, Mauricio Carvallo, and John T. Jones, "Implicit Egotism," *Current Directions in Psychological Science* 14, no. 2 (April 2005): 106–10.

19. See, for instance, James R. Bettman and Barton A. Weitz, "Attributions in the Board Room: Causal Reasoning in Corporate Annual Reports," *Administrative Science Quarterly* 28 (1983), 165–83.

20. See, for instance, Kathleen M. Eisenhardt, "Agency Theory: An Assessment and Review," *Academy of Management Review, 14* (1989), 57–74; and Stephen A. Ross, "The Economic Theory of Agency: The Principal's Problem," *The American Economic Review, 63* (1973), 134–39.

21. "Management by Walking About," http://www.economist.com/node/12075015, September 8, 2008.

Chapter 7: Take Care of Yourself

1. Sandra L. Robinson and Denise M. Rousseau, "Violating the Psychological Contract: Not the Exception but the Norm," *Journal of Organizational Behavior* 15 (1994): 245–59.

2. David Cassilo, "For College Scholarship Athletes, Injury Can Spell Financial Disaster," *Daily Caller*, November 9, 2011, http://dailycaller .com/2011/11/09/for-college-scholarship-athletes-injury-can-spell -financial-disaster/.

3. http://abcnews.go.com/Health/kevin-ware-injury-draws-attention-ncaa -healthcare debate.

4. The prevalence of at-will policies is well known. See, for instance, Cynthia L. Estlund, "Wrongful Discharge Protections in an At-Will World," *Texas Law Review* 74, no. 7 (June 1996): 1655–92.

5. Louis Uchitelle, *The Disposable American: Layoffs and Their Consequences* (New York: Random House, 2007).

6. Alvin W. Gouldner, "The Norm of Reciprocity: A Preliminary Statement," *American Sociological Review* 25, no. 2 (April 1960): 161–78.

7. Joseph Henrich and Natalie Henrich, *Why Humans Cooperate: A Cultural and Evolutionary Explanation* (New York: Oxford University Press, 2007).

8. Peter Belmi and Jeffrey Pfeffer, "How 'Organization' Can Weaken the Norm of Reciprocity: The Effects of Attributions for Favors and a Calculative Mindset," *Academy of Management Discoveries* 1, no. 1 (2015): 93–113.

9. Erich Fromm, *Escape from Freedom* (New York: Ferrar and Rinehart, 1941).

10. Jean Lipman-Blumen, *The Allure of Toxic Leaders: Why We Follow Destructive Bosses and Corrupt Politicians—and How We Can Survive Them* (New York: Oxford University Press, 2004).

11. Neil Torquiano, "Anchorage Workers Protest Firing of Men's Wearhouse Founder," KTUU.com, June 23, 2013, http://articles.ktuu .com/2013-06-23/south-anchorage_40151242.

12. Ibid.

13. James Surowiecki, *The Wisdom of Crowds* (New York: Random House, 2005).

14. Dale T. Miller, "The Norm of Self-Interest," *American Psychologist* 54, no. 12 (December 1999): 1053–60.

15. Rebecca K. Ratner and Dale T. Miller, "The Norm of Self-Interest and Its Effects on Social Action," *Journal of Personality and Social Psychology* 81, no. 1 (July 2001): 5–16.

16. Adam Grant, *Give and Take* (New York: Viking, 2013).

17. Ibid., 4.

18. Jennifer A. Chatman and Sigal Barsade, "Personality, Organizational Culture, and Cooperation: Evidence from a Business Simulation," *Administrative Science Quarterly* 40, no. 3 (September 1995): 423–43.
19. Warner Wilson, "Reciprocation and Other Techniques for Inducing Cooperation in the Prisoner's Dilemma Game," *Journal of Conflict Resolution* 15, no. 2 (June 1971): 167–95.
20. http://www.bartleby.com/73/417.html

Chapter 8: Fixing Leadership Failures: You *Can* Handle the Truth

1. Niall Doherty, "The Stockdale Paradox," *Disrupting the Rabblement* (blog), March 19, 2010, www.ndoherty.com/stockdale-paradox/.
2. Peter Burrows, "HP's Carly Fiorina: The Boss," *BusinessWeek*, August 2, 1999.
3. Esther Addley, "Rebekah Brooks: A Ruthless, Charming Super-Schmoozer," *Guardian* (U.K.), July 8, 2011.
4. Robert A. Caro, *The Path to Power: The Years of Lyndon Johnson* (New York: Knopf, 1982).
5. Quoted in Roderick M. Kramer, "The Great Intimidators," *Harvard Business Review*, February 2006.
6. Seymour Hersh, *The Price of Power: Kissinger in the Nixon White House* (New York: Summit, 1983).
7. Tim Dickinson, "How Roger Ailes Built the Fox News Fear Factory," *Rolling Stone*, May 25, 2011, www.rollingstone.com/politics/news/how-roger-ailes-built-the-fox-news-fear-factory-20110525.
8. Steve Forbes and John Prevas, "The Price of Arrogance," *Forbes*, June 18, 2009, www.forbes.com/2009/06/18/alexander-great-hubris-leadership-power.html.
9. Curt Gentry, *J. Edgar Hoover: The Man and the Secrets* (New York: W. W. Norton, 1991).
10. Joshua Kendall, "The Temper Tantrum: The Key to Smart Management?," *Fortune*, November 22, 2013, http://fortune.com/2013/11/22/the-temper-tantrum-the-key-to-smart-management/.
11. Ibid.
12. Ibid.
13. Elizabeth Kolbert, "How Tina Brown Moves Magazines," *New York Times Magazine*, December 5, 1993.
14. John P. Kotter, "Leading Change: Why Transformation Efforts Fail," *Harvard Business Review*, May 1995, 59–67.

15. Geraldine M. Leydon et al., "Cancer Patients' Information Needs and Information Seeking Behaviour: In Depth Interview Study," *British Medical Journal* 320, no. 7239 (April 1, 2000): 909–13.

16. Elizabeth Warren, *A Fighting Chance* (New York: Metropolitan Books, 2014).

17. Quoted in Gretchen Morgenson, "From Outside or Inside, the Deck Looks Stacked," *New York Times*, April 26, 2014.

18. Nicole Perlroth, "Solving Problems for Real World, Using Design," *New York Times*, December 29, 2013.

19. Henry Mintzberg, *The Nature of Managerial Work* (New York: Harper-Collins, 1973).

20. Fred Luthans, Stuart A. Rosenkrantz, and Harry W. Hennessey, "What Do Successful Managers Really Do? An Observation Study of Managerial Activities," *Journal of Applied Behavioral Science* 21, no. 3 (July 1985): 255.

21. Warren Bennis, *Why Leaders Can't Lead: The Unconscious Conspiracy Continues* (San Francisco: Jossey-Bass, 1989), 14.

22. Robert Kramer, "Book Review: 'Why Leaders Can't Lead: The Unconscious Conspiracy Continues,'" *Journal of Management* 16, no. 4 (December 1990): 869–79.

23. Atul Gawande, *Complications: A Surgeon's Notes on an Imperfect Science* (New York: Profile, 2010).

24. Sam Borden, "Where Dishonesty Is Best Policy, U.S. Soccer Falls Short," *New York Times*, June 15, 2014.

25. Ibid.

26. John T. Scott and Robert Zaretsky, "Why Machiavelli Still Matters," *New York Times*, December 9, 2013.

27. Doris Kearns Goodwin, *Team of Rivals: The Political Genius of Abraham Lincoln* (New York: Simon and Schuster, 2005).

28. Michael Ignatieff, "Machiavelli Was Right," *The Atlantic*, December, 2013, 42.

29. R. Reiser, "Oversimplification of Diet: Coronary Heart Disease Relationships and Exaggerated Diet Recommendations," *American Journal of Clinical Nutrition* 31, no. 5 (May 1, 1978): 865–75.

30. Deborah H. Gruenfeld, "Status, Ideology, and Integrative Complexity on the U.S. Supreme Court: Rethinking the Politics of Political Decision-Making," *Journal of Personality and Social Psychology* 68, no. 1 (January 1995): 5–20.

31. This quote is widely available on the Internet, albeit not always in the identical form, as it is used in Christian and Buddhist teaching and writings. This version comes from www.co

32. Jim Collins and Jerry I. Porras, *Built to Last: Successful Habits of Visionary Companies* (New York: HarperBusiness, 1994).

33. Charles L. Bosk, *Forgive and Remember: Managing Medical Failure*, 2nd. ed. (Chicago: University of Chicago Press, 2003).

34. John A. Byrne, *Chainsaw: The Notorious Career of Al Dunlap in the Era of Profit-At-Any-Price* (New York: HarperBusiness, 1999).

35. Jonathan Mahler, "The Coach Who Exploded," *New York Times Magazine*, November 6, 2013.

36. Ibid.

37. Fred Luthans and Robert Kreitner, *Organizational Behavior Modification* (Glenview, IL: Scott, Foresman, 1975).

38. David Carr, "Why Not Occupy Newsrooms?," *New York Times*, October 23, 2011.

39. Andrew Ross Sorkin, " 'Tainted,' but Still Serving on Corporate Boards," *New York Times*, April 23, 2012.

40. Ibid.

41. Susan Craig and Peter Lattman, "Companies May Fail, but Directors Are in Demand," *New York Times*, September 14, 2010.

42. Steven M. Davidoff, "Little Accountability for Directors, Despite Poor Performance," *New York Times*, April 5, 2013.

43. Steven M. Davidoff, Andrew Lund, and Robert J. Schonlau, "Do Outside Directors Face Labor Market Consequences? A Natural Experiment from the Financial Crisis," *Harvard Business Law Review* (forthcoming), available at http://dx.doi.org/10.2139/ssrn.2200552.

44. Andrew Ross Sorkin, "A Reputation, Once Sullied, Acquires a New Shine," *New York Times*, February 18, 2013.

45. Ibid.

Index

About the Author

JEFFREY PFEFFER is the Thomas D. Dee II Professor of Organizational Behavior at the Stanford Graduate School of Business, where he has taught since 1979. Pfeffer has authored or coauthored fourteen books on topics including power, managing people and human resource management practices, organizational design, and evidence-based management. He is also the coauthor of *The Knowing-Doing Gap*. Pfeffer has presented seminars in thirty-eight countries throughout the world and has been a visiting professor at London Business School, Harvard Business School, Singapore Management University, and IESE in Barcelona. Pfeffer has served on the board of directors of several human capital software companies as well as other public and nonprofit boards. He won the Richard D. Irwin Award for scholarly contributions to management, received an honorary doctorate from Tilburg University, is listed in the top twenty-five management thinkers by Thinkers 50, and has received numerous other awards for books, articles, and his scholarly career.